Frame Work in Language and Literacy

CHALLENGES IN LANGUAGE AND LITERACY

Kenn Apel, Barbara J. Ehren, Elaine R. Silliman,
and C. Addison Stone, *Series Editors*

Frame Work in Language and Literacy

How Theory Informs Practice

Judith Felson Duchan

Series Editors' Note by
Elaine R. Silliman and C. Addison Stone

The Guilford Press
New York   London

© 2004 The Guilford Press
A Division of Guilford Publications, Inc.
72 Spring Street, New York, NY 10012
www.guilford.com

Printed in the United States of America

This book is printed on acid-free paper.

Last digit is print number: 9 8 7 6 5 4 3 2 1

Library of Congress Cataloging-in-Publication Data

Duchan, Judith F.
     Frame work in language and literacy : how theory informs practice /
Judith Felson Duchan.
        p. cm. — (Challenges in language and literacy)
     Includes bibliographical references and index.
     ISBN 1-57230-949-0
     1. Language and languages—Study and teaching. 2. Frames
(Linguistics) 3. Language acquisition. 4. Language disorders in
children. 5. Literacy. I. Title. II. Series.
P53.4116.D83 2004
418'.0071—dc22

                                                    2003018779

To Elaine R. Silliman, for her support on this project
and many others in the past

About the Author

Judith Felson Duchan is Emeritus Professor at the State University of New York at Buffalo. She has published widely on language pathology and development, with particular emphasis on autism, pragmatics, normal language acquisition, and aphasia. Much of her early work indirectly addressed issues related to the influence of frames on clinical and educational practices. This book is the first she has written that elaborates on the frame work done by professionals. For a sampling of her past and current interests and publications, visit her website at *http://www.acsu.buffalo.edu/~duchan*.

Series Editors' Note

We are pleased to introduce Judith Duchan's fine book as the first volume in The Guilford Press's new series, *Challenges in Language and Literacy*. As Professor Duchan notes in the Preface, this book stems from the journey of discovery she has undertaken over many years in questioning beliefs about models and practices that many of us take for granted. In this volume, Professor Duchan reflects on the myriad conceptions of language, literacy, and disability that populate the scholarly and professional fields that focus on children at risk for problems in language and literacy development. We resonate with Professor Duchan's argument that frames and metaphors play powerful roles as both organizers and blinders for those who work, often unwittingly, within them in the name of these children. The arguments that she presents are especially important in this time of transition, a time when the fields of speech–language pathology, education, and special education are becoming increasingly juxtaposed, and when, within the speech–language field, the traditional medical model is being challenged by a sociocultural model. Given these trends, it is increasingly important that both scholars and professionals reflect carefully on the issues raised by Professor Duchan. It is her distinct gift that she can present such complex arguments clearly, and that she can bring alive the many implications of the points she makes.

First and foremost, this is a book about perspectives, or frames, that guide how we interpret the individual differences that characterize all children, but, more specifically, those children who continuously struggle with the language of learning. These same frames, which may not be overtly known to us, are then reflected in the clinical and educational practices applied to support children in the language and literacy domains. The frames on which we hang our beliefs directly shape how diagnostic descriptions about individual children are arrived at and how the processes of assessment, intervention, and the evaluation of progress are conceived. These same beliefs influence the ways we teach, what children learn, whether they come to value themselves as competent learners, and what they learn about the meaning of learning.

Professor Duchan's book embodies many of the themes of the *Challenges in Language and Literacy* series. The aim of this series is to integrate interdisciplinary perspectives on language and literacy with empirically based components for promoting effective learning outcomes in diverse students. The series is based on the premise that oral and written language skills are functionally intertwined in individual development. Understanding the complexity of this relationship requires the collaborative contributions of scholars and practitioners from multiple disciplines. The series focuses on typical and atypical language development from the preschool years to young adulthood. The goal is to provide informative, timely resources for a broad audience including practitioners, academics, and students in the fields of language science and language disorders, educational psychology, general education, special education, and learning disabilities.

We trust that readers of this volume, whatever their background, will find the rich food for thought that then provokes the kind of reflective journey serving as the impetus for this book. We hope the book will also serve to stimulate more conversations across the disciplinary and subdisciplinary boundaries that Professor Duchan describes so effectively.

ELAINE R. SILLIMAN
C. ADDISON STONE

Acknowledgments

This book grows out of changes in thinking that I experienced in various periods of my professional life. There are many who have contributed to those changes—people who provided me with dialog and perspectives for reflecting on new and old models and practices. Those early on in my academic career were Bill Brewer, who introduced me to what was happening in psycholinguistics, why Osgood was wrong, and why it seemed important to examine the advantages of cognitive over behavioral approaches. Klaus Witz allowed me to explore ideas and methods coming from frames outside traditional cognitive and behavioral frameworks.

A bit later I worked with Nan Lund to elaborate a linguistic-based frame for assessing the linguistic underpinnings of children's language disabilities. At the same time, Joe Oliva and I examined the richness of microinteractional video analyses and the temporal coordination between verbal, intonational, and movement systems during a person's speech and language production. The methodology in those studies with Joe Oliva was applied wonderfully by Barry Prizant in his dissertation study of illocutionary acts underlying the echolalia of children with autism.

The multilevel coordination of timing within and across individuals also combined well with the phenomenological frame that Jim Palermo introduced me to. This very rich reality frame, which I have called the subjective reality frame in this book, has been particularly useful in my work with colleagues in a narrative discourse research group. The aim of the research group was to capture the felt sense of space, time, and ego orientation (what we and others have called deictic perspectives) in narratives produced by children and adults. I have been especially influenced by David Zubin, Erwin Segal, Gail Bruder, Mary Galbraith, and Lynne Hewitt from that narrative group, and by my cousin Nancy Felson, who worked with us and who added to my ideas about deixis.

I am also indebted to Dana Kovarsky for providing conversation, and a forum for exploring social participation and social interaction frames, drawn from sociolinguistics and anthropology. Dana brought to my attention, and to the attention of many others in the field of speech–language pathology, a rich literature on social and cultural frames and a grounding in qualitative research methods. He helped me open up my research to include clients' and students' perspectives.

Along with the many people who influenced changes in how I framed my research questions and methods, were those who influenced how I thought about people with disabilities. Of particular importance were the respectful practices and insights of Jeff Higginbotham, as he explored various interactive aspects of augmentative communication users; of Tamar Jacobson, who introduced me to the intricacies of anti-bias approaches in early childhood education; and of Rae Sonnenmeier and Michael Mc-Sheehan, who have provided me and the profession with sensitive, creative, and inclusionary ways of working with children with severe communication disabilities.

My foray into politically framed practices came from my exposure to facilitated communication, a method that made sense within my phenomenological frame, but not within an objective, scientific frame. I thank Elaine Silliman for allowing me venues within which to voice and frame my politics, and Rae Sonnenmeier, Sylvia Diehl, Steve Calculator, Annegret Schubert, Michael McSheehan, and Gary Cumley for providing the exchange that clarified the political issues.

I would also like to acknowledge the influence of my colleagues in the United States and London, who have been working within a social engagement frame to create a world that is more accessible and livable for those who have communication disabilities. Of particular importance to my recent thinking are the discussions and research I have been engaged in with Sally Byng, Susie Parr, Carole Pound, Aura Kagan, and Nina Simmons-Mackie.

Besides the many who have contributed to my frame growth over the years, there are a few who have given invaluable help as I tried to grapple with writing about frames. Especially noteworthy are two of the editors of the series in which this book appears: Addison Stone and Elaine Silliman. They took their job of editing very seriously, and this is a better book as a result.

Throughout all these years of my doing frame work, my husband, Alan Duchan, and my sister, Elaine Vanzant, have been there to watch, listen, and provide sustenance. They have created the conditions for me to live so happily in my common-sense, everyday, reality frame.

Preface

In this book I will try to illustrate how frames permeate and dictate much of what is done on behalf of children with communication and literacy difficulties. Teachers and clinicians might want to argue that they are not influenced by frames, but rather that they base their teaching or clinical decisions on "what works." However, I hope to be able to show that even opinions about "what works" are biased according to what one takes to be "progress." That is to say, I will be arguing that the most mundane of judgments made by teachers and clinicians are grounded in, and influenced by, the point of view behind the judgment.

So it should come as no surprise that this book has also been influenced by frames. The very nature of its organization reflects my choice of a medical frame over an educational one. The chapter titles—focusing on diagnosis, assessment, intervention, and evaluation—are framed in the medical model, as are terms such as *clinician, therapy, client.* That is, they are founded on a causal logic that is problem-based. The logic of the book's structure casts diagnosis in a key role, and sees therapy as a way to fix the diagnosed problem.

However, I do not embrace this medical model wholeheartedly. Indeed, while I try not to be judgmental when I talk about various frames underlying everyday clinical and educational decision making, I have the most difficult time talking about the medical model in a neutral way. I wish that I did not feel the need to begin this book about children with language and literacy disabilities with a chapter on diagnosis. But what would that other book have looked like? I found it impossible to go against the grain of a clinical/medical model, given that my goal has been to reveal the frames underlying existing professional thinking about children with disabilities—thinking that is deeply entrenched in a medical way of thinking.

Nor is the medical model the only frame bias in this book. My examples of different methods used to meet the needs of children with speech, language, and literacy problems have favored those used by speech–language pathologists. My bias is also evidenced in the way I have placed literacy in its own circumscribed chapter, rather than integrating it into the other chapters. I did not set out to emphasize frames of speech–language pathologists over those of educators. Rather, my decision to do this had to do with where I locate myself professionally. I am optimistic that as both speech–language pathology and education work toward the common goal of inclusionary practices, I, and the speech–language pathologists and teachers toward whom this book is geared, will have an easier time thinking and talking about one another's frames and understanding the frame-based origins of one another's practices.

Finally, and perhaps most importantly, I have adopted a subjective view of reality as opposed to an objectivist view. Indeed, this notion that reality—in this case, a view of services provided to children with language and literacy disabilities—can exist outside any biasing frames is the main thesis against which I will be arguing. I will try to show throughout the book that the real world surrounding a child with language learning and literacy disabilities is a mirage. Rather, views of children so identified are socially constructed ones—ones that emerge from the frames that professionals and family members use to understand children. We see children's problems differently depending upon what frames we look through.

I begin, in the first chapter, by distinguishing between reality frames, models, and metaphors and giving examples of each. In later chapters I talk about how some frames are nested in one another, and how frames associated with particular educational or clinical practices merge and/or clash with one another. I end this book by talking about the advantages of becoming more cognizant of the frames underlying practice and how professionals might go about discovering their hidden worlds and evaluating them.

Contents

ONE

Interpretive Frames

Books and articles on language and literacy disabilities express a point of view. While the authors of such scholarship typically do not lay claim to a select perspective, they write with a set of assumptions that represent a particular take on what communication is, what children are doing as they learn to communicate, and what children with communication problems are like. For example, authors are more likely to represent communication as a way for speakers and listeners to exchange information than to see it as a way in which participants become socially engaged. A focus on informational aspects of communication leads writers to describe children's communication problems in terms of their difficulties with linguistic knowledge rather than in terms of difficulties the children may be having because of lack of opportunity or social barriers.

Similarly, professionals such as classroom teachers and clinicians such as speech–language pathologists[1] must also interpret

---

[1] I will be using the terms *speech–language pathologist* and *clinician* interchangeably throughout this book. While *clinicians* ordinarily refer to specialists who work within a medical model (occupational therapists, physical therapists, psychologists), I will be referring mostly in this book to speech–language pathologists. The term *clinician* allows me to distinguish them from teachers and special educators without having to call them by their full and somewhat cumbersome name.

1

communication from a select perspective. This perspective is not always conscious. For example, when teachers plan a reading lesson, they are not aware of the assumptions they are making about the nature of reading or of children's learning. Rather, their assumptions may be hidden from their psychological view, as is much of what we take for granted as we go about our everyday activities.

This book is aimed at uncovering hidden points of view that are lurking in the clinical and educational literature and the practices of those engaged with children who have language and literacy disabilities. Commonly used assessment, therapy, and teaching methods are described and analyzed for their underlying assumptions. One hoped-for result of this undercover operation is that it will open up more avenues for supporting and advancing children's use of oral and written communication. Another hope is that seeing a clearer picture of the ideas behind current practices will allow professionals within the same discipline to better communicate their purposes and practices to one another. Such clarity would also foster better understanding and communication between professionals from different disciplines who are working within different conceptual frames.

There are many well-worn methods that clinicians and teachers use with children with language and literacy disabilities. This book analyzes some of the main ones for their core ideas. It differs from other books on therapy and teaching methods in that it focuses not only on the practices themselves but also on how those practices are viewed by those who carry them out and write about them. The analyses used to discover ideas underlying current practices are drawn from an emerging literature on interpretive frameworks. That literature exposes the significant role that conceptual models play in how people understand and engage in the activities of everyday living (e.g., Goffman, 1974; Lakoff & Johnson, 1980, 1999; Leary, 1990; Reddy, 1979). Included in those studies are analyses of reality frames, models, and metaphors.

INTERPRETIVE FRAMES:
WHAT ARE THEY? WHERE ARE THEY?

Research in linguistics and cognitive science over the last couple of decades has revealed just how rich language systems are. Unlike previous renditions that located language meaning in the semantics associated with lexical items and their relations, more recent research has treated language like a Rorschach ink blot—something that provides a hint of what meanings can be read into it.

For example, suppose you are at the library and you pass this note to a friend: "Are you coming to Jane's birthday party tonight?" Because you didn't write "Are you going to Jane's birthday party tonight?" you were inadvertently indicating to your friend that you intend to be there. You were already imagining yourself as located at the party and you used the verb "come" to describe your friend approaching where you see yourself being. You chose the verb based on your spatial frame of reference that included you, your friend, and the birthday party. In addition, your use of the word "tonight" carries with it a temporal anchor that requires that you and your friend know when the note was written in relation to when the party is to take place. And, of course, you both need to know who you mean when you say "Jane."

These sorts of invisible aspects of language have been called "frames," or "mental models." In the above example, the spatial and temporal frames that were used to interpret the words allowed you and your friend to understand one another. Someone reading your note without access to the frame, say, a custodian who finds your note in the wastebasket the next day, would not be able to understand it, even though he would be able to understand the words in it. He would not know who Jane is, or where or when the party is to be held.

By the same token, one uses frames to render and describe communication itself. If I asked you what that note was about, you might answer that you were passing a message to your friend. This description is based on a "message-passing" view of communication. When you describe your note as a message, yourself as its sender, and your partner as its receiver, you are drawing upon a large and complex concept that depicts communication as a message passing enterprise.

This message-passing view of communication is an interpretive frame that has been called a "conduit metaphor of communication" (Lakoff & Johnson, 1980; Reddy, 1979). It portrays communicators as senders and receivers of messages, whether the messages be in written, oral, or gestural form. Speakers, for example, communicate with listeners by sending them oral messages through an invisible air stream—similar to an electrical conduit (Reddy, 1979).

The conduit view of communication involves a decontextualized, serial, to-and-fro exchange of information. In so doing, it may be leaving out other aspects of communication captured by other interpretive frames. For example, it does not easily depict how communicators use the current situation to create meaning, or how communication serves an interactional function, or how partners go about collaborating together to create common meaning.

The intention of this book, then, is to discover and explicate the hidden frames in the language and activities of clinicians and teachers when they write about children with language and literacy disabilities and when they describe their educational or clinical approaches. Let me give some examples of what I mean.

The Medical Model: An Example of an Interpretive Frame

Interpretive frames have long been recognized as being influential in clinical and educational practices, even though they have not been called that. Speech–language pathologists, for example, have struggled with the assumptions of what has been called "the medical model." School-based speech–language professionals who are involved in school inclusion are likely to experience the limitations of such medically based thinking when they focus on providing classroom support to teachers and nondisabled children as well as those with disabilities. Speech–language pathologists who use the vocabulary of their host profession may be inadvertently distancing themselves from the other professionals at the school. Their very title, "pathologists," "therapists" or "clinicians," rather than "teachers," may be unintentionally conveying an image of themselves as "other," as "different," or even as "superior."

Besides casting speech–language pathologists as "clinicians" rather than as "teachers," the medical model leads school clinicians to use different labels to describe themselves and what they do. They might be inclined to call their students "clients" or "patients," or to refer to their teaching as "therapy." They are likely to see their teaching as "remediation" or "rehabilitation" of deficits rather than as educational. They are thereby inclined to focus their teaching on individual children's clinical goals rather than on educational plans that are associated with the curriculum.

The different terminology is not just a difference in vocabulary. It represents a deeper differential conceptualization of the entire work enterprise. Speech–language pathologists working within the medical model, even if they were to call themselves "speech teachers," would not see themselves as educators. Rather, they would still see themselves as clinicians, working to lessen the impact of their clients' communication disorders. Their assessments of children, if governed by the medical model, are designed to discover those children's deficits rather than their achievements. Their therapy plans, even when they represent them in "Individualized Education Programs" (IEP), are not seen as part of the curriculum. Instead they are regarded as plans for remediating the deficits caused by each individual child's communication impairment. (See Table 1.1 for a comparison of concepts used in educational and medically based clinical frameworks.)

Table 1.1. Conceptual Comparison between Professionals in Schools Using Educational and Medical Models

Domain of comparison	Educational model	Medical model
Their perceived role	Teacher, educator, tutor	Clinician, therapist, pathologist
How they regard children in their charge	Student	Patient/client
How they regard and assess children's performance	As levels of achievement (competence)	As severity of problem (deficit)
What they call their professional activities	Teaching/instruction, using different teaching approaches	Therapy/remediation, using different remedial approaches
What the label "language or literacy disabilities" implies to them	An educational classification used in making placement and educational programming decisions	A diagnosis, offering an etiology and prescribing certain therapies
Their professional aim	To teach the curriculum to all children in the class	To remediate communication skills of individual children in the class

TYPES OF INTERPRETIVE FRAMES AND HOW THEY WORK

Frames work like rose-colored glasses. They provide a way of looking at the world, a way of making sense of what is going on. There are a number of different types of interpretive frames that have been occupying the thoughts of cognitive scientists who study the effect of frames on people's interpretations of the world. At least three types can be identified. One is a frame that operates on the level of rose-colored glasses worn throughout an experience. I will be calling this type a *reality frame*. A second type of frame I will term *models*. Models are sometimes referred to in other ways, for example, as "paradigms" or "schemas." They provide an overall structure and organizational coherence to segments of experience. They too work like rose-colored glasses, but ones that are taken on and off more readily. Finally, frames such as *metaphors* or analogies can operate at a more fine-grained rather than at a general level of interpretation. They serve to create meanings at the level of components or elements of a larger frame such as individual words or phrases—they are like rose-colored glasses put on and removed repeatedly during an event. (See Table 1.2 for some clinical and teaching examples of frames at each of the levels.)

Reality Frames

Reality frames have to do with broad perspectives on reality. A narrative, say, if engaging, requires the reader or listener to shift into another world, the world of the story. This perspective shift brings with it new reference points. The words "here" and "now" when part of the story world is no longer referring to the place and the time of the storyteller and the listener. Rather, they are located in a different reality frame in the realm of the story. (Shifting realities from the here-and-now of the present to another imaginary here-and-now in the world of the story has been called a "deictic shift" [Segal, 1995].)

But that's not the end of the story about narratives and reality frames. The narrative also can have other reality frames embedded within it. For example, stories are often told from the worldview of one or more characters in the story. The exchange between Little Red Riding Hood and the Big Bad Wolf requires a shift in perspective on reality from someone who is astounded by the physical changes she perceives in her grandmother ("What big eyes you have, Granny!") to someone who is busy thinking about his upcoming dinner ("The better to see you with, my dear"). Their perspective is

Table 1.2. Examples of Dfferent Types of Frames Found in the Clinical and Teaching Literatures on Childhood Language and Learning Disabilities

Reality frames

Everyday taken-for-granted reality: The reality frame that is seen as the most basic kind of reality against which everything else is framed (see below for a description of an "as-if" reality frame). This frame is what is used to interpret everyday-life, unselfconscious events. It is the reality that one is talking about when one talks about the "real world" and "everyday life contexts."

Objective reality: A reality frame that construes the world in terms of directly perceivable or measurable events.

Subjective reality: A reality frame in which the world is seen from the perspective of a particular person and one that includes the person's beliefs or feelings.

"As-if" reality: The reality frame that underlies demonstration teaching, practicing, authentic assessment, and role play, where the activities are experienced and grounded in everyday reality but are not the same as everyday reality (e.g., demonstrating how to do something rather than "really doing it," practicing for the "real world," assessing in contexts that simulate "reality," engaging in pretense, an imagined story, not a "real" one).

Meta-reality: The reality frame that one experiences when critically evaluating the taken-for-granted everyday reality (e.g., reflecting critically on one's teaching or clinical practices, determining what frames are underlying one's practices).

Models/paradigms/schemas

Medical model of clinical practices: A frame in which adults in schools see their main role as being to remediate clients' problems.

Education model of teaching practices: A frame in which adults in schools see their main role as being the education of students.

Social model of disability: A frame that focuses on the social origins, barriers, and opportunities offered to those with disabilities.

Information-processing model of communication: A frame in which communication is analyzed in terms of psychological processes required to receive and interpret incoming information and to translate ideas into a communicative (usually portrayed as linguistic) form.

Linguistic model of communication: A frame that focuses on the linguistic structuring of communication, whether it be oral or written.

Social participation model in teaching or clinical practice: A frame that places social participation in a central role when working with those who have disabilities. It is often used to guide school inclusion approaches.

(continued)

Table 1.2. continued

Experimental research paradigm: A frame in which the world is construed in terms of variables that need to be controlled or manipulated and that cause other variables (dependent variables) to change.

Reading readiness frame: A frame that focuses on decoding when first teaching children to read. The aim is to provide children with the skills needed to read.

Emergent literacy frame: A frame that focuses on interpretive context when teaching children to read. The aim is to provide children with the life experiences required to interpret written materials.

Economic model for service delivery: A frame often used by administrators to allocate resources and evaluate programs in terms of relative costs and benefits.

Metaphors

The conduit metaphor: A frame that treats teaching and communication as consisting of messages being passed over an invisible conduit from one person to another.

The container metaphor: A frame that treats learning and listening as involving a process of receiving and storing information (in a mental container) for later retrieval.

The attunement metaphor: A frame that treats children's learning and communication as a means for them to feel engaged with people and activities.

The functional metaphor of communication: A frame that depicts communication as the expression of communicative intent. It has to do with how communicative tools (e.g., gestures, words, utterances) are used to express desires.

The exercise metaphor: A frame that sees repetition and practice as a way to "strengthen" newly formed skills. This assumes that practicing skills, like exercising muscles, results in better performance.

a subjective one in that it allows an interpreter to call on the inner realities of the characters in the story.

Understanding the quotes of Little Red Riding Hood and the Big Bad Wolf requires taking each of their subjective perspectives on reality. Most of the literature describing language and literacy disabilities depicts reality as *objective*, as a truth outside subjective perspectives. So children's language is described in diagnostic reports, articles, and IEPs in objective terms. Results of tests and observational assessments are portrayed as data that exists in a reality that is separable from the interpretive frame representing the points of view of the children who use the language or of the adults who assess those children. Several chapters in this book include discussions of the reality frames of authors as they go about depicting various activities associated with children's language and learning disabilities.

Another reality frame that is often used by teachers and clinicians working with children with language and learning disabilities is what might be termed an *"as-if"* frame. In this frame, those engaging in an interaction involving practicing or demonstrating something know that what they are doing is preparing for another reality, often called the "real world." Teachers have children act "as if" they were "really" doing what they are practicing.

And yet another commonplace instance of clinicians and teachers shifting their reality frames occurs during reflection. In this case they are "thinking about" how things are going, or how things went, or how things might have gone better. This requires a mental shift to a *reflective reality frame*—one that stands outside the everyday taken-for-granted reality.

Models

Models are different from reality frames in that they relate to the ingredients of a structure rather than to the overall way the structure is cast. A model for a particular play activity, for example, would be like a script that governs the selection and arrangement of the play components and that provides a logical structure for understanding how the components relate meaningfully to one another (Duchan, 1991). The reality frame for play, on the other hand, would have to do with how play, as a whole, is seen as "nonserious" (Bateson, 1972).

Models can help explain the "reading wars" that have arisen between those who subscribe to a reading-readiness view of early reading and those who see reading as emergent literacy. The *reading readiness model* depicts reading as a process of identifying written symbols and interpreting their meaning. Indeed, reading is sometimes described as "decoding." Within this frame, teaching a child to read begins with teaching him or her to sound out letters in the alphabet. Some versions of the reading readiness model presume that for children to understand this difficult decoding task they need to be directly taught, and that children are not usually ready to grasp the concepts involved until age 5 or so.

The *emergent literacy model,* on the other hand, depicts reading in a broader way. It is seen as part of one's life experience, not unlike learning to play or to dress oneself. In this model, learning to identify letters, involves the same sorts of understandings as learning to identify objects. It results from figuring out how things work in everyday life. A recognition of an "m" is likely to be picked up from those double yellow arches found everywhere well before it is taught in the curriculum.

Another model that is commonly found in the literature related to children with language and literacy disabilities is the one that portrays children's language as information processing (e.g., Aram & Nation, 1982; Duchan & Katz, 1983; Stark, Tallal, & McCauley, 1988). This *information-processing model* sees communication in terms of information being processed by speakers and listeners. Speakers, in order to convey information, need to process their ideas into sounds or letters, words, and syntax. Listeners, when interpreting information, process spoken messages by identifying speech sounds or letters, recognizing words, analyzing the syntax, and interpreting and storing the information in memory. Nonspoken messages such as gestures and facial expressions require a different sort of processing from senders and receivers, but processing nonetheless.

Models that seem very complex and well integrated are sometimes called *paradigms* (Kuhn, 1996). Kuhn, in his classic book, *The Structure of Scientific Revolutions,* defines scientific paradigms as "universally recognized scientific achievements that for a time provide model problems and solutions to a community of practitioners" (1996, p. viii). The dominant scientific paradigm used by researchers in education and clinical disciplines such as speech–language pathology employs a hypothesis-testing, experimental research design. In this experimental paradigm researchers test hypotheses by identifying, controlling, and manipulating observable variables so that they can measure the causal effects of different variables on one another. Experimental research on children with language and learning disabilities has been carried out to discover diagnostic categories and to assess the impact of various therapy and teaching methods.

Typically, the experimental model governs research practices, the educational model governs teaching practices, and the medical model governs clinical practices. Each of these models provides the users with a logical structure for conceiving of and carrying out their work. Their work will differ depending upon the model used. For example, controlling and manipulating variables will be a focus for researchers using the experimental model, diagnosis and therapy will be focused on by professionals who use the medical

Just as for syntax, higher order frames can influence one's choice of lower order frames, and the same lower order frame may be interpreted differently when embedded in different higher order frames. In several chapters I talk about a *functional metaphor*. While its general meaning is the same in its varied manifestations, this metaphor is applied differently in different contexts. When embedded in a communication context, *functionality* refers to the use made of communicative acts such as gestures or a piece of writing. For example, a gesture can function as a refusal and a letter can function as an invitation. When applied to behavioral therapies, functions have to do with units such as stimuli and responses. A stimulus functions as a discriminative stimulus for its associated response.

Frames can also merge in other ways. They may be combined as parallel, complementary, structures by being added together rather than embedded in one another (e.g., row 2 in Figure 1.1). Linguistic and discovery models may be combined in teaching children to read by aiding them to find the linguistic rules underlying rhyming words or prefixes and suffixes. The finding of the rules involves a discovery model and the linguistic nature of the rule fits a linguistic model.

A recent communication model forwarded by Prizant, Wetherby, and Rydell (2000) provides an interesting example of a model containing different frames added together. This additively constructed composite is further embedded in a medical model in that the authors use it to individualize treatment with children who are diagnosed as having autism spectrum disorders. It is called SCERTS, an acronym standing for social Communication, emotional regulation, and transactional support, areas that are considered as "core deficits observed in children with [autism spectrum disorders]" (Prizant et al., p. 207).

The social and communication components (or "SC") of the SCERTS model draw from a functional metaphor of communication. In this approach, communication is seen as being in the service of a communicative intent. Specifically, children's gestures or oral communications are analyzed for which of three functions they serve: behavior regulation, social interaction, or joint attention. Interventions are then designed to expand the type and frequency of a child's existing communicative intents.

The emotional regulation component (or "ER") of the SCERTS model has to do with how well a child can "control or modulate his or her level of emotional arousal" (Prizant et al., 2000, p. 211). This idea is based on an energy or electricity metaphor. Emotions

model, and academic skill and knowledge building will be focused on by those who work within the educational model.

Metaphors

Conceptual metaphors are a third level of interpretative frame that pervade clinical and educational practices. Lakoff and Johnson (1999) have described them as "mappings across conceptual domains that structure our reasoning, our experience, and our everyday language" (p. 47). For example, the familiar experience of seeing liquids flow through a tube or pipe is used to understand and depict what is going on in communication. Information is talked about as "flowing" from one source to another through an invisible conduit.

A metaphor commonly associated with children's communication is that involved in the understanding of things placed in a container. This container metaphor borrows a schema of "in-ness" and confinement of objects in a container and extends its use to how information or knowledge is imparted to and learned by children (Lakoff & Johnson, 1999, pp. 31–32). Communication is treated as information that is transported from the mind (container) of one partner to that of another, where it is stored. Similarly, learning is treated as the imparting of knowledge. Teachers teach children by giving them knowledge and children receive the knowledge by storing it in their minds.

Many other metaphors have been used to depict children's learning and communication. One that is currently in favor is an "engagement" metaphor wherein communication is seen as emotional attunement or involvement rather than as a message-passing activity (e.g., Stern, 1985). The emphasis is on affective aspects of communication involving social connection and cooperation.

Metaphors, like models, can be blended together into larger and more complex frames (Coulson, 2001; Fauconnier & Turner, 2002). The conduit and the container metaphors blend together under the information-processing model. In the complex rendition of communication, information or messages are portrayed as being passed from one person to another (via an imagined conduit) and as being processed and stored in longterm memory for future use (via an imagined container).

I have been arguing throughout this chapter that frames differ from one another in fundamental ways. Some are broad, general, and have a pervasive influence on the perceptions and practices of those using them. Others are more localized, more specific, with less of an influence. And still others fall somewhere in between. I have forwarded a tentative taxonomy in which I named the three kinds of frames, proceeding from the most general and pervasive to the most specific and least influential: reality frames, models, and metaphors (see Table 1.3 for a summary of these core terms). I have also provided some examples of each of these frame types (see Table 1.2, pp. 7–8, for a listing). What I have yet to address is how frames of different types or of the same type might work together or against one another.

FRAME MERGERS

My approach in this book, for the most part, is to talk about frames as if they are isolated from one another. I occasionally go on to show

Table 1.3. Summary of Terminology Used to Understand and Differentiate Types of Frames

Frame

A conceptual structure used to make sense of and construct realities. Frames can be classified into types, depending upon their scope. Reality frames tend to have the widest scope, models next, and metaphors have most narrow scope. Frames of one type can easily slide into another type, depending upon their specific uses.

Reality frame

A broad conceptual frame that serves to situate someone in a particular reality. For example, when understanding a narrative one needs to shift from the here and now reality into the reality of the story world. Reality frames has to do with how one views all that is going on—that is, the entire reality of the experience.

Model

A conceptual frame that offers a way to make sense of a set of aspects of experience. The elements of models work together logically to provide coherence as one makes sense of what is going on. Models have also been called paradigms, schemas, scripts, and scaffolds.

Metaphor

A frame in which conceptual interpretations from one domain of meaning are applied to another domain. Metaphors tend to be smaller in scope than reality frames and models, applying to selected elements within an experience.

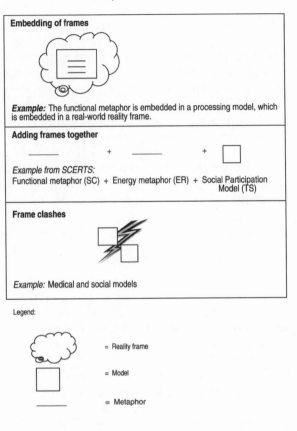

Figure 1.1. Graphic representation of frame types, mergers, and clashes.

how these isolable frames combine with one another—in what I have called "frame mergers."

Metaphors, models, and reality frames, perhaps because of their differences in scope, can often be found nested within one another. For instance, information-processing models typically contain a conduit metaphor and assume an objective stance toward reality. These frame mergers work something like the elements involved in syntax, in which lower order localized structures, such as lexical items, are embedded in higher order structures, like phrases, which, in turn, are embedded in yet higher order structures, like sentences. (The top row in Figure 1.1 illustrates this nested relationship between metaphors, models, and reality frames.)

are viewed as a kind of energy, residing in the body, that can be aroused or activated in a variety of ways. When emotions get out of control, as is often the case for children with autism spectrum disorders, they can be distracting and interfere with children's ability to attend or to problem-solve. At these times, emotions need regulation, much like one would regulate heat using a thermostat. Prizant et al. (2000, p. 212) offer some suggestions for how to help a child regulate emotions: for example, when one child is distressed as indicated by vocalization, bodily tension, or agitated movement, a partner may respond by speaking in a slow, calm voice, and by hugging or giving a child some deep pressure on the shoulders or arms.

A third component of the SCERTS model is transactional support (the "TS" of the acronym). The notion of transaction pertains to the interaction between the environment and the child. The particular slant Prizant et al. take on transactional support involves social participation in events. They describe it as having to do with how family members and peers think about and interact with the child who is diagnosed with a type of autism. The authors then draw their third component from a social participation model. They recommend ways of engineering events and creating social exchanges that promote positive and more normal participation with children with autism.

In summary, the SCERTS model contains three differentiable frames; a functional metaphor, an energy metaphor, and a social participation model. Together, they offer teachers and clinicians a variety of things to do to support children with autism spectrum disorders. All three models of SCERTS are combined in a parallel relationship and all three are nested, side by side within a medical model that involves an individualized, remedial approach based on the deficits of children with a particular diagnosis. (See Figure 1.1 for a graphic representation of the SCERTS frame.)

FRAME CLASHES

One of the ways that frames can come to light in the course of ordinary clinical or educational practices is when they clash with one another (see a graphic illustrating these relationships in row 3 of Figure 1.1). These clashes may occur for different reasons. One source of incompatibility is in the frames themselves, requiring that practitioners choose between them when representing a child's difficulties or program goals. A second source is that frames that in theory are compatible may be brought into conflict because of the practical need to choose one over the other. Third, frame clashes may occur because professionals who now need to plan together have grown up in different disciplines with different theoretical and practice frames. Finally, conflicts can become obvious when an institution's frames run counter to the ones held by teachers, speech–language pathologists, and families working with those institutions. Examples of these different conflicts will show how frames play a part in many of the conflicts experienced in everyday professional practices.

Incompatible Frames

It is obvious to anyone who takes sides in a conflict between frames that some frames are not easily merged. Two such frames are the medical and the social models of disabilities. In the medical model, the focus is on the individual, and the causal structure relates to what, in the person or in his or her history, is causing "his or her problem." Remediation in the medical model consists of individualized therapy or teaching—fixing the person's impairment.

The social model, on the other hand, emphasizes the social origins of a person's disability, examining the barriers and access opportunities that are provided by the society for its citizens. (Note the use of a navigation metaphor with such words as "barrier" and "access.") The focus is on eliminating barriers to a child's social participation and on providing support and participation opportunities in everyday life contexts.

Proponents of the two frames often see them as incompatible, since each is associated with different practices and each construes the source and remedy of the problem differently. But even for these obviously conflicting paradigms, one can find similar practices. For example, someone from a social model might see hearing aids as a way of supporting a person's participation and eliminating barriers, and someone from a medical model would see the same practice as minimizing the impairment.

Compatible but Impractical Combinations of Frames

Sometimes frames are compatible in theory, but incompatible in practice. For example, subscribers to the whole language approach are sometimes pitted against those who take the phonics approach to teaching reading. The two combatants are incompatible because the methods arising from the models are incompatible. They each dictate different places to begin teaching reading (whole language beginning with meaning, phonics beginning with sounds), and they offer different outlines of how a reading curriculum should progress. The whole language approach progresses from interpreting meanings and whole words to a later analysis of words into letters and associated sounds; the phonics approach begins with sounds and progresses to words and textual meanings.

There have been efforts to blend these apparently incompatible approaches to reading. For example, reading researchers have recently advocated "balanced teaching" in which children are asked to sound out words during a whole language lesson (Pressley, 1998).

Professionally Based Frame Clashes

Professions are based on different frames. For example, clinical professions tend to draw heavily on a medical frame that begins with identifying problems in individuals, and then working to diagnose and remediate them, often in the context of one-on-one sessions. Teaching professions do not assume that individual children in their charge have problems. Rather, their educational model emphasizes how best to impart knowledge to groups of children in the classroom and how best to implement the school curriculum. The IEP, until recently, has been structured around a medical model in which children's problem areas are identified and therapies and interventions prescribed for improving the child's performance in those areas.

The clashes between the medical and the educational models can be found throughout the professional literatures in the disciplines of both education and speech–language pathology. A recent display of a clash can be found in the Report of the President's Commission on Excellence in Special Education (U.S. Department of Education, 2002), in which there is a call for altering what have been impairment-based IEPs (a medical model) to make them more curriculum-based (an educational model).

Institutionally Based Frame Clashes

A common concern of teachers and school speech–language pathologists is how to carry out their services in the context of budgetary exigencies. Their preferred textbooks, commercial materials, or teaching programs may be too expensive for their allocated budget, and they often need to choose other, less expensive ways of delivering their services. Classes may be too large for teachers to provide the support needed for children with language-learning problems. There may be too few speech–language pathologists in schools because of budgetary constraints, resulting in excessive caseloads for those who are there.

These economic constraints placed on professionals by school administrators often prevent teachers and speech–language pathologists from doing what they want to do. Because of large classes and too few service providers, school professionals may not be able to afford the time needed for team planning and collaboration.

The economic model within which school professionals are forced to work often comes into direct conflict with other models that professionals would otherwise use to carry out their curricular and therapeutic practices. In this way, specialty services and models for delivering them must be continually prioritized, with some being supported and others not. Teachers and speech–language pathologists must negotiate with administrators to argue for why more money needs to be spent for their program. They may find themselves, in the course of their discussions, not only arguing for their approach on its own merits, but also arguing for it on the basis of its cost-effectiveness, making their case on economic grounds.

Resolving Frame Clashes

One way that is often recommended for resolving frame clashes is to advise people to pick the frame that is compatible with their personal values and that can best achieve their long- and short-term goals. But to do this, professionals must know what frames they have to choose from, to understand their own values and goals, and to understand how their frames fit with those of their fellow professionals and their institutions. I make the case throughout this book, but especially in the final chapter, that reflective practices are essential for revealing frame bias, for evaluating the usefulness of frames, and for resolving frame conflicts.

QUESTIONS TO BE ADDRESSED IN SPECIFIC CHAPTERS IN THIS BOOK

This book addresses a variety of questions related to interpretive frames. Chapter 2 examines what frames are used in the diagnosis of children with language and learning problems. Chapter 3 addresses frames of assessment. Chapter 4 examines frames used in intervention, instruction, and support of students with language and literacy disabilities. Chapter 5 outlines frames used in designing outcome measures for evaluating change in both students and teachers. In Chapter 6, I outline some frames used in the evaluation and teaching of literacy to children with language and learning disabilities, and in the course of that discussion I compare the educational and clinical approaches to literacy. In Chapter 7, I ask how institutions impact clinical and educational practices and examine specific public school practices, such as the use of an IEP, for how those models have influenced services. I try to pull things together in Chapter 8 by reflecting on ways interpretive frames can positively affect clinical and teaching practices and by considering how reflective practices also carry with them potential frames. I will be advocating for the idea that we need to add a critical frame to our clinical and educational approaches, one that examines practices for whether or not they are empowering. The frame in this case will be one that involves a critical analysis, such at that used by Apple (2000), Giroux (1983), and Wink (2000) in the field of education.

Throughout this book I make the case that clinical and educational practices have often been done as if those carrying out the practices were wearing analytic blinders. I will also argue that it is crucial to be aware of one's interpretive frames since the way we see children, the diagnostic and assessment instruments we choose to use, and the teaching methods we employ are all influenced by such frames. Further, one's sense of success and judgments about whether therapies or teaching approaches "worked" will differ depending upon the evaluative frames one uses to judge children's progress.

If I am right that practices will differ depending upon the interpretive frames brought to bear, how can individuals determine what works best? Subjective evaluations about children's improvement are cast within a particular evaluation perspective. Even therapy outcomes that confine themselves to objective measures are based on particular ways of looking at things. And scientific efficacy studies, usually considered impervious to bias, are also based on a particular worldview—that having to do with variables and observable measures. If practices and research contain interpreter bias coming from interpretive frames rather than being grounded in an objective "truth," how do we decide the best ways to go about diagnosis, assessment, therapy, or evaluation? I try to find answers (not a single answer) to these difficult questions and point to some future directions and new frames that will help professionals deal with the dilemmas posed by the relativistic perspective that results from examining one's interpretive frames.

TWO

Diagnostic Frames

Diagnosis was, in days of yore, the responsibility of physicians. They identified symptoms and determined what was causing them. The result was a diagnosis, a label, a classification, an etiology.

Now many professionals, borrowing from the medical model, do diagnoses. They see the symptoms as being caused by the diagnostic condition—the so-called etiology. They, like their medical predecessors, treat the etiology as an explanation of the symptoms. They are likely to cast biologically based diagnoses as more explanatory, as deeper, as more primary than psychological or social ones. They often design treatments based on causal logic associated with the diagnosis: they would rather get rid of the causes than treat the symptoms.

This medical–causal frame is often used by professionals engaged in the process of evaluating children to determine whether they have language and literacy disabilities. Its goal is explanatory and predictive, a different goal from that used in assessment evaluations. In assessment, the goal is to describe a child's problems associated with a diagnosis rather than to explain it. (For much more on assessment, see Chapter 3.) A diagnostic evaluation results in a diagnosis, an assessment evaluation results in a description of a child's strengths and deficits. Like for all frames, these two ways of doing evaluation can, in some contexts, become blurred (I will have more to say on this topic later).

Imagine encountering a child in a third-grade classroom who has unusual facial characteristics, who seems lethargic, who is not yet reading, and whose speech is unintelligible. You immediately wonder what is wrong with him. You look in his school record to find out. What are you looking for? Most likely, you would be satisfied with some sort of diagnosis that would explain all of his unusualness—his physical differences, his learning problems, and his speech difficulties. You could then understand how those differences fit together—that is, you would see that they are all caused by the same condition, perhaps fetal alcohol syndrome (FAS). If you were a teacher or therapist responsible for the children in that classroom, you would then need to get on with the business of what to do about this child's reading and speech problems, and maybe explore ways to help him overcome his lethargy.

In order to find out how best to work with the child, you might research FAS and find out whether there are some practical suggestions in the literature for working with such children. You discern that children with this diagnosis can learn to read, and they can improve their speech, even though they may also be diagnosed as mentally retarded (Gerber, 1998; Jung, 1989; Shprintzen, 1997; Sparks, 1984). You would begin to understand that your child's learning difficulties are probably due to brain damage and not to a lack of motivation to learn. You might even find an article or two on therapy or teaching approaches that have been successful with children with FAS. You then proceed to assessing this child's skills and designing an IEP based on what you, the child's family, and your colleagues consider to be the best practices to use with children with this diagnosis.

This scenario places diagnosis at center stage for working with children with special clusters of symptoms. A diagnosis, such as FAS, can provide an *interpretive frame* for identifying and understanding how a child's symptoms fit together. Learning about other children with FAS will give you a sense of what sorts of things to assess and will provide you with some ideas concerning how to go about supporting a particular child. Learning about FAS will give you an idea about what this child's future might bring, and how you can prepare him for it. Learning the diagnosis also may provide you with insights about the child's social–cultural circumstances. For example, FAS is caused by preterm alcoholism of the mother and is commonly found in Native American and Alaskan American communities (Pore & Reed, 1999, p. 37). This information might prompt you to promote community education programs aimed at disseminating information that could increase understanding and help prevent FAS in children (e.g., those education and prevention programs described by Gerber, 1998, and Paul, 2001).

The above scenario presents a picture of a child from one particular frame, a medical one. It is a frame that places diagnosis on center stage and motivates thinking about the child in terms of deficits caused by the diagnosis. Even though the frame is a medically based, diagnostic one, it allows for a choice of certain alternatives in how it is acted on. The medical model, like other models, has a certain flexibility. For example, the medical model can contain different types of causal reasoning. This chapter discusses four different but related causal frames that are associated with the medical model and that are used by professionals to reason about why children with language or learning disabilities do what they do.

The causal frames that are tucked into the medical model are classified in this case as metaphoric ones, since they are derived from notions of physical causality. In the physical world, causes have to do with bodily forces changing something physically by direct contact (Lakoff & Johnson, 1999). Also, the causal frame in diagnosis qualifies as a metaphor since the ideas of diagnostic causality are specific in their scope, applying to particular related elements. This specificity distinguishes them from the more wide-reaching frames associated with models and construals of reality described in Chapter 1.

CAUSAL FRAMES ASSOCIATED WITH DIAGNOSES

Different types of causal interpretations can grow out of knowing a child's diagnosis. One type of interpretation involves viewing symptoms as comprising a *syndrome*, a group of symptoms that are all associated with a particular preexisting disease or disorder. The diagnosis, once made, is regarded as the cause of the syndrome. The frame does not require drawing a relationship between the different symptoms in the syndrome, as would be the case for frames associated with assessment (see Chapter 3). In the case of child with FAS, his physical differences do not need to relate logically to his reading difficulties in order for both to be part of the syndrome.

A second sort of causal frame that results from a diagnosis is *symptom prediction*. In this case, the causal logic works from the general to the specific, by looking for symptoms commonly associated with a particular diagnosis. This differs from the causal logic used to make the diagnosis in the first place. In that case the direction of logic is to work from the symptoms to infer the disease or disorder. In the case of symptom prediction, a child is viewed as having the potential to develop a particular set of problems, and it is up to the professional to be on the lookout for them. The third-grade child with FAS may have difficulty with writing short essays since children with FAS are known to have difficulties with discourse (Coggins, Friet, & Morgan, 1998). The notion of "at risk" captures the symptom prediction frame: children with a particular diagnosis are at risk for certain symptoms, which one needs to be on the lookout for.

There is yet a third type of causal frame associated with diagnoses, one having to do with the relationships between multiple diagnoses. This frame associates diagnoses with one another through a *causal chain metaphor*. The chain metaphor arranges causes in a sequence of links. The links involved in FAS, for example, would involve the mother's alcohol consumption during pregnancy, which caused brain damage in the fetus, which in turn caused the condition of FAS, which includes mental retardation, which caused the child's speech, language, and literacy difficulties. The links in the causal chain are temporally ordered and two-faced, with each link functioning as both a result of the previous cause, and a cause of the next item in the chain.

A fourth causal frame involves *fault finding*. If a child's diagnosis originates with something that the mother did prenatally, then the mother may feel responsible for the child's disability. If the problem is genetic in origin, the parent who supplied the "bad genes" may feel guilty. Doctors are also implicated. There is an etiology especially reserved for them, *iatrogenic etiology*, in which the child's condition is produced by something the doctor did. Most iatrogenic etiologies are inadvertent, caused by a doctor's lack of knowledge or mistakes that are bound to occur in the normal course of clinical practice. One of the best known examples of iatrogenic etiology occurred when doctors prescribed thalidomide to women who were pregnant, not realizing its effect on fetuses, who were born deformed as a result of their treatment. (See the discussion below for other iatrogenetic diagnoses associated with language and literacy disabilities.)

In summary, there are several sorts of causal frames drawn from the medical model and used in conceptualizing diagnoses. They work as metaphors because they originate in notions of physical causality in which one event—for example, a physical force such as a push—causes another event to happen—for example, a fall. Causal metaphors used in diagnoses serve to explain and predict symptoms. This leads to different sorts of causal logic. There is the causal logic involved when using a single diagnosis to explain a group of symptoms, a syndrome. This is the basis for the notion of "at risk." There is the causal logic in which future symptoms are predicted by the diagnosis. Causal logic can work in cause–effect chains in which symptoms of previous causes can themselves cause new symptoms. And there is the causal logic involved in fault finding, in which people and circumstances are blamed for causing the child's symptoms. Let's look at each in more detail.

Syndrome Frames

In order to test your knowledge of diagnostic syndromes, you might consult a checklist of known diagnoses, such as the ones found in Shprintzen (1997). When looking at such a list, you might first sort out the diagnoses that you know from those that you haven't heard of. You might then subdivide the diagnoses that you know about into those that are common and those that are rare. Or you might just identify those diagnoses that have been associated with children you have known and ignore the others. Or you might have just met a child who is quite involved and you want to see if there is a syndrome that fits her symptom profile. In that case, you would go to a more detailed etiology list that contains information about the problems associated with different etiologies and sort it on the basis of common problem areas.

These various sortings, done to accomplish your particular purposes, are not the same as those used by the people who make up the etiology lists. Rather, scholars and authors discussing etiology typically frame their etiology listings biologically. For example, the diseases or disorders with genetic origins are categorized into one superordinate group, those having to do with the sensory system are classified together in another, and so on. This *taxonomy* or lists of groupings, provides a biological frame for understanding a particular disease. So a particular disease, such as Down syndrome, is understood as chromosomal in origin and therefore inherited, in contrast with others that have different sorts of causes.

Syndrome Classifications Based on Etiologies

Table 2.1 provides the biological classifications of several authors who have studied the etiologies of speech, language, and hearing problems. Their taxonomies pay attention to (1) whether the etiology is inherited or acquired (inherited/congenital, environmental); (2) when it occurred (e.g., perinatal); (3) which neurobiological systems are implicated (e.g., neurological, metabolic, sensory, anatomical); (4) whether the specific chromosomes of inherited abnormalities are identifiable (in chromosomal terms they are; in genetic terms they are not); (5) what type of disease it is that is causing the acquired disorders (e.g., cancers, burns, infections); and (6) whether the etiology was caused by something done by the mother during pregnancy (teratogenic) or by the doctor (iatrogenic).

Genetic and Chromosomal Etiologies

Some authors have distinguished chromosomal from genetic etiologies (see Gerber, 1998, and Paul, 1998, 2001, in Table 2.1), but this distinction is only meaningful if the term *genetic* is taken to refer only to family inheritance. That is, a syndrome (referred to in the genetic literature as a *phenotype*) can be classified as genetic just on the basis of evidence that there is a history of the condition running in families. But the term genetic also implies that there is a gene made up of chromosomes that cause the syndrome. So all genetic syndromes, in this sense of "genetic," are, by definition, chromosomal. (For a recent lucid review of the literature on genetic correlates of language and literacy disabilities in children, see Gilger & Wise, in press.)

There is a new optimism among researchers who are trying to discover the genetic bases of language and literacy disabilities. The optimism derives from recent dramatic advances in molecular genetics and brain imaging (Bates & Dick, 2000; Gilger & Wise, in press; Lai, Fisher, Hurst, Vargha-Khadem, & Monaco, 2001; Pinker, 2001; Rice, 1996). This search for genetic etiologies comes with its own set of interpretive frames for looking at childhood language and literacy

Table 2.1. Groupings of Biologically Based Etiologies for Syndromes That Include Communication Disorders

Pore and Reed (1999)

Inherited and congenital disorders or abnormalities
Neurological disorders
Metabolic and endocrine disorders
Musculoskeletal and connective tissue disorders
Sensory disorders
Head and neck cancers
Infectious disease
Burns

Sparks (1984)

Chromosomal disorders
Single-gene disorders
Multifactorial genetic disorders
Environmental birth defects
Perinatal and iatrogenic birth defects

Gerber (1998)

Disorders of chromosomal origin
Disorders of genetic origin
Infections, intoxicants, iatrogens
Trauma
Complex craniofacial disorders
Respiratory disorders
Metabolic disorders

Jung (1989)

Chromosomal syndromes
Single-gene syndromes
Polygenetic–multifactorial syndromes
Sporadic syndromes
Environmental syndromes

Paul (2001; based on Gerber, 1990, and Shprintzen, 1997)

Chromosomal
Genetic
Metabolic
Teratogenic

disabilities. Rice (1996) outlines what it is that researchers look for when searching for relationships between genetic events (genotypes) and physical or behavioral events (phenotypes) in their efforts to discover the genetic bases for language disorders in children:

> Essentially, the search for a genetic contribution to language requires the identification of variation in an individual's linguistic capability that corresponds to variation at the level of genes. (p. xiv)

Those involved in discovering the genetic bases for symptoms of specific language impairments in children must first decide on the specific variables (also called "traits," "behaviors," and "phenotypes") to associate with the genes. The variables that make up the phenotype should have certain characteristics. They should be measurable. They should be cross-cultural (genes must be cross-linguistic in order to allow children from all cultures to learn language). It would also be helpful if the variable defining the phenotype would be what Rice (1996) calls "a pathognomonic marker" (p. xxi). That is to say, good variables are unusual and peculiar to the disorder being studied. As Rice admits, there are no such markers for specific language impairment (p. xxi), nor are there such markers for any other type of complex language–learning–literacy disability (Snow, 1996). As one can tell from the stringent criteria in Rice's list, the symptoms that make up a genetic phenotype are likely to be different from those that go into a clinical or education definition of a disability. For example, children who are having difficulty reading, as indicated by their low achievement scores, would qualify in Rice's list as having a reading disorder even if their difficulties are due to cultural or environmental differences.

Despite the difficulties in finding variables that remain stable across individuals and groups with speech–language–literacy disorders, there has been considerable progress in recent years in the search for a genetic cause for speech and language disabilities (Gilger & Wise, in press; Lai et al., 2001; Pinker, 2001). For example, researchers in England have identified a 34-member intergenerational family in which 15 of the members have severe speech, motor, and language disabilities. By testing the genetic makeup of all the living members of the family (referred to as the "KE family"), researchers found a genetic regularity. They discovered that the 15 members with speech and language disorders, and none of the others, showed a developmental disruption of a specific gene: FOXP2. Another individual, known as "CS" who had similar speech and language impairments similar to the 15 KE family members also showed irregularity of this gene.

Speech and language tests that were used to identify which KE family members had speech and language disorders included phonologically based tasks (rhyming, repeating meaningful words and nonsense words, articulation testing, identifying basic speech sounds), memory tasks (digit repetition, sentence repetition), measures of literacy (reading, spelling), grammar tests (test of morphological inflections, comprehension of relative clauses, judging grammaticality), motor tests (following directions to carry out actions of the tongue), and IQ tests (Verbal and Performance) (Vargha-Khadem et al., 1998).

This set of tests is based on a linguistic and information-processing view of language and language disorders. Omitted from this list are tasks involving social and pragmatic competence. While the researchers (Lai et al., 2001) and commentators (Pinker, 2001) are cautiously optimistic that the gene is one that underlies all speech and language disorders, their concerns have to do with the state of the art in genetics and not about whether the model of language that underpins their testing program is the best one to use.

Metabolic Etiologies

Another category used in the classification of etiologies is metabolic, such as thyroid conditions or enzyme deficiencies that result from the child being unable to process certain chemicals. Gerber (1998), Shprintzen (1997), and Paul (2001) identify a subtype of metabolic etiology knownas teratogenic syndromes. These are ones that result from diseases or toxins encountered by the fetus *in utero*. Prenatal diseases of the mother include rubella and AIDS; toxins consumed by the mother during pregnancy include alcohol or cocaine.

Unknown Etiologies

The symptoms of most children with language and literacy disabilities have no known etiologies. The biological taxonomies in Table 2.1 do not include categories for diagnoses such as specific language impairment, autism, or learning disabilities—diagnoses whose biological origins have yet to be discovered (Akshoomoff, 2000; Leonard, 1998; Rice, 1996). These categories, if included in a biological taxonomy, are placed under the rubric "unknown etiologies" (e.g., Paul, 2001, p. 107) or "developmental disorders" (e.g., Pore & Reed, 1999, pp. 29, 58).

Naming and Framing

How do disorders get named? If we take names at face value, we can guess what the person naming them had in mind. Some based the names on a normal standard (e.g., learning disability, intellectual disability—formerly called "mental retardation," or "developmental disability"); some focused on a special difficulty (autism—aloneness; attention deficit disorder—attention difficulties, hyperactivity); some chose biological names for the condition (cleft palate, cerebral palsy, fragile X syndrome); and some named a disorder after themselves, the person(s) who first identified and described it (Down, Asperger, Tay and Sachs).

One often finds diseases or disabilities with several names, depending upon what different namers took to be important. Specific language impairment (SLI), for instance, has had its name changed several times. It was called "congenital aphasia" by those who were emphasizing parallels between childhood and adult language disorders (Eisenson, 1972; Myklebust, 1952) and "delayed speech development" by those who were focusing on normative comparisons (Froeschels, 1918/1980; Van Riper, 1939). The term SLI is favored by researchers who want to emphasize that this subtype of language impairment does not co-occur with other conditions—it is a deficit that is specific to language. This allows the researchers to study language in a pure form, unaffected by other confounding biological or psychological variables (Leonard, 1998).

It is often the case that children with severe speech–language–literacy disorders have multiple diagnoses, each serving different purposes. For example, a parent with a child diagnosed with pervasive developmental disorder, not otherwise specified (PDD NOS) sometimes described her child as having a "kind of autism" when talking with those who did not know about PDD NOS, and other times as having attention-deficit/hyperactivity disorder (ADHD), when wanting to minimize the severity of her child's disability (Galasso, in press).

Once a condition is diagnosed and given a name, the name takes on additional status. It no longer labels an aspect of a child's condition as would be the case of a child with red hair being called "Red." Named diagnoses carry causal connotations. For example, when an excessively active child is diagnosed as having hyperactivity, the diagnosed condition is regarded as causing the symptom: hyperactivity (the diagnosis) causes a child's hyperactive behavior (the symptom). This and other types of causal interpretations happen because a diagnosis comes in a causal package. Interpreters of diagnoses are required to make inferences. They often infer, for example, that diagnoses cause abnormal behaviors and that the diagnosed condition has an etiology—a prior cause—even when that etiology is not known.

Symptom Prediction

Unlike the identification of diagnostic syndromes, which is based on an inductive logic proceeding from the symptoms to the diagnosis, symptom prediction works deductively from the diagnosis to the symptoms. A child who is diagnosed as mentally retarded could be predicted to have a language disorder. Much of the research about language and literacy disabilities is aimed at finding new symptoms for children in particular diagnostic categories. Do children with autism also have auditory processing problems? Are children with SLI at risk for reading problems?

Today's textbooks on childhood language and literacy disabilities often talk about how etiologies are typically not determinable. For this reason, they argue against classifying children into etiological-based frames, and instead favor a descriptive approach that focuses on assessment rather than diagnosis. However, they still may provide a review of the research literature on a few select etiological classifications. Why do they do this? I suggest that their focus is on identifying which children are likely to have language and literacy disabilities rather than on which children have particular etiologies. That is to say, their focus is one involving prediction rather than explanation.

Table 2.2 lists the etiological classifications provided by four commonly used textbooks in the field of childhood language disorders. None of the authors takes responsibility for the myriad of diagnostic categories that cause language disorders in children. All opt for selecting a few commonly occurring diagnoses that have been well studied. Owens (1999), for instance, justifies his selections as follows:

> I have chosen not to discuss some categories because of the small numbers of children or the paucity of research data. I have omitted other categories because language disorders are tangential to the primary disorder. Finally, some categories . . . have such pervasive communication problems as to be beyond the scope of this book. . . . (p. 21)

The diagnoses in common for all the authors in Table 2.2 are learning disabilities, mental retardation, autism, and hearing im-

**Table 2.2. Syndromes That Are Included in Basic Texts
That Deemphasize Etiologies**

Basic texts	Etiologies
Bernstein and Tiegerman-Farber (2001)	Learning disabilities
	Mental retardation
	Autism
	Hearing impairment
Nelson (1998)	Central processing factors (e.g., mental retardation, specific language disabilities, autism, acquired brain injury)
	Peripheral sensory and motor system factors (e.g., hearing impairment)
	Environmental and emotional factors (e.g., neglect and abuse)
Owens (1999)	Mental retardation
	Language learning disability
	Specific language impairment
	Pervasive developmental disorder/autism
	Brain injury (traumatic brain injury)
	Early expressive language delay
	Neglect and abuse
Paul (2001)	Mental retardation
	Sensory deficits (e.g., hearing impairment)
	Environmental components (e.g., substance abuse, maltreatment)
	Psychiatric disorders (autism)
	Acquired disorders of communicative function (e.g., traumatic brain injury)
	Specific language disorders

pairment. Each of the authors listed in Table 2.2 talks about the inadequacy of what they term the "etiological approach" (Owens, 1999), "the categorical model" (Paul, 2001), or "biological maturation theories" (Nelson, 1998). Among the limitations and cautions levied at the biologically framed categories are the following:

1. Knowing the etiology does not help in knowing what the child's language will be like.
2. Some children with language problems have no known etiology.
3. Assigning a child to an etiological group implies incorrectly that a language disorder has only one cause.
4. The classification of a child into an etiological group does not help in determining appropriate assessment or intervention approaches to use with the child.

These four criticisms are interesting to analyze in themselves because they reflect what clinicians and teachers would ask from a diagnostic frame that classifies childhood language and literacy disabilities. They want it to be based on the children's language differences, since that is their focus, and they want it to provide a guide to what to do next, since that is their job. The authors who express dissatisfaction with a biologically based frame advocate for another interpretive frame, one that is grounded in information about normal language development and one that is more focused on description of a problem than it is on explanation or prediction of problems. This has been called the "descriptive developmental model" and its focus is on assessment rather than diagnosis (Naremore, 1980; Paul, 2001). (See Chapter 3 for details on how this developmental approach is used for language and literacy assessment.)

Even though these authors advocate for another frame as a substitute for the biological one, they still see advantages to looking for biological etiologies within the medical model. They justify this position by pointing out that:

1. Services are allocated in certain settings according to etiological classifications.
2. Clinicians and teachers need to know the biological underpinnings of childhood language disorders in order to communicate with the medical establishment, which is based in the biological framework.
3. A few biologically based diagnoses, such as hearing impairment, are closely associated with assessment and intervention practices (e.g., in-depth hearing testing and amplification).

4. Knowing the biological origin of a child's language disorder may provide hints about what to expect from that child.

I suggest that the fourth point is the primary reason why these authors want to retain certain etiological classifications. They cannot ignore a large and relevant research literature in childhood language and literacy disabilities that identifies the possible symptoms of given etiologies. In order to present this literature, Owens (1999), for example, associates lists of symptoms with his selected etiological categories. While his symptoms are cast in a descriptive–developmental model, including linguistic and information-processing problems, they are presented as symptoms of biologically based etiologies.

Causal Chains and Causal Networks

There are seldom instances in which a diagnosis carries with it a single cause. Rather, language disorders have many causes, even in the same child. Paul (2001) has identified multiple causality as a problem for diagnosticians:

> Whenever we think that we have found the cause of something, we can always ask, "Well, what caused that?" If we discover that eating large amounts of sugar causes dental caries, we might ask, "Well what causes the sugar to cause the caries?" If we find that sugar increases tooth decay by altering the acidity of the oral cavity to provide a more conducive environment for bacterial growth, we could ask, "Well, why is that level of acidity so conducive to growth of bacteria?" You get the picture. Now, we face the same problem in language pathology. (p. 98)

The description in Paul's paragraph arranges causes in a causal chain where each link in the chain causes problems for the next link in the chain. One might also read into her description the implication that the goings-on at different links are of equal explanatory value. Finally, the example provided presumes the same causal chain for anyone with the diagnosis. The causal chain metaphor may thus misrepresent multiple causes of a language disability for a child whose causes are not temporally linear, are not of equal influence, or whose problem originates in the social context (e.g., poor instruction) rather than from an impairment in the child.

Some investigators have conceptualized a causal frame that extends beyond a set of specific cause–effect relations into a complex of such relations. These frames, because of their structural complexity, resemble models more than they resemble metaphors.

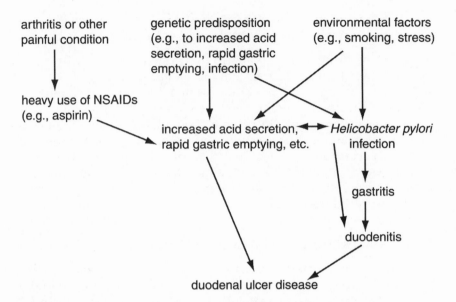

Figure 2.1. Thagard's depiction of a complex causal frame to explain duodenal ulcers. From Thagard (1999, p. 115). Copyright 1999 by Princeton University Press. Reprinted by permission.

Thagard (1999) has offered a model for depicting causality in multiply caused conditions. His example, in Figure 2.1, is a causal network representing several possible causal factors involved in the condition of duodenal ulcers. The network is used to figure out the particular causal patterns for a particular patient:

> For a patient with stomach pains, a physician can start . . . by determining whether the patient takes large quantities of nonsteroidal anti-inflammatory drugs (NSAIDS). Different instantiations can take place on the basis of tests to determine whether the patient's stomach is infected with H. pylori bacteria. . . . The physician might [also discover] that a patient has a hereditary inclination to excess acidity. . . . (p. 114)

Treatment is then based upon where the patient fits in the causal constellation.

Silliman, Butler, and Wallach (2002) have also argued for a complex causal model when arriving at an explanation for why some children have language or reading disabilities. They critique a unidirectional chain that is proposed by some: that language and reading disabilities are caused by a phonological deficit (e.g., Shaywitz, 1996). In place of a unidirectional single causal explanation, they forward a "distributed causality model." Their complex causal model is comparable to Thagard's casual constellation. In it they expand the domains of causality, suggesting that various areas of language difficulties (e.g., phonological, semantic, discourse) can lead to difficulties in other areas, thereby causing general language and literacy difficulties (Silliman et al., 2002, pp. 9–15).

Blaming as Framing

A diagnosis, when received by a family, is often catastrophic. Family members, even those who suspect that a child has difficulties, describe the moment of diagnosis as a shocking experience (Killilea, 1952; Maurice, 1993).

> We were jolted out of the mainstream and were entering into another time and place, one whose scope and boundaries were still unknown to us, but which surely resonated with the dark tones of grief. (Maurice, 1993, p. 26)

The diagnosis sometimes produces a watershed experience requiring a dramatic reframing of their ideas about their child: "My little one whose eyes once upon a time smiled up into mine—where was she? Who was she?" (Maurice, 1993, p. 29). "Stripped of our illusions, we found Anne-Marie to be suddenly alien" (Maurice, 1993, p. 31). For the diagnoses of conditions that require prolonged intervention, family members have been described as going through stages of acceptance of the child and themselves that are not unlike stages describing acceptance of the death of a family member (Blacher, 1984).

Part of the adjustment to a diagnosis involves coping with feelings of blame and shame associated with a family member's newly named disability. (See Table 2.3 for examples of parents' depictions of blame.) The questions that commonly follow upon recognition that the child has a disability, such as "Why did this happen to me?" or "What did I do to deserve this?," are typically asked using interpretive frames of blame and punishment (Coats, 2001; Killilea, 1952). Marie Killilea describes her and her husband's reaction to her daughter's diagnosis of cerebral palsy and mental retardation: "Privately each considered the other's family—was it hereditary? Or worse—somehow is it my fault? Of what am I guilty?" (p. 36). And Catherine Maurice (1993), mother of two children with autism, comments: "Still, if I reacted defensively and with anger to other people's facile psychoanalysis, I nonetheless heaped guilt and blame aplenty on my own head. . . . The problem just had to reside with me. I was a stay-at-home mother. . . . So theoretically I should have been able to give my kids lots of wonderful, nonstressed motherly attention" (p. 13).

Along with this reaction of self-blame, and not necessarily incompatible with it, are reactions of relief, as when families suspect retardation and the doctor confirms the suspicion:

> Another early warning sign was [Jay's] plain dullness. . . . His pediatrician . . . seemed to pooh-pooh my concerns. . . . Had it not been for Dr. Neal Aronson, the neurologist who leveled with me, the entire staff of Johns Hopkins Hospital might have kept me in eternal ignorance. . . . He let me know so gently that all I felt was absolution, the soft vanishing of my present and past anxiety. (Turnbull, 1985, pp. 109–110)

Table 2.3. Various Manifestations of Parental Blame

Mary Akerley (1985) worked with two psychiatrists on issues related to her son's diagnosis of autism, "neither of whom ever came right out and said, 'You caused the problem,' even though both based everything they said on that premise" (p. 25).

Michael Berube (1996) felt blamed for his child's existence by those who advocate abortion for children with Down syndrome (pp. 40–95).

Beth Kephart (1998) attributed her son's developmental delays to her social isolation as a parent: "no play groups, aunt to no nieces or nephews, with a personal calendar absurdly stark and bare" (p. 10).

Marie Killilea (1952) and her husband privately considered whose family might be to blame as a possible genetic cause of their child's newly diagnosed cerebral palsy (p. 35).

Catherine Maurice (1997) worried that her overprotection caused her daughter's slow development: "I knew what the problem was! I had been coddling her too much, overprotecting her" (p. 12).

Annabel Stehli (1991) blamed herself for her daughter's autism at first, agreeing then with Bruno Bettelheim's view that autism was caused by mothers ignoring their children (p. 35).

Leah Ziskin (1985) tried to find a cause for her daughter's retardation: "I mentally reviewed what I had done, persons I had been in contact with, what types of exposure I had possibly had to things that could not be tested for" (p. 68).

Besides having to deal with their own reactions to what caused their child's disabilities, family members must persistently contend with being blamed by others for their child's diagnosis and associated difficulties. For example, professionals who see alcoholism as a willful immorality may blame mothers directly for their child's FAS. Mothers may also have negative reactions to being given prescriptions to enroll in parent training or counseling programs to help them cope better with their child's disability or to help them improve upon their interactions with their child or with other family members (Maurice, 1993, p. 54; Schulz, 1985).

> The current concept of parent training is extremely insulting. Some colleagues told me of an encounter with a young mother and her two boys, aged seven and twelve, both mentally retarded and blind. My associate suggested that parent training was indicated. I wondered at the time who we knew that could tell this mother anything. In fact, I immediately wanted to meet and learn from a woman who had raised children with such complicated problems. (Schulz, 1985, p. 6)

Ironically, a causal frame associated with diagnosis can serve not only to engender blame, but also to redirect and assuage it. For example, children's abnormal behaviors can be explained as being due to the disease or disorder rather than being caused by a lack of home discipline. The disability rather than poor upbringing can be blamed for their children's misbehavior in public or at school. And the disability, rather than poor motivation or outright disobedience, can be seen as the cause of a child's lack of school success.

Finally, there is the element of physician blame associated with the diseases or disorders inadvertently caused by the doctors—the iatrogenic group of diagnoses listed in Table 2.1. For example, a recent article describes potential side effects of various drugs given to children and adults with pervasive developmental disorders, including those with autism. The authors comment:

> Though psychotropics have a role in the management of some symptoms of autism, clinical trial evidence for the use of psychotropics is in its infancy and needs close monitoring. . . . It is also important to recognize that psychotropics can sometimes worsen behaviour, and can produce iatrogenic symptoms. (Santosh & Baird, 2001, p. 427)

In summary, the medical model and its associated ideas related to diagnosis are grounded in various types of causal metaphors. The medical model invites the following kinds of thinking:

1. Abnormal behaviors and sickness are symptoms of underlying disease located in an individual.
2. Abnormal behaviors or sicknesses can occur as identifiable groups, or syndromes.
3. The cause of symptoms or syndromes are called etiologies; once identified, they become the diagnosis of the symptom.
4. There may be several etiologies for a particular set of symptoms that interact in a causal network.
5. In the case of multiply caused syndromes, the patient is said to have several diagnoses, with some serving as primary and the others as secondary.
6. Etiologies can be classified together into similar groups, based upon their biological commonalities (e.g., genetic diseases, infectious diseases).
7. Diseases can sometimes be treated or cured physically with medicine or surgery, or they can be dealt with psychologically with therapies carried out by physicians themselves or prescribed by them for others to carry out.
8. The aim of medical interventions is to establish or restore physical, emotional, and psychological health to the person with the disease.

The first five elements of the medical model are based on causal reasoning: symptoms and syndromes are caused by single or multiple etiologies, some of which are more influential or primary than others. The medical model also favors biologically based interventions founded on the understanding that biological remedies will cause changes in behavior and help to eliminate symptoms of diseases or disorders and thereby promote a healthy physical or psychological state.

I am arguing, then, that the use of causal reasoning based in biological knowledge is what gives the medical model legs to stand on. There are other elements of the medical model that are not directly associated with causality or biology. For example, it presumes that the patient is a passive recipient of medical services (hence the name "patient"). It requires patients to assume a "sick role" and doctors to assume an authoritative role as the ones who know how to cure the sickness or disease. The medical model is, then, a highly complex interpretive frame based on a combination of ideas built from a blending of different models and metaphors, especially those involving biological diagnosis and causal logic.

THE IMPACT OF DIAGNOSES ON CLINICAL AND TEACHING PRACTICES

The medical model has been seen by some speech–language pathologists and teachers as a thorn in their sides. There is a considerable teaching and clinical literature arguing against the biological determinism that can be associated with the medical model, and against educating children in terms of their diagnostic labels. Indeed, the inclusion movement is based on providing equal access to the curriculum for all children, regardless of their biological or psychological classifications. However, there are many instances in which teachers and clinicians are required to think about children in terms of their biological diagnosis, and there are often occasions when this kind of thinking is illuminating.

Often diagnostic reports that are based in a biological/medical model will be included in a child's school or hospital record. The medical report will not only describe an etiology (if it can be identified) but may also contain prescriptions related to specific deficit areas in need of remediation. So children who have been diagnosed as having a biologically based condition prior to school entry bring with them a dictate to regard that child in terms of his or her medical history and biological diagnosis.

Clinical and school assessments also can have elements that draw from a causal frame of the medical model. Family members are interviewed to obtain a "case history." During this process the interviewer typically asks questions aimed at discovering any biological or psychological sources that may have caused or be still causing a child's symptoms. The case history approach is grounded in a biological medical frame involving a search for a diagnosis. In this case of children with potential language or literacy difficulties, the diagnosis would be of a speech–language, hearing, or literacy disability.

A typical assessment report written by a speech–language pathologist is logically structured to fit the medical model. The first section describes the problem, as presented by the family or referral source. The problem is usually stated in terms of symptoms and concerns to be explained via a diagnosis. A case history section provides birth, medical, and developmental history information that would point to a cause for the problem. The test results are provided in terms of areas of deficits that are then summarized as one or more diagnoses (Duchan, 1999).

The therapy approaches of speech–language pathologists are often designed to fit a child's diagnosis. For example, clinicians might draw from the considerable literature on the specific practices recommended for children diagnosed with autism, mental retardation, hearing impairment, or learning disabilities and plan their therapies or classroom activities accordingly.

Similarly, classroom teachers also must deal with a child's biology. Children may be medically fragile, requiring a program for administering medication or curtailing activities. Or they may have a hearing loss, requiring special seating and an amplification system. Or they may have a diagnosis associated with particular symptoms that are not under the conscious control of the child. For example, a teacher may see a child's outbursts as a result of an attention deficit disorder rather than as an intentional attempt by the child to disrupt the class.

So while the medical model in many respects is alien to school professionals who favor an educational or social model, it nonetheless intrudes on them. It behooves both teachers and speech–language pathologists to examine their ways of thinking and to evaluate how and when they are using the medical model and its associated causal metaphors. In this way they will be better able to determine whether its use is enlightening or blinding for understanding children with language and literacy disabilities.

CONCLUSIONS

This chapter has focused on interpretive frames associated with the diagnostic process. I have argued that causal thinking is central to the diagnostic process, and I have identified four causal metaphors that affect how people go about doing diagnosis and interpreting and acting on diagnoses once they are made:

1. Causes of symptoms—inferring a diagnostic etiology from known symptoms.
2. Prediction of symptoms—predicting potential symptoms from a known etiology.
3. Causal chains and networks hierarchies—arranging multiple causes according to direction of influence.
4. Fault finding—assigning causal blame for different diagnoses.

I have talked about the role of causal frames in the enterprise of doing diagnosis and have concluded that diagnosis would not be diagnosis without causal frames. Finally, I have examined the effect that biological causal thinking in diagnosis has on clinical and educational practices, and I have shown that it is ever present despite the discomfort that some speech–language pathologists and teachers feel about "medicalizing" their practices and the children they work with.

What I have yet to talk about is another way to define and interpret children's language and learning disabilities, one that has been called an "assessment approach." This approach is different from a diagnostic one in that it is not as associated with underlying causality, it is not so conceptually tied to a search for biological origins, and it has more to do with description than explanation or prediction. In the next chapter, on frames of assessment, I detail the elements of one such approach, a developmental descriptive approach, and the frames within which it is understood.

THREE

Assessment Frames

In the last 50 years several new models have come into use, either working alongside or serving as a replacement for the medical model. These new models have been developed to do what clinicians call *language assessment*. Assessment is more focused on describing the psychological or linguistic areas in which a child has difficulty than on explaining them by discovering their biological origins. (See Chapter 2 for more on this distinction.) Because assessments result in identifying deficits, they are sometimes treated as diagnoses. That is, they are used as explanations, rather than as descriptions of a child's difficulties. An assessment might find, for example, that a child has a problem in a particular area of language processing, such as auditory memory or sound blending, with the result that the defined problem area is then interpreted as the cause for the child having difficulties with auditory memory or sound-blending tasks. But the cause, in this case, is based on the child's processing or knowledge differences or difficulties rather than on a condition outside the domain of deficit. When the descriptive label resulting from an assessment is in the same conceptual domain as other difficulties being described in that domain, it has its feet in the assessment frame. This is the case even when the label is used to explain rather than to describe the condition. So when a child's problem is classified as being due to hyperactivity or language–literacy disabilities from the results of an assessment protocol, the label can serve both as a diagnosis, explaining the symptoms of hyperactivity or learning difficulties, and as a label, describing the types of problems the child has.

Two primary models that been used to assess children with language and literacy disabilities. Assessments resulting in the identification of processing problems are based on a *processing model*. Besides identifying processing problems, assessments are often done to identify areas of knowledge in which a child is deficient, such as syntax or phonology. Assessment of knowledge domains are carried out at different linguistic levels, such as phonology, morphology, syntax, semantics, or pragmatics. These sorts of assessments are governed by a *linguistic model*.

Assessing a child's language knowledge results in discovering what linguistic knowledge domains are less developed than would be expected. More detailed assessment results in a description of what the child knows or doesn't know about language in that domain. For example, a child might have difficulty understanding relative clauses in the domain of syntax.

Once the deficiencies are identified, IEP goals are developed. Table 3.1 contains examples of the IEP goals that were established for a child with a cochlear implant following a linguistic assessment. The goals identify the deficit area and focus on particular structures within that area that require development.

The areas identified by the information-processing and linguistic knowledge frames have been called "specific abilities." Assessments done to ascertain children's competence in these areas are thus said to have a *specific abilities* orientation (Lahey, 1988, pp. 92–121). There are various ways of going about assessing information-processing and linguistic knowledge, depending upon what version of an information-processing or linguistic model is used.

INFORMATION-PROCESSING MODELS

One commonly used model for assessing children's language and literacy skills focuses on how well they process information. Information-processing models typically depict various abilities that go into language processing. The abilities are often placed in separate boxes with labeled directional arrows linking the boxes to one another (see Figure 3.1). The boxes in these "box-and-arrow" render-

Table 3.1. IEP Goals Resulting from Assessments of a Child's Language at Different Linguistic Levels

Phonology (articulation)

Annual goal: Child will complete dissolution of phonological processes.

Short-term objective: Child will eliminate syllabic structure processes by producing final consonants in 20 different contexts with a 50% level of accuracy.

Morphology

Annual goal: Child will develop the understanding and use of verbs.

Child will develop the understanding of an appropriate use of the present progressive tense as well as singular/plural auxiliary verbs by constructing sentences properly utilizing "is" + verb + "ing" with a 50% level of accuracy.

Short-term objectives: Child will develop the understanding and proper use of regular past tense verb forms by constructing sentences properly using regular past tense verb forms with a 50% level of accuracy.

Child will develop the understanding and correct use of irregular past tense verbs by properly using irregular past tense verbs in conversational speech with a 50% level of accuracy.

Semantics

Annual goal: Child will improve understanding and responses to "wh" interrogatives.

Short-term objective: Child will improve comprehension, formulation and responses to "who" questions by formulating "who" questions regarding a presented picture with a 90% level of accuracy.

Note. Data from Itsy Bitsy Webs (2002).

ings (Baker, Croot, McLeod, & Paul, 2001) are often arranged in both vertical and horizontal rows showing the pathways of travel for information. One pathway is usually portrayed as beginning at the bottom level of the right side of the model where peripheral (sensory) processing takes place. It proceeds to the top level, which involves central (conceptual) processing abilities. A second pathway for information processing begins at the middle top of the model and travels down the right side, ending in motor production. The left side of the model is the input side, depicting information reception; the top middle is the cognitive component, depicting comprehension; and

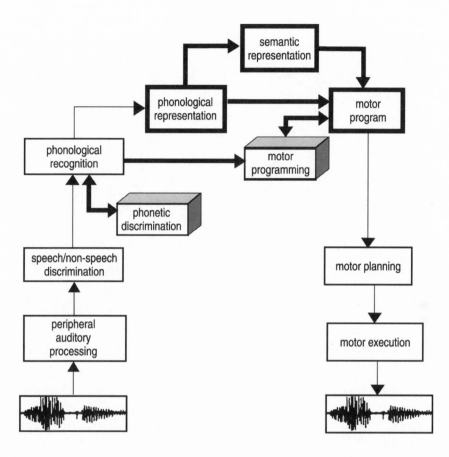

Figure 3.1. Stackhouse and Wells's speech processing model. From Stackhouse and Wells (1997, p. 350). Copyright 1997 by Whurr. Reprinted by permission.

the right side depicts the processes involved in speech or language expression.

Some information-processing models are more specialized, showing the details of a particular kind of processing. For example, Baddeley (1998) has developed a model for working memory (see Figure 3.2). This area of processing would be but one box in a larger information-processing picture, a box that would be located early in the reception pathway of information processing.

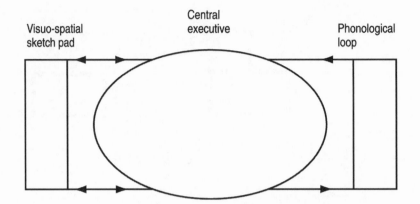

Figure 3.2. Baddeley's information-processing model of working memory. From Baddeley (1998, p. 52). Copyright 1990. Published by Allyn & Bacon. Copyright 1998 by Pearson Education. Reprinted by permission of the publisher.

Metaphors Used in Information-Processing Models

Information-processing models combine the imagery of several metaphors (see Table 3.2). One primary metaphor is a *spatial* one, as can be seen in depictions of processing at the bottom and top. The "top" and "bottom" in the descriptions refer to the placement of the boxes and arrows. Processes taking place in the boxes at the top of the model have been called "higher order" processes. They have also been described as "deeper" processing, with steps up the processing system being described as requiring increasing "depth of processing" (Craik & Tulving, 1975). The spatial metaphor is also the source of the "bottom-up" and "top-down" terminology used when describing the flow of information through the system. Finally, there is a spatial representation for each of the boxes. They are depicted as containers of information or as storage locations, with some models even depicting the way the information is spatially organized within a box (e.g, Morrisette & Gierut, 2002). In order to get the information out of the box, one must "go to" the box, find or "access" the desired information in it, and then "retrieve" the information for use—all notions that depend upon a spatial metaphor related to a storage space.

Table 3.2. Metaphors Found in Information-Processing Models and Examples of Their Use

Metaphor	Examples of the metaphor's use
Spatial metaphor	Higher order processing Bottom-up versus top-down processing Depth of processing Storage of information in memory Need to "go to" memory storage to retrieve information.
Flow and pathway metaphors	Processing pathways Processing channels
Energy metaphor	Energy overload
Temporal metaphor	Temporal capacity Temporal processing abilities Speed of processing abilities Slow processing problems
Computational metaphor	Serial processing Parallel processing Input and output modalities Knowledge networks

There are also *flow* and *pathway metaphors* that are used to support the ideas in an information-processing system. Information "flows" over pathways from lower to higher (bottom-up) and from higher to lower (top-down) destinations.

Several different metaphors have been employed to express a general notion of the scarcity of resources available for processing information. This notion of limitations on processing resources has been used to account for children's communication difficulties in several ways. The processing boxes and the system that they are part of are depicted as having a finite capacity that can become overloaded, causing processing breakdowns. Some theorists and practitioners convey the limitation as a problem of limited *energy* similar to what would happen if fuel runs out or electrical circuits short out (Kirsh, 2000). The notions of "load" and "overload" can be associated with this energy metaphor. Others portray the limited capacity in *spatial* terms wherein memory storage space is exceeded (Gathercole & Baddeley, 1990). *Temporal* limitations are also used to account for children's language or communication difficulties. In this case the speed at which the system responds to information is regarded as being too slow to keep up with the speed of incoming information. This results in special difficulties processing stimuli of brief duration (Catts, Gillispie, Leonard, Kail, & Miller, 2002; Ellis Weismer & Hesketh, 1996; Leonard, 1989; Tallal, 1976). The speed hypothesis has also been used when accounting for the difficulties children with specific language impairment have in speech production, resulting in an inconsistency in their use of grammatical inflections such as plural endings or the past tense (Bishop, 1994).

Another frame common to information-processing models is the *computation metaphor* (Sternberg, 1990). The processing work that takes place in the boxes is frequently likened to computing. Discussions of children's language problems are sometimes rendered in terms of "parallel processing," to describe processing activity going on in different regions of the processing model at the same time, and as "serial processing," to describe sequential steps in a processing pathway. Parallel processing is seen as having advantages over serial processing because it allows for faster computation and offers new kinds of programming, relying less on the use of hierarchical structures (Thagard, 1986). On occasion, "online processing," or language processing that goes on in "real time," as the language is being experienced, is contrasted with processing that takes place "off line," before or after one hears or says something (e.g., Stackhouse & Wells, 1997).

Comparison of Different Information-Processing Models

Different information-processing models used in assessment have different labels on the boxes, reflecting the theoretical emphasis of the person doing the assessing. One model that often appears as a historical reference point in basic textbooks on childhood language disorders is an adaptation of the model developed by Charles Osgood (1953). Osgood's model, intended to represent language processing in humans, was based on behaviorism, a theory of behavior having to do with the associations between stimuli and responses. Osgood regarded language processing as a series of different types of stimulus–response connections. The types varied depending upon the sensory or motor channel or pathway used (auditory, visual, tactile, motor, etc.), the level of representation at which the associations were made (sensory, perceptual, or representational), and whether the stimulus–response connections involved reception, organization, or expression of information.

Osgood's students, Samuel Kirk and James McCarthy, used Osgood's model to develop a test called the Illinois Test of Psycholinguistic Abilities (ITPA; Kirk & McCarthy, 1961). They took some of Osgood's information-processing boxes and designed a subtest to go with each one so they could evaluate children's competencies in that particular area of information processing. There were subtests to assess a child's abilities to process visual or auditory stimuli, to associate the stimuli with learned responses or learned representations, and to produce motor or verbal responses. The resulting profile of ITPA assessment was used by clinicians and teachers as a focus for their intervention. Commercial programs were designed to fit the ITPA model, with suggested activities to remediate the child's problems in different areas of processing (Karnes, 1968; Minskoff, Wiseman, & Minskoff, 1972).

Baker et al. (2001) have compared different box-and-arrow models for speech processing. They show how boxes might represent different things—they may depict the steps through which speech sounds get interpreted, or the steps involved in interpreting words, or the steps that are involved in translating articulatory movements into spoken words.

A more recent, elaborate, and influential speech-processing model has been proposed by Stackhouse and Wells (1997) (see Figure 3.1, p. 45). It, like its predecessors, separates boxes involving processing of incoming information (peripheral auditory processing, speech–nonspeech discrimination, and phonological recognition) from those boxes that involve processing of output information (motor planning, motor execution). The Stackhouse and Wells model differs from other models in its middle section. Here they have an elaborate set of boxes that do what Stackhouse and Wells call "offline" processing (the bolded and shaded boxes, including phonetic discrimination, phonological representation, semantic representation, and motor programming). These middle processes are nonobservable, meditative processes that occur after speech sounds are heard and before they are spoken.

The Stackhouse and Wells model also differs from earlier ones in that the model is less unidirectional in its information flow, and more particular and detailed in what it covers. Finally, Stackhouse and Wells give the middle or higher order part of information processing a more prominent role than did many of their predecessors.

Another recent example of an information-processing model focuses on one area of processing: working memory. This model, offered by Baddeley (1998), is an active information-processing unit that temporarily stores and manipulates information. It is made up of three components: a central executive component, a phonologi-cal loop, and a visual–spatial scratch pad (Baddeley, 1998; Gathercole & Baddeley, 1990). (See Figure 3.2, p. 46.) The phonological loop and the visual–spatial scratch pad serve similar functions: to process in-formation when the central executive component is overloaded. The loop and the scratch pad store information just after it enters the system, for very short periods of time. The primary role of the phono-logical loop is to aid children in learning new words. This loop serves to keep unfamiliar sound patterns active while the higher order memory records them for more permanent storage (Baddeley, Gath-ercole, & Papagno, 1998).

Summary of Information-Processing Assessment Models

The models discussed above can be summarized as follows:

1. The emphasis of processing models is on activity as opposed to knowledge representation. The processing models involve actions performed on information, such as identifying it, transforming it, storing it, retrieving it, and remembering it. Processing is to knowledge as verbs are to nouns, as action is to thing, as bouncing is to ball.
2. Processing approaches to assessment regard encoding and decoding information as being a critical part of communica-tion.
3. The aim of assessment based on information-processing mod-els is to discover what types (boxes) of processing are deficient.
4. Assessment of the different areas of a child's processing is done separately, with little focus on how the areas integrate, although some writers are uncomfortable with this division (e.g., Butler, 1975).
5. Information-processing models presume that a child's prob-lems in one or more areas of processing can cause general communication problems.

THE LINGUISTIC MODEL

The linguistic model is an alternative to the information-processing model of assessment. Using linguistic frames for assessment is a fa-miliar system to those in the fields of children's language and liter-acy. The linguistic model has been used to determine whether children know what they need to know about the linguistic rules that govern their speech, language, and literacy performance. The types of rules vary, depending upon the level of linguistics and modality being examined. The linguistic levels include phonology, morphology, syntax, and some parts of pragmatics. Semantics and other parts of pragmatics have not been found to be particularly amenable to linguistic renderings (e.g., the structuring of discourse or social interactions).

A rule is usually depicted as a deep-structure algorithm or formula that takes an underlying linguistic form and changes it to make it ready for linguistic interpretation or production. Phonological rules simplify words; morphological rules add words or meaningful forms together to create more complex words; and syntactic rules combine words into phrases and sentences, creating the hierarchical tree structures that make up the grammatical system.

Phonology Assessment

Speech and Phonological Rules

The use of phonological rules to assess children's mispronunciations is relatively new to the field of speech–language pathology (Ingram, 1976; Lund & Duchan, 1978). Prior to its development, children's speech problems were typically described by comparing errors in the production of sounds (substitutions, omissions or distortions) to the correct production of sounds. The typical assumption when a misarticulation was found was that the child had a problem somewhere in his or her perceptual motor system, causing him or her either to misperceive the sound (perceptual), to misarticulate it (motor), or both.

The phonological approach, on the other hand, describes the errors by hypothesizing conceptual rules that children might be using that result in their incorrect speech productions. This shift to a linguistic-based conceptualization of children's speech errors from a perceptual–motor one created a minor revolution in the field (Baker et al., 2001; Camarata, 1995). The name of these children's difficulty was changed from "articulation disorder" to "phonological disorder." The attributed source of the difficulty also changed. The previous view was that speech problems arose from perceptual or motor difficulties that caused problems with learning individual sounds or features of sounds. In comparison, the phonological view portrays speech problems as arising from the use of a conceptually based phonological rule that applies to groups of sounds.

Table 3.3. Practice Differences between Linguistic and Perceptual–Motor Models of Speech Problems

	Linguistic view	Perceptual–motor view
Name of the problem	Phonological disorder	Articulation disorder
Nature of the speech problem	A phonological disorder results from problems with the application of linguistic process rules	An articulation disorder results from problems with perception or motor production of speech sounds or features
The unit in focus	Words and groups of sounds—the units to which the phonological rules apply	The individual phoneme or place, manner, or voicing features of phonemes
Assessment approaches to discover the child's specific difficulties	Phonological process analysis of a naturally occurring speech sample or of a child's performance on a picture-naming test	Error analysis of phoneme production on a picture-naming articulation test for substitution, omission, or distortion of sounds or of sound features
Normative data	Age norms of phonological process acquisition	Age norms of acquisition of individual phonemes or phoneme features
Therapies	Activities that promote rule induction (focused stimulation, minimal pair contrasts, auditory bombardment)	Activities that promote articulatory accuracy (phonetic placement, imitation of sounds, practice drills of sounds in isolation, syllables, words, discrimination drills)

(See Table 3.3 for a comparison of linguistic and perceptual–motor models of speech problems.)

Clinicians who assess the phonology underlying children's misarticulations aim to identify abstract phonological rules or processes governing children's speech errors. The phonological process view of speech sound production classifies children's errors into phonological processes that operate like a formula to change adult phonological forms. The rules are sometimes called "simplification processes" because they serve to make the words easier to say. For example, children under age 4 often use the phonological processes of fronting (they substitute sounds produced using the front of the mouth, such as /t/ or /d/, for sounds using the back of the mouth, such as /k/ or /g/) or stopping (they substitute stop sounds, such as /t/ or /d/, for fricative sounds, such as /s/ or /z/).

In order to discover the child's speech errors, speech–language pathologists may give the child a test, such as having him or her name objects or pictures that have targeted sounds in them (Hodson, 1980), or they may encourage the child to talk so that spontaneously produced errors are revealed (Ingram, 1976). Once the errors are collected, they are then analyzed for their patterns. Some of the patterns governing children's errors are typical of children of certain age groups. For example, the fronting error is usual for children below 4 years of age, but is considered abnormal when used by children who are 5 and older. So errors are assessed as phonological problems only if they are below what is expected of children in the child's *cohort group* (i.e., children who are the same age or at the equivalent level of development). This developmental criterion is integral to all assessment. It contains underlying assumptions that follow from yet another frame: a growth model (see below).

Reading and Phonology

Phonological understandings in reading, like speaking and listening, are treated as fundamental to success. Children's phonological awareness, for example, is often assessed as a means for predicting reading success or as a way to identify the source of a child's reading difficulties. Phonological awareness, a kind of linguistic knowledge, includes such things as (1) awareness of the constituent syllables of words, (2) awareness of the beginning (onset) and endings (rime) of words, and (3) awareness of the individual sounds in words. Similarly, the alphabetic principle and a child's ability to decode words require that the child associate sounds with different letters and letter combinations, a skill that is sometimes depicted as linguistic in nature. So, like for speech errors, assessing children's reading errors can provide a teacher with valuable information about their phonological understandings and misunderstandings, thereby accounting for their reading mistakes (K. Goodman, 1965; Y. Goodman, 1986).

Writing and Phonology

One of the most interesting recent developments in children's literacy has been the study of the linguistic logic underpinning children's invented spellings (Treiman & Bourassa, 2000). Some linguistically based examples of their creative misspellings are the following:

1. They often use a letter name rather than letter sounds to spell their words. For example, "light" is spelled "LIT," using the pronunciation of the vowel name "I" ("eye").
2. They insert a vowel in each syllable of a word in order to mark the unit as a syllable—for example, by spelling "miss" as "mes."
3. They insert letters where they don't belong in words, following their observation that sometimes letters are silent.

Morphology Assessment

Morphology and Spoken Language

When assessing children's oral language, speech–language pathologists typically focus on what linguists have called "inflectional morphology." That is, they examine the children's grammatical markings of prefixes or suffixes, with a particular focus on word endings, such as plural markers for nouns (cat/s̲/, dog/z̲/, or glass/e̲z̲/) or third-person-singular markers on verbs (hit/s̲/, give/z̲/, bounc/e̲z̲/).

In order to discover whether the child has difficulty in forming the common word endings required in English, speech–language pathologists collect and examine the child's use of word endings with a particular focus on errors. Collection of endings may involve elicitation procedures such as giving a child a sentence completion task (Mary has a book. John has two _____.) (Berko, 1958). Or speech–language pathologists might create more open contexts and engage the child in a talking event such as a conversation, storytelling, or a picture description activity (Lund & Duchan, 1993; Rice & Wexler, 2001). The child's language is audio- or videorecorded and later transcribed and analyzed for how the child expresses word inflections (e.g., Lund & Duchan, 1993; Miller, 1981). The emphasis in standardized morphological tests is to test for inflections that are frequently used and that are early to develop. Owens (1999) puts it this way: "Most tests emphasize suffixes, such as tense markers, plurals, possessives, and comparators, because of their high usage and relatively early development" (p. 82).

Once a pattern of errors is discovered, it is compared with those produced by typical children in an age or stage comparison group to see whether it is similar to or below what would be expected. Roger Brown (1973b), in his classic study of three children's development of morphology, for example, provided a developmental picture of 14 commonly occurring morphemes, most of which are inflectional morphemes. Assessments of children's morphological development have been geared to the discovery of those same 14 morphemes in children, to compare their development with Brown's developmental norms as well as norms in subsequent studies (e.g., de Villiers & de Villiers, 1973).

Studies of typically developing children revealed that they did not learn inflectional morphemes all at once but in a predictable order. The sequential order of acquisition was represented by comparing the acquisition of the morphemes to the length of the sentence in which they occurred. This index, commonly known as an *MLU* (mean length of utterance in morphemes), divided children's language development into five stages, ranging from an MLU of one morpheme to an average of five or more morphemes per utterance (Brown, 1973b).

The ages at which typical children arrive at the different stages have been used as a comparison standard for children's morphology development. Children who perform below what would be expected for their age are identified as having *morphological deficits*—that is, as not being where they need to be in their learning of morphological rules. The linguistic model, therefore, when used to assess whether children are developing as they should, has a *normative model* built into it, tying it to a *growth model* (see more on this below.)

Morphology and Written Language

When children spell, they are helped considerably by their basic morphological understandings. If they do not have a full grasp of inflectional morphology, they are likely to leave off word endings in their writing or to misspell them. For example, unless they understand past tense structuring, they will not understand the linguistic logic underlying the different spelling of "round" and "owned." Another key to later spelling is the morphological patterns found in the derivation of words such as "electric"/"electricity."

Syntax Assessment

Children's syntactic performance is based on the rules that children use to combine words into phrases and sentences. Just as with assessing phonology and morphology, assessing children's syntactic knowledge requires collecting examples of syntax in use. In this case the samples are of phrases and sentences. Methods for sampling syntax production have included picture descriptions (Lee, 1971), sentence imitation tasks (Carrow, 1974), and naturally occurring language such as conversation, storytelling, and event descriptions (Lund & Duchan, 1993; Miller, 1981).

Children use syntactic rules to interpret as well as to produce syntactic constructions. Syntactic rules parse strings of words by grouping them into phrases, clauses, and sentences. The syntactic groups are related to one another hierarchically, with some groups embedded in others. This is often depicted metaphorically as a tree or as a set of nested boxes. Syntactic trees have nodes (joints at junctures of branches) at different levels. Nodes at a higher level branch into nodes at a lower level. (The trees are really more like roots since they grow down, with a central "trunk" or node usually depicted at the top.) The relationship between the nodes in the tree is one of governance or control. Higher level or "mother" nodes control lower level or "daughter" nodes.

This *vegetation metaphor* involving trees, branches, and roots is used to describe the shape of the linguistic structure. The *kinship metaphor*, involving mother, sister, and daughter nodes, describes their nested relationships. These metaphors have been adopted by linguists to aid in their own and others' conceptualization of the relationships between linguistic categories.

Syntax begins for typically developing children when they first combine words into two- or three-unit strings (Bloom, 1973), and continues to develop until children can produce complex, multiply embedded, clausal structures. Children who do not meet the expected syntactic level of children in their age or developmental group are identified as having syntax deficiencies. Such identification results from combining the linguistic assessment model with a normative one.

Semantic Relations: Are They Rules?

Semantics is that area of linguistics that involves meaning interpretation. Semantics includes single- and multiple-word meanings, sentence meanings, and discourse meanings. Children's acquisition of semantic knowledge does not fit the linguistic model if the latter is defined as rule-based. For phonology, morphology, and syntax, there are identifiable rules that serve to create or transform linguistic components into new forms. Sometimes the rules simplify, as in the case of phonological rules that produce phonological errors. In other cases the application of rules results in more complex structures. Morphological inflectional rules do this by adding forms together to create a new amalgam, while syntactic rules do this by creating complex tree arrangements out of simpler ones. It would be nice if there were semantic rules that took meaning forms and translated them into simpler or more complex versions, but the efforts of linguists working out a theory of generative semantics to discover such rules has been deemed unsuccessful (Matthews, 1997).

One of the reasons that meanings are difficult to characterize using formal rules is that the unit of language that carries semantic meaning is hard to identify. Many researchers and clinicians focus on meanings associated with morphemes when they go about determining young children's acquisition of semantics. Others analyze semantic features of words in particular semantic domains, sometimes referred to as "prototypes" (e.g., Rosch, 1981). Still others call upon conceptual strategies rather than linguistic ones to explain children's semantic learning. For example, Markman (1990) hypothesizes that children approach the task of early word learning by assuming that any new word will refer to whole objects rather than to parts of objects or to qualities of objects.

Another reason for the difficulty in assigning linguistic rules to semantics is that word combinations carry more meaning than the individual words that make them up. Interpreting an utterance such as "mommy's sock" does not involve adding up the meanings of "mommy" and "sock." Rather, the phrase means something beyond its components: the sock is an object that is owned by, belongs to, or is associated with mother. Similarly, meanings of sentences are something more than the meanings of the individual words that are used in the sentences.

The closest an analyst can come to ascribing linguistic rules to children's semantic learning is to focus on children's two-word utterances. For example, when a child says two words, such as "mommy sock," she is considered to be using a combinatorial semantic rule that somehow marks "mommy" as an attribute, in which case she would mean "This sock is mommy's." Or she may be applying a rule to depict "mommy" as an agent, in which case she would be meaning "Mommy, put my sock on me." (See Bloom, 1970, for details on this particular example, used by her 2-year-old subject, Kathryn.)

There are some 10 of these two-word semantic relations that have been found in children's two-word utterances (Bloom & Lahey, 1978; Brown, 1973a). With surprisingly little variation, this list seems to represent the meaning of children's first words whatever their language or culture. Thus, the list of semantic relations and relational rules has become a universal checklist for evaluating children's two-word utterances all over the world.

A typical approach for discovering the semantics of a particular child's two-word utterances is to take a sample of the child's spontaneous language, and then to determine which of the meanings in the checklist the two-word utterances best fit. The use of checklists of semantic relations involves taking on the idea that semantic combinations work like syntactic ones. Word meanings for words in combination are derived through the use of predictable, productive rules. These checklists therefore presuppose a linguistic model.

Where Does Pragmatics Fit In?

If semantics seems to be a stepchild of linguistic approaches, not quite fitting into the linguistic model that associates abstract deep-structure rules with their surface forms, pragmatics is even more so. Modern-day pragmatics originated in the discipline of philosophy in the late 1960s with speech act theory (Austin, 1962; Searle, 1969). Speech acts have to do with the utilitarian function of utterances. For example, when a child points to an out-of-reach-object and says "want," he is using his language to request an object. Or if a child pushes an object away and says "no," she is using her language to refuse an object. The speech or communicative act serves to attain a goal or objective. It is thereby described using a *tool metaphor* or a *functional metaphor*. Utterances, like hammers, are used as tools to accomplish a purpose. Different utterances serve different functions (purposes).

The early work in pragmatics involved identifying the functions or purposes of the first communicative attempts by children. Researchers classified children's earliest communicative gestures and utterances into groupings based on common functions, such as requests, comments, greetings, and so on (Dore, 1973, 1975; Halliday, 1975). (See Chapman, 1981, for a detailed summary of these studies.)

These groupings of single communicative acts, later termed *communicative intents* or *communicative functions*, were employed in the design of assessment tools aimed at discovering whether children with suspected language learning difficulties used the same types of intents as normal language learners, and, if not, how their intents differed (Coggins & Carpenter, 1981; Prizant & Duchan, 1981). Efforts were also made to discover the intents underlying unconventional behavior, such as echolalia in children with autism (Prizant & Duchan, 1981) and nonverbal aberrant behavior in those with severe communication disabilities (Donnellan, Miranda, Mesaros, & Fassbender, 1984).

Communicative acts are among the first communications attributed to children. They begin at age 9 months or so when children develop notions about how to attain their goals (Bates, Camaioni, & Volterra, 1975), and they continue to develop into elaborate and subtle manipulations (Tough, 1977). As for other, more linguistically based, aspects of language development, developmental stages and inventories of communicative acts have been documented. However, unlike for phonology and syntax, these acts are not presumed to be derived from linguistic rules. Rather, they can even be carried out nonverbally, originating in understandings of accomplishing goals.

Since its emergence in the 1970s, pragmatics has sprouted. It does not fit into a formal linguistic framework having to do with language-based rules, so it has less stringent requirements for what sorts of entities fit within its domain. With ill-defined boundaries, pragmatics has come to include many non-rule-like aspects of communication.

Pragmatics is now an umbrella term covering areas as disparate as social and interactional competencies and discourse abilities. For example, assessments of children's pragmatics abilities might include their use of politeness forms, their ability to accomplish appropriate conversational turn taking and repairs if the conversation breaks down, their ability to initiate and maintain topics in conversation, and their ability to assume the other's perspective when they engage in discourse (see Prutting & Kirchner, 1983, for discussion of these and other domains that have been classified as part of pragmatics).

Unlike most areas of pragmatics, there are a couple that have been represented as rule-governed in a linguistic or grammatical way. One is the area of narratives, with the most well-known being Stein and Glenn's (1979) use of tree structures to generate stories. These authors have hypothesized a linguistic tree structure to represent children's recall of Aesop's fables. The trees have branches that stem from nodes. At one end, usually the top, is a single node, the story. Then the tree branches into two or more branches, to become a setting and episodes. Each episode, in turn, consists of a string of elements or lower level branches: an initiating event, the main character's internal response, the character's plan, the character's attempt to solve the problem, the consequence of the plan, and the character's reaction to the events of the story. Multiple-episode stories are depicted as nested structures that may hold temporal, additive, or causal relationships with one another (Stein & Glenn, 1979).

A second linguistic rule-like domain found in pragmatics is discourse markers. These linguistic cuing devices, such as "so," "and," "anyway," or "however," signal the logical relationships between different segments of discourse. For example, a "so" at the end of an expository or narrative, marks the next segment as a summary or conclusion (e.g., Schiffrin, 1987; Segal, Duchan, & Scott, 1991) and a "then" indicates a shift in perspective (Duchan, Meth, & Waltzman, 1992).

Characteristics of the Linguistic Model: A Summary

The linguistic model, when used to guide assessment practices in the field of language and literacy disabilities, does the following:

1. Focuses on what children know about their language and how they represent that knowledge to themselves.
2. Depicts information, whenever possible, at different levels of language in terms of rules. The levels or domains of language are phonology, morphology, syntax, semantics, and pragmatics.
3. Usually treats linguistic levels separately, rather than as an integrated system, although there is an acknowledgment by some that the separate areas interrelate (e.g., Bloom, 1978; Chapman et al., 1992; McGregor & Leonard, 1995).
4. Assumes that linguistic problems in one modality, say, speaking, will be manifested in other areas, such as writing and reading.

A BLEND OF INFORMATION-PROCESSING AND LINGUISTIC MODELS

Information-processing and linguistic assessment models are often blended into what has been dubbed a *descriptive developmental framework* by Paul (2001, p. 17) and the *communication–language orientation* by Bloom & Lahey (1978) and Lahey (1988, p. 121). Others have referred to such combined models as *psycholinguistic models,* with the psychological side being the boxes involving information processing and the linguistic side being the levels of linguistic knowledge and rules being processed (Baker, et al., 2001).

Two of the more popular blends of information-processing and linguistic models have been used to depict *central auditory processing* and *language processing*. Let's look at each in turn.

The information-processing side of central auditory-processing models focuses primarily on auditory processing (for early examples, see Myklebust, 1952, and Eisenson, 1972). The emphasis on auditory over other modalities is due to the focus of speech–language and audiology professionals on spoken communication conveyed auditorily.

The auditory-processing models are reminiscent of the information-processing approaches discussed above, but they are confined to the auditory modality. Because of their specialization, they tend to represent auditory information in more specified ways than do the more general information-processing models. The

Table 3.4. Auditory Models of Central Auditory Processing

American Speech–Language–Hearing Association (1996b)

1. Sound localization and lateralization
2. Auditory discrimination
3. Auditory pattern recognition
4. Temporal aspects of audition, including temporal resolution, temporal masking, temporal integration, temporal ordering
5. Auditory performance decrements with competing acoustic signals
6. Auditory performance decrements with degraded acoustic signals

Aram and Nation (1982): Auditory operations

1. Auditory attention
2. Auditory rate
3. Auditory discrimination
4. Auditory memory
5. Auditory sequencing

Sanders (1977): Aspects of auditory processing

1. Awareness of acoustic stimuli
2. Localization
3. Attention
4. Differentiation between speech and nonspeech
5. Auditory discrimination
   a. Suprasegmental discrimination
   b. Segmental discrimination
6. Auditory memory
7. Sequencing
8. Auditory synthesis

most advanced areas of auditory processing represented in these models have been referred to metaphorically as *higher-order process-ing* or *central auditory processing*. Also, unlike the more general information-processing models that describe both comprehension and production, input and output, auditory-processing models usually confine their attention to the input side.

Central auditory-processing models vary considerably. Some are represented as box-and-arrow models, arranged serially (Aram & Na-tion; 1982, Osgood, 1953), others in parallel (e.g., Bishop, 1997). Still others are in the form of short unordered lists of different audi-tory skills (Aram & Nation, 1982; American Speech–Language–Hear-ing Association, 1996b; Sanders, 1977). Audiologists usually forward models that are confined to processing of auditory signals, with less emphasis on language knowledge (e.g., American Speech–Language–Hearing Association, 1996b; also see Table 3.4). Indeed, audiologists often make an effort to differentiate auditory processing from lan-guage processing and to distinguish children with central auditory disorders from those with language disorders.

Speech–language pathologists, on the other hand, typically see auditory and language processing as part of one model, operating in either serial or parallel ways. They sometimes call their models *language-processing models* or *psycholinguistic models* as a way of distinguishing them from the central auditory-processing models that do not include phonological, morphological, or syntactic rule representations (Butler, 1983; Duchan & Katz, 1983). Language-processing models are different from linguistic models in that they go beyond linguistic rule representations to consider how those rules are processed. These models are likely to have a place for pro-cesses such as attention, memory, and cognitive strategies, along with a representation of linguistic knowledge (Butler, 1983).

Recent language-processing models, for example, have included *working memory*, drawing from Baddeley's theory of information processing (Baddeley, 1998; Dollaghan & Campbell, 1998; Ellis Weismer & Hesketh, 1996). Working memory qualifies as a language-processing model rather than as an auditory-processing one because it has a phonological loop that provides individuals with the ability to rehearse linguistic units for up to 2 seconds af-ter they are heard.

Various methods in the research literature have been developed to assess children's working memory. Such assessments have been offered as a way to determine whether children have memory-processing defi-cits, and also as a way to discover the source of difficulties with learning new words (Ellis Weismer, 1996) and with sentence comprehension (Montgomery, 1996). Tasks in these assessment approaches include having the children repeat nonsense words (Dollaghan & Campbell, 1998; Ellis Weismer, Tomblin, Shang, Buckwalter, & Jones, 2000) and varying the rate of presentation of words in word-learning tasks (Ellis Weismer & Hesketh, 1996).

As has been seen, the information-processing and linguistic models have been blended in different ways. Some have the linguistic knowledge involved in all levels of language processing, from peripheral sound detection (knowledge separating speech from noise, or knowledge of linguistic features involved in phoneme recognition) to discourse interpretation. Others reserve the language analysis components for the highest order levels of processing and assign the lower order processing jobs to a nonlinguistic auditory component (Duchan & Katz, 1983). While these different blends are often the subject of controversy, sometimes represented as clashes between top-down versus bottom-up versions of processing, they both are built upon the same two frameworks: information-processing and linguistic models.

VERSIONS OF THE GROWTH MODEL

A big part of assessment is to ascertain whether the child being assessed is developing normally. The concept of "normal" contains a notion of comparison. What is considered normal and what kinds of departures from normal are taken as signs of abnormal depend (You guessed it!) on the frame used to judge "normality."

Notions of normality, when associated with age and development, are grounded in a conceptual model having to do with growth. "Normal growth" is what children who are successful in school do. Children with difficulties are seen as growing in abnormal or below-normal ways. A *growth model* takes on different characteristics depending upon how one conceives of growth and what it is that is seen as growing.

One common way of measuring that growth is in terms of *biological maturation*. According to this version, growth is seen as a biological unfolding of abilities. The metaphoric parallel has to do with what goes on with physical growth of limbs and fingers (Ingram, 1989, Ch. 2). The child's development is seen as evolutionary, having more to do with genetic and biological determination than with environmental influences.

A second way growth has been depicted is from a *constructivist view*. In this type of growth model the child is conceptualized as an active learner, an acquirer of knowledge. The child takes what he or she knows and constructs new knowledge based upon his or her environmental context.

A third type of growth model used to assess normality and developmental progress is a *behavioral one*. This model regards children's gains in proficiency as the addition of new responses or the generalization of stimulus–response associations to new contexts.

The Maturational Growth Model

Subscribers to a maturational view of growth see language development as being governed by innate factors, similar to those involved in physical growth. By virtue of being human, a child has an inborn kind of knowledge that matures with age. This must be the case, it is argued, since basic linguistic competencies, such as hearing differences between sounds and understanding basic grammatical relations, require knowledge that is not available in the perceived world. This maturational model, most famously forwarded by Noam Chomsky (1975) in defense of his transformational grammar, brings with it the notion of specialized and separable components of knowledge that are biologically based. These components, called "language modules," presume that different areas of language, such as syntax and phonology, operate independently, for the most part, and that they mature in predetermined ways.

Chomsky's notion of separate modules later evolved into a full-blown "modularity theory" forwarded by Fodor (1983). Fodor argued that language modules are biologically innate and encapsulated areas of knowledge responsible for handling a specific type of representation, such as syntax and phonology.

This *modular view* of what matures in language growth is one that is compatible with information-processing as well as with linguistic frames. Both frames have boxes, or modules. In the information-processing models the child gets better at doing different kinds of processing: attending to and discriminating speech sounds, using working memory, or controlling the speech musculature. In the linguistic models the child accrues knowledge in each linguistic box. A child's progression at each level is assessed and compared with what would be expected for children of the same age or developmental level.

The strict form of the modularity hypothesis presumes a predictable growth pathway for all children. Norms are gathered to

ascertain the growth paths for each module, and assessment procedures are developed to determine the degree to which a child con-
forms to expectations.

The modularity version of development leads to questions about
the relative rate of growth for different modules. Do children with language problems manifest those problems in particular modules? Are
there modules that are more delayed than others? How does delay in
one module affect growth in another? These are questions that are un-
available to those who subscribe to a more generalist and nonmodular
view of development such as constructivists following in the theoretical footsteps of Piaget (1955) or Vygotsky (1981).

At one level, the answer to whether children can be in different developmental stages at the same time is obvious. The very act
of identifying a child as having a problem in one area, such as syntax, but not in others, provides evidence for the separateness of
modules. Indeed, much of the research in language and literacy
disabilities by linguists and psychologists has presumed the existence of separate modules by virtue of analyzing one at a time.
There has been very little effort to see how the areas relate.

The clearest expression of the modules' separateness is in the recent work of theorists who are looking for evidence of modularity
theory. For example, studies of autism have been carried out with the
aim of isolating a "theory of mind" module (for a review, see Tager
Flusberg, 1994). Children with specific language impairments are of
particular interest to researchers because their isolated language
problem argues for the existence of a language-learning module (for
a review, see Bishop, 1997, Ch. 9; and Leonard, 1998, pp. 55–71).

Until now we have been talking about modules that make up
language. But one can also think of the language and cognition domains as separate modules. This separation has been a long-standing assessment issue because it allows diagnosticians to decide
whether children's language disorders are part and parcel of their
cognitive impairment. It also provides clinicians and administrators with a counter to what has been called the *cognitive referencing
hypothesis* for service provision.

The cognitive referencing hypothesis portrays a child's performance in a particular domain as a part of his or her cognition, not
separate from it. It therefore carries with it the expectation that
children should be developing in all areas that are consistent with
(neither below nor above) their general cognitive abilities. For example, children whose motor levels are commensurate with their
cognitive levels are judged ineligible for special services. Occupational and physical therapists operating under the cognitive refer-

encing hypothesis would reason thusly: cognitive referencing is "an approach to service provision that predicts that children with motor delays that are commensurate with their cognitive abilities will not benefit from intervention to the extent that children with motor delays and higher cognitive abilities will benefit from intervention" (Muhlenhaupt, 2001).

Cognitive referencing, when used to determine service eligibility for children with language disabilities, argues that children's language performance level "must be assessed as being less than is expected for their cognitive level before they would be eligible for speech–language intervention services" (Casby, 1992, p. 199). In order to justify services for children whose language and cognition are comparable, one needs to argue that language is separate from cognition, not dependent upon it. One type of powerful evidence for the nondependence of language on cognition is to find children whose language abilities exceed their cognitive abilities (Casby, 1992). There is such a group of children, those who are diagnosed as having Williams syndrome. These children have advanced syntax and social abilities even though most qualify as being mildly mentally retarded (National Institute of Neurological Disorders and Stroke, 2001).

Constructivist Growth Models

A less strict form of the maturational view of growth depicts children as having developmental options, depending upon their learning experiences and interests. These more flexible approaches, sometimes referred to as "constructivist," allow children some options in development. One aspect of assessment, then, is to examine innovations that individual children make. The children are portrayed as builders, constructors, or acquirers. That is, they are active creators of their language knowledge and use.

A well-developed example of the constructivist growth model is that of Piaget (1955). In his theory, learning is seen as active, involving processes such as assimilation of experience to existing knowledge, which he calls "schemas," and accommodation to experience by changing those schemas.

Piaget's conceptualization of growth is also in keeping with the maturational model because the processes of assimilation and accommodation are prescribed genetically. It is not in keeping with a modularist view, however, since Piaget saw language learning as symbol formation, and as a part of general learning affecting all aspects of knowledge.

As do all versions of constructivism, Piaget's version uses a *building construction metaphor*. Schemas, or knowledge structures, are described as "building" upon one another. Some schemas are foundational. New, more complex schemas are constructed from them. The idea of construction goes beyond putting blocks or schemas on top of one another, however. Rather, it is more like an artistic construction in which new structures are created out of given materials. In Piaget's terminology, the known schemas "accommodate" to meet the needs of the construction worker.

Constructivism, then, involves growth from simple to complex schemas through a process of active learning. Piaget posited, for example, that symbolic knowledge is constructed gradually building upon sensorimotor schemas. The process evolves through six sensorimotor stages and takes around 2 years. This construal of prerequisite knowledge or "readiness" as being like building blocks for later learnings has been an important one in language assessment. Assessments done in this vein have involved looking to see whether a child who has difficulty with complex constructs knows the conceptual prerequisites needed to understand the complex structures. For example, has a child who is not yet engaging in symbol formation reached Piaget's Stage 4 of sensorimotor knowledge? This knowledge was seen by Piaget and others as requisite for understanding symbols.

Besides Piaget's, there is another well-developed rendition of constructivism, that developed by the Russian scholar Vygotsky (1981). Vygotsky's child constructs new concepts from what is provided to him or her in the social context. The new concepts are created in collaboration with others, using real-life experience that falls within a child's conceptual grasp. Vygotsky calls this area of conceptual grasp "the zone of proximal development."

Assessments grounded in Vygotsky's approach focus on the child's learning potential under different conditions rather than on what it is that he or she has already acquired. The assessment approaches in this Vygotskian version of constructivism are called *dynamic assessment* to distinguish them from the more static approaches of the maturationists or the Piagetian-type constructivists (Brown & Ferrara, 1985; Feuerstein, 1979; Gutierrez-Clellen & Pena, 2001; Olswang, Bain, & Johnson, 1992).

The Behavioral Growth Model

The behavioral model treats growth as the acquisition of behaviors that are copied from what is seen and heard in the world outside the child. Learning is thereby driven by external real-world experiences rather than by internal biologically determined maturation or internal constructions.

Behaviorists regard children's language learning as working like a copying machine or, in today's mechanical parallel, an electronic scanner. Language stimuli are presented to the child, copied by him or her through imitation, and then stored for future use. The learner not only makes associations between external stimuli and his or her copied responses, but also between stimuli in the real world that have temporal or spatial contiguity. Stimuli that are regularly followed by other stimuli become associated with each other, as do stimuli that are located near one another. The result is the creation of *associative chains*—a metaphor that conjures up linear strings of linked events. Similarly, associations are made between behavioral responses and the following positive or negative reinforcements. The associations between responses and subsequent reinforcements affect the likelihood of the responses occurring on future occasions or transferring to new contexts.

Since the main focus of the behavioral growth metaphor is on the accumulation of learned associations, there is little concern for how associations get organized once they are learned. The approach, therefore, unlike modularity theory or constructivism, does not theorize about the child's internal processing. Learning is seen as a process of growing new associations and associative chains rather than as a process of construction of new conceptual edifices.

Behaviorism also depicts growth in terms of a *container metaphor*. Children store their new learnings or stimulus–response associations alongside their old associations in a conceptual container. Newly made associations are added to the container contents or repertoire for later use. Assessment of learning involves comparing a baseline of behaviors that were in the response repertoire prior to a learning experience with what is there following a learning task.

The behavioral growth model also incorporates a *functional metaphor*. Functional relations are associations made between stimuli, responses, and reinforcement. Specifically, responses are seen as functions of stimuli and of reinforcements. This functional metaphor is drawn from mathematics and is what is meant when one describes Y as being a function of changes in X. In the case of behavioral functions, the second element of an association is a function of the presence of the first element.

The most frequent use of behavioral models in doing assessments is to analyze a child's unwanted behaviors, sometimes referred to as "aberrant" (e.g., Donnellan et al., 1984) or "challenging" behaviors (e.g., Reichle & Wacker, 1993). These are acts performed by children with disabilities that are judged by those around them as inappropriate or interfering. In order to change the children's behaviors, or to get rid of them, behaviorally trained clinicians assess the conditions surrounding the behaviors, doing what has been called *applied behavioral analysis* (ABA).

ABA involves examining the functional relations between the stimulus conditions that precede an unwanted behavior (sometimes referred to as "the discriminative stimuli"), the behavior itself (seen as a response in this model) and the reinforcement conditions or consequences of the behavior. These three things, when analyzed together, have come to be called an "ABC analysis" (antecedents, behavior, consequences). The focus of the analysis is not just on the three conditions, but on the functional or causal relations between the conditions. In the example below provided by Halle and Spradlin (1993), the antecedent stimulus conditions are the cookie and Mom, the behavioral response is a tantrum, and the consequences are that the mother gives the child a cookie. Halle and Spradlin describe the functional cause–effect relationships that are inferred from the juxtaposition of these ABCs.

> If in the presence of a cookie and Mom, a child has a tantrum that produces access to the cookie, then the motivation for the tantrum is positive reinforcement and the stimulus complex "cookie and Mom" is discriminative for positive reinforcement. (p. 84)

Interestingly, when behavioral principles are applied to situations in order to eliminate undesirable behaviors, such as a tantrum in the above example, growth is seen as a decrease in associations. That is, the discriminative stimulus becomes dissociated with the response.

SUMMARY OF ASSESSMENT MODELS

Language assessment has come into its own in the last 50 years or so. It requires moving away from a diagnostic or medical model to models that represent children's knowledge or processing abilities. Predominant among the assessment frames have been ones that represent a child's information-processing abilities or linguistic knowledge. Together these two frames have blended to become a new discipline: psycholinguistics. In these frames, speech and language are usually depicted as surface manifestations of underlying psycholinguistic processing or knowledge rules. The assessment effort is to find these underlying processes or rules for particular children and then to compare the processing abilities and rule knowledge of those children with the processing abilities and rule knowledge of their age or stage cohorts. The assessment question involves knowing whether or not the child's processing or knowledge of linguistic rules are within expected ranges.

The larger frames of the information-processing and linguistic models contain a number of smaller metaphors. (See Table 3.5 for a review of the frames described in this chapter.) The metaphors,

Table 3.5. A Summary of Models, Blends, and Metaphors Used When Assessing Children's Areas of Language and/or Learning Deficits

Frame type	Examples
	Assessment models
Specific abilities models	Information-processing model
	Linguistic rule model
	Metaphors associated with assessment models
Information-processing model	Spatial metaphor (bottom and top)
	Flow metaphor (down from top and up from bottom)
	Energy metaphor—finite resource metaphor (spatial and temporal limitations)
	Computational metaphor (online, executive component, working memory)
Linguistic rule model	Rules (phonological, morphological, syntactic, narrative)
	Vegetation metaphor (linguistic trees, branches, roots)
	Kinship metaphor (mother–daughter nodes)
	Spatial metaphor (deep and surface structures)
	Tool metaphor (communicative intents)

(continued)

Table 3.5. continued

Frame type	Examples
	Blended models
Information-processing and linguistic rule models	Aram and Nation (1982)
Auditory-processing and language-processing models	Butler (1983) Duchan and Katz (1983)
	Growth models
Maturational growth model	Developing modules of different types of learning
	Disparities in growth (cognitive referencing)
Constructivist growth model	Growth via active thinking based on assimilation and accommodation (Piaget, 1955)
	Growth through dynamic learning (Vygotsky, 1981); this idea is related to dynamic assessment methods
Behavioral growth model	Growth happens through the storage of new associations (container metaphor)
	Increase (in the case of learning) or dissociation (in the case of extinction) in functional relations between stimuli, responses, and reinforcements

while separable from the models, are helpful in spelling out the details of the more general frames.

The notion of growth is basic to assessment. This notion, however, comes in different versions, depending upon the growth model used. One group sees growth as normal maturation, a second group sees it as normal active learning, and a third group sees growth as the acquisition of desirable speech and language behaviors or a reduction of undesirable misbehaviors. These three models of growth that frame the assessor's judgments of normality are even more crucial in the determination of what to do when a child is found to be below normal. It is to these issues surrounding intervention decisions that I now turn.

FOUR

Intervention, Instruction, and Support Frames

Three terms can be used to describe what specialists or teachers do as they work with children in school contexts. Each conjures up a different set of teaching practices. Each is based in a different teaching framework. The first term, *intervention*, describes teaching that is aimed at remedying deficits in children. Intervention connotes individualized therapies, often carried out in a separate area, away from what is going on in classrooms. Intervention approaches are typically based on a child's diagnosis or the results of a speech, language, or literacy assessment. It is a term, along with therapy, describing what speech–language pathologists usually do when they work with children with language or literacy disabilities. It best fits a medical model of service provision.

Instruction, on the other hand, is a term that is most often used to describe what teachers do in classrooms. It is not confined to remediation, but rather is something that teachers ordinarily do with typical as well as with atypical children as they work to achieve their curricular goals. Instruction arises out of the educational model of service provision.

Support is a term for yet a third way of providing services to children with or without special needs. It can refer to what anyone does to facilitate children's participation in everyday life activities. Support derives from a model of participation and engagement and is a relatively recent way that speech–language pathologists and teachers describe what they do.

This chapter outlines and compares frames associated with each of these three modes of teaching. The particular emphasis will be on how the terms describe different ways of thinking about and working with children who have language and literacy disabilities.

INTERVENTION

Intervention, like therapy, is a term most often used by those who work within the medical model. When a professionals call what they do "intervention," they are likely thinking of it as something that is designed to remediate a diagnosed problem. Teachers, parents, or clinicians who see themselves as carrying out intervention are probably working to minimize a child's deficits in a particular area identified as deficient.

There are many different types of interventions that speech–language pathologists and teachers can choose from as they endeavor to remedy a child's speech or language difficulties. The choice may depend upon the frames used in the diagnosis and assessment, upon the results of evaluations, or upon other factors, such as the child's age and abilities and the clinician's explicitly or implicitly held notions about how children learn.

Interventions often have particular names, in order to identify them and distinguish them from one another. The act of naming an intervention requires a framing, of sorts. First, one needs to pick an attribute from the many available that best characterizes the intervention. Second, one needs to group the instances of the intervention type in order to name and frame them into one generic type. For example, to name an intervention as "drill," one must know the sorts of thing that that name describes.

Some names of interventions are based on *what* is to be taught (e.g., semantic therapies, narrative therapies, phonological awareness approaches), other names are based on *who* is being taught (family-centered programs, parent-training programs), and still others are based on *the method* being used (behavioral approaches, providing contextual support).

Often interventions are classified into two opposing categories, emphasizing broad differences in types of approaches. For example, interventions have been dichotomized into unstructured versus structured approaches, child-centered versus adult-centered approaches, holistic versus analytic approaches, didactic versus naturalistic approaches, whole language versus phonics approaches, and context-based or participation versus impairment approaches.

While opposing classifications are common, those working with the dichotomies often find them inadequate. This is evidenced in practitioners' observations that certain interventions have features that fit one category of the dichotomy and other features that fit into the other category of the dichotomy. Interventions, for example, may be structured in some respects and not in others. Some parts of an intervention may be under the child's control, while other parts are under the adult's control. A particular approach may contain both holistic and analytic elements. And an approach may be didactic and intrusive in some respects but naturalistic in others.

Mark Fey (1986) has offered a solution to this problem of what to do with middle-ground interventions by reframing the dichotomous model, placing the two contrasting approaches at different ends of a single continuum. When describing adult- and child-centered interventions, for instance, he placed each at a different end of a "continuum of naturalness." Fey and his colleagues later renamed (and thereby reframed) this naturalness continuum, calling it a "continuum of intrusiveness" (Fey, Catts, & Larrivee, 1995).

At the negative end of the naturalness–intrusiveness continuum are approaches that are selected and directed by adults—the least natural and most intrusive. At the positive end of the continuum are approaches that are controlled by the child. (See Table 4.1 for features of the two approaches. For other features see Kovarsky & Duchan, 1997, and Norris & Hoffman, 1990.)

Fay (1986) names the approaches in the middle of the continuum "hybrid approaches." For example, in a focused stimulation approach the adult provides the child with many models of a targeted structure conforming to the adult specifications and, at the same time, follows the child's lead in the carrying out of an activity (Fey, 1986; Leonard, 1981).

Fey offers an example of focused stimulation in which a mother and a clinician provide the child with several models of the targeted structure "can't," as shown in the following transcript from Fey (1986, p. 210):

Table 4.1. Feature Comparison of Adult-Centered and Child-Centered Intervention Approaches

Features of interventions	Adult-centered intervention	Child-centered intervention
Control of event	Adult picks and leads event	Child picks and leads event
Role of adult	Teacher	Facilitator
Origin of context	Designed by adult	Arises naturally from child's activities
Type of activities	Lessons, highly structured activities	Conversations, stories, child-directed play activities
Naturalness	Low	High
Techniques	Drill, structured activities, scaffolding	Responsive modeling, indirect language stimulation
Sample programs	Drills in lesson formats	Hanen program, using interactive approach with conversational response techniques

Clinician: I have a dog that can fly.

Child: Doggie not fly.

Mother: Doggies can't fly.

Clinician: Can't doggies fly?

Child: No.

Clinician: I think they can.

Child: Nope. Bird fly.

Mother: Doggies can't fly. Birds can fly.

Clinician: Oh, that's right. Doggies can't fly. They don't have wings.

The language of the adults controls the conversation, resembling the didactic teaching role. This qualifies the interaction as being at the intrusive, nonnaturalistic end of the naturalness continuum. However, the interaction also has some characteristics of a more natural interaction in that the talk has an open conversational quality and both teacher and mother respond with interest to the child's contributions, without correcting him directly. This interaction, with features of both adult- and child-centered approaches, qualifies as something in-between, what Fey refers to as "hybrid."

Two other examples of a hybrid approach are *milieu teaching*, developed by Hart and Risley (1968) and their colleagues (for reviews, see Hart & Rogers-Warren, 1978; Warren & Kaiser, 1986; and Kaiser, Yoder & Keetz, 1992), and the *activity-based approach* developed by Bricker and Cripe (1992).

Milieu teaching, sometimes called the "incidental teaching approach" (Warren & Kaiser, 1984), is built upon a behavioral frame involving antecedent, behavior, and consequent (ABC) contingency principles. Teaching programs built on these behavioral principles prior to 1968 used strict adult-centered therapies in a drill format. The milieu approach departs from this highly constrained method by allowing the child more control. In the milieu approach adults provide language prompts that are in keeping with the child's interests as he or she engages in naturally occurring activities. The "milieu teacher" interacts with the child in his or her own milieu, watches what he or she is doing, and then prompts the child to provide target language related to the ongoing activity. The prompts may be of various types, including tempting the child with a desirable object (stimulus manipulations), focusing the child's attention on an object (focused attention), waiting until the child responds (time delay), telling the child what to say (mand model), partial prompting (request for partial imitation), and confirming a correct response (confirmation) (Hart & Risley, 1968).

Proponents of milieu teaching have described its characteristics as involving (1) following the child's lead or interest, (2) providing multiple examples, (3) prompting a child's production of forms, (4) providing natural consequences when the child produces forms correctly, and (5) embedding the teaching in ongoing interactions (Kaiser, Yoder, & Keetz, 1992, p. 9).

Bricker and Cripe's *activity-based approach* is another intervention method that is classified as hybrid, falling somewhere between the more natural and the less natural approaches. It was designed for preschoolers with disabilities or who were at risk "to develop functional skills that capitalize on the daily interactions of children with their social and physical environment" (Bricker & Cripe, 1992, p. 2). In activity-based intervention, the goals for individual children are embedded in everyday events, whether they be routine activities, teacher-planned activities, or child-initiated activities. Teachers or clinicians build upon aspects of the event in order to promote children's goals—for example, by asking questions to build vocabulary or encouraging more exchanges to increase social

Table 4.2. Hybrid Approaches, Falling between Adult-Centered and Child-Centered Approaches

Features	Focused stimulation	Milieu teaching	Activity-based intervention
Control of event	Adult controls much of the responsive discourse, child controls event in other ways.	Adult follows child's attentional lead when offering prompts. Child controls what is said and done.	The activity dictates what all participants do.
Role of adult	Adult provides child with multiple examples of the target stimuli.	Adult prompts child to produce target.	Adult structures environment to elicit target.
Selection of context/activity	Clinician offers topics to talk about.	Child-directed play.	Child selects activities offered by clinician.
Type of activities	Conversational exchanges.	Open-ended play activities.	Routinized activities, such as ritualized games.
Naturalness	Clinician's talk unusually repetitive. Activity, however, is from everyday life.	Activities are characteristic of play activities directed by the child.	Activities are naturally occurring routines.
Techniques	Auditory bombardment in which child is "bombarded" with many examples of targeted stimuli.	Stimulus manipulation, focused attention, time delay, confirmation of correct response.	Use of sabotage[a] techniques. And use of labeling of objects during preset routines that are part of the school or home culture.

[a]The adult blocks the execution of part of the activity (sabotages or interrupts it) in order to get the child to do something to keep it going.

interaction. The approach therefore incorporates teacher-directed discourse in everyday events.

As can be seen from the feature analysis of hybrid approaches in Table 4.2, the focused stimulation, milieu, and activity-based approaches are considered hybrid for different reasons. In the focused stimulation approach, the adult controls the discourse but the child can choose what is going on. For the milieu approach, the adult does the prompting but follows the child's lead during child-directed, open-ended play. In the activity-based intervention, the adult works on a child's communication goals during naturally occurring classroom or home activities.

The term *naturalness*, when applied to intervention approaches, can be used not only to describe a general type of intervention (e.g., natural interventions vs. didactic interventions), it can also be used as a way to evaluate a particular intervention approach. Fey (1986) suggests that approaches be evaluated for their "similarity to everyday situations in which the child has frequent opportunities to communicate" (p. 63).

The metaphor of naturalness used by Fey is one that pervades the intervention literature in speech–language pathology and education, taking on different meanings depending upon its context. While complex in the domains it is applied to, the naturalness metaphor applies similarly to different aspects of those domains, one at a time (e.g., the naturalness of a location, of participants, of classroom instruction). In this sense, it is somewhat narrow in its application, qualifying it as a metaphor rather than as a more complexly formulated model.

The Naturalness Metaphor

Fey (1986) defines an activity that is low on a "naturalness continuum" as one in which a child is required to practice target behaviors "while looking at pictures or observing the clinician's manipulations of objects. The child is not required to use her target behavior during the course of some broader social activity; the target behavior *is* the activity" (p. 64). At the other end of the continuum, Fey describes a child and father washing dishes together, a context that can offer naturally occurring opportunities for practicing a target behavior, such as requesting someone to perform an action ("Give me the soap").

Fey's naturalness idea takes as its source of comparison the reality frame involved in everyday life. The most natural therapies are the ones that look as if they are everyday reality, even though they are not. Interventions, in this case, are taken to be something other than real-life experiences. That is to say, they are carried out in an *"as-if" reality frame.*

Fey distinguishes three dimensions along which naturalness can vary: the activity, the physical context, and the social context (see Table 4.3 for examples of each), and provides a means to quantify an activity according to its location on the naturalness continuum. Activities that earn zero points are the least natural. The most natural are 2-point activities. Fey's example of zero-level naturalness is a drill activity carried out by a clinician in the clinic, with all three dimensions of naturalness having a zero point value. The most natural activity in Fey's model is one that is a daily activity carried out at home by the parents. It would receive a point value of 6 (2 points for each of the three dimensions).

Fey's model is designed to describe teaching situations. The social context presupposed in this model is a one-on-one situation involving an adult (whether it be a parent, teacher, or clinician) as teacher and a child as learner. In Fey's description, naturalness is blended with a behavioral model in that it incorporates the idea of generalization sometimes referred to as "transfer." Fey promotes

Table 4.3. Dimensions of the Naturalness Continuum

Dimensions	Least natural (0 points)	Middle-level natural (1 point)	Most natural (2 points)
Activity (what participants are doing)	Drill, lessons	Organized games	Everyday, openly structured activities
Physical context (where activity takes place)	Clinic	School	Home
Social context (which adults are engaged with child)	Clinician	Teacher	Parents

Note. Adapted from Fey (1986, p. 63). Copyright 1986. Published by Allyn & Bacon. Copyright 1986 by Pearson Education. Adapted by permission of the publisher.

natural approaches in order to enhance transfer of learning from a teaching context to an everyday life, or "natural," context. Camarata (1995) adds another justification for natural activities to Fey's generalization. "Social validity" is another reason, argues Camarata, for favoring natural over didactic approaches to intervention. That is, learned responses should be "noticeable by family members, teachers, peers, and other conversation partners" (Camarata, 1995, p. 67).

Camarata, also working within a behavioral framework, suggests that interventions be made more naturalistic by (1) embedding imitative prompts into conversational contexts (e.g., by asking a child to say "red block" when he picks up a red block) and (2) by using natural reinforcers (e.g., rewarding a request for an object with the object) (p. 72). He offers an even more radical third suggestion to achieve interactive naturalness when he recommends that interventionists eliminate imitative prompts and overt reinforcers from their procedural practices (p. 72). He justifies his recommendation by arguing that these procedures have a potentially negative impact in that they "interrupt the natural flow of interaction" (p. 69).

Another intervention method that promotes natural interaction is the "floor time" approach of Greenspan and Weidner (1998, 1999, 2000). These authors recommend that parents sit with their child on the floor eight or more times a day and engage the child intensively in interaction for 20–45 minutes. The approach is aimed at fostering intimacy and attentional "focus" in children with autism spectrum disorders. These authors recommend eliminating any elements in interactions with children that seem like didactic teaching. The adult's job in an interactive sequence—what Greenspan and Weidner call "circles of communication"—is to pick up on the emotional and physical content of what the child is doing and respond accordingly rather than to intrude on the child's naturally occurring, emotionally motivated affect to teach him or her something. Greenspan and Weidner (2000) provide an example of a circle of communication between a father and his son:

> The father put his hand on a toy car very gently as his son was exploring it and pointed to a particular part, as though to say, "What's that?" but, in pointing, the father actually moved the car, so the son felt the car moving in his hands and noticed his father's involvement without becoming upset. The son took the car back but looked at where the father had touched it with his fingers. . . . The son's interest in the car and the father's point to a spot on the car and moving it a little opened a circle of communication. (p. 292)

Another metaphor used to describe naturalness in practices is *authenticity*. This word, authentic, is sometimes used when describing approaches that simulate naturally occurring conditions. The opposite of "authentic activities" are "contrived activities" that look like they are intended solely for purposes of practice.

To recap, naturalness has become a frame within which various interventions have been identified, described, and evaluated. The frame is a complex one, and includes a variety of dimensions. The underlying concept, one that gives the frame its coherence, is that therapies and educational approaches designed to achieve intervention goals should be unobtrusively embedded the in everyday life activities of a child—that is, the activity should look and feel "natural" to the participants. Or, if this is not feasible, the approaches should be conducted in situations that simulate typical circumstances of everyday life.

The Functional Metaphor

The term *functional* is commonplace in the intervention literature. It is used to describe (1) clinical approaches ("a functional approach"), (2) how components work within a system ("working memory functions as part of the information-processing system"), (3) children's overall performance ("he is high functioning"), (4) children's communication abilities ("her communication is very functional"), (5) aspects of children's communication ("his gestural system is functional, but his vocalizations are not"), and (6) individual or types of communicative acts ("she expresses four communicative functions").

The term *functional* in all of these instances is used metaphorically to mean *use* or *usefulness*. This "use" or "instrumental" metaphor is used in two main ways in the language intervention literature. In the first, an entity is described as "functional" in the same way that a tool is "functional": it is used as an instrument to achieve an ultimate end. This is the way Bloom and Lahey (1978) have described communicative acts such as requests. Children use them to achieve an ultimate goal. They function as means to an end. It is this meaning of functional that is used when referring to functional intervention approaches, that serve the purpose of improving a child's life. It is what Camarata (1995) has referred to as the criterion of "social validity."

A second use of the term *function* has to do with how well something is working. Children, like machines, are said to function well or poorly, or somewhere in between. This version of function carries with it the notion of level—high or low, competent or incompetent. The child, as a whole, can be described in these terms ("he is a low-functioning child"). This machine version of the functional metaphor can also be used to describe the child's performance in different domains ("she functions well in oral language but is a terrible speller") or in different contexts ("she functions better in the mornings").

Robert Owens (1999), the author of a popular text in the field of language disorders, describes his functional approach using both the instrument and machine senses of the functional metaphor:

> A functional language approach to assessment and intervention, as described in the text, targets language as it used or as it works for the language user as a vehicle for communication [vehicle = tool, instrument]. In clinical practice, a functional approach is a communication-first approach. The focus is the overall communication of the child with language impairment and of those who communicate with the child. As stated, the goal is better communication that works in the client's natural communicative contexts [that works = machine]. (p. 5)

Like the metaphor of naturalness, the functional metaphor takes on different forms when embedded in different frames. In a linguistic frame, the term *function* is associated with *speech act theory*. Communicative acts are associated with children's intentions—they function to achieve the child's communicative goals. This is the meaning of function that Owens draws from when describing how language works for the language user as "a vehicle" (see above).

Within a behavioral approach, sometimes described as *the* functional approach, the term has to do with the how elements relate to one another. Stimuli function to elicit responses, reinforcements function to strengthen or weaken responses (strengthening and weakening are metaphors related to physical exercise). Another use of functional phraseology in behavioral approaches is that responses are functions of stimuli. In this use, one that originates in mathematics, a set of responding variables are said to be "functions" of another set of influencing variables. When values of one dimension of a variable change in response to changes in the values of a variable in another dimension, the affected dimension is described as being "a function" of the first. X is a function of Y, tantrums are a function of overstimulation.

Learning Models

Models differ as to the purposes they best serve. Some models, such as a behavioral one or a constructivist one, are designed to represent mechanisms or principles of learning. This has to do with the "how" of intervention. Learning principles provide a guide for how to promote learning in children. Other models have more to do with the content of learning, or the "what" of intervention.

The "How" of Intervention

The *behavioral model* uses principles of stimulus presentation and reinforcement. The *constructivist model* uses principles of discovery learning, inferencing, and abstracting rules from surface data. (For more on these models, see Chapter 3.) The focus of a learning theory has more to do with the factors involved in learning rather than what specifically is to be taught or learned.

The *behavioral model* is sometimes called a "learning theory" because of its attention to principles that govern the acquiring of new behaviors or the extinguishing of unwanted behaviors. Behavioral principles have been developed to depict relationships between stimuli, responses, and reinforcements, and, in so doing, they provide a rational means of carrying out intervention. Interventions are designed, for example, to alter the antecedents and consequences of undesirable behaviors in order to extinguish them. Or, when teaching a new behavior, discriminative stimuli are increased, to offer the child lots of opportunities to imitate (learn) them.

Methods such as focused stimulation and auditory bombardment are used to teach a child new sounds, concepts, or grammatical structures. These behavioral methods focus on altering the stimulus targets. They provide children with discriminative stimuli in the hopes that they will imitate the stimuli. In so doing the children will be adding the imitated response to their behavioral repertoire.

Behavioral principles also argue for providing multiple opportunities for practicing targeted goals. Recitation-based learning, often in lessons or drill formats, is aimed at strengthening responses. This notion of strengthening draws from an *exercise metaphor* that casts learning as parallel to doing exercise. Muscles (speech or language skills) are strengthened through practice; the more practice, the stronger the skill. This exercise metaphor is not only used to govern intervention involving muscle-based elements, such as tongue or lip strengthening for better speech sound production, it is also applied to work with nonmuscular skills such as strengthening morphological endings or sound–letter associations.

An alternative to the behavioral model, and one often seen as conflicting with it, is the *constructivist model* of learning. In the constructivist model, the task of learning goes beyond copying or imitating a stimulus. A learner's job is to study the stimulus and infer rules or meanings from it. That is to say, the child constructs information from the data available. The child learning phonology must infer phonological processes from speech sounds he or she hears as well as from what he or she already knows about the phonological system. Similarly, the child learning grammar must infer underlying morphological and syntactic structures from surface word order and other information at his or her disposal. The child learning semantic relations must figure them out by inferring meaningful relationships between words based on contextual cues and background knowledge.

The "What" of Intervention

Some models depict the content of intervention, or what it is that is being taught. The targets of intervention, like the methods used to achieve them, will differ depending upon the frame used to create them. A linguistic model leads to the creation of therapy programs designed to teach linguistic rules. Many language therapy programs have been developed to teach various aspects of phonology, morphology, syntax, semantics, and pragmatics.

Blends of "How" and "What" Models

And, as one might have guessed from earlier chapters, models have been developed that blend the two emphases, focusing both on the "what" *and* the "how" of learning. For example, an information-processing model might be used as a way to represent an area of knowledge, such as by selecting phonological awareness as an area to work on (the "what" of learning). It can also be used to decide how to present information, such as to reduce task complexity in order to enhance processing (the "how" of learning). (See more on this below.)

The information-processing model feels slippery. For example, processing goals, even though they serve to identify the content of an intervention, have a "how" focus: how to process information. But in this case the "how" of processing becomes the "what" of the teaching program. Processing is what it is that is being targeted, and processing is how one goes about getting and storing information.

Clinicians and teachers who create processing goals must still figure out how to achieve their processing goals. That is, they need to decide between learning models such as behavioral or constructivist ones to teach the processing content. So a child who has been identified through an information-processing model as having a central auditory processing deficit may be placed in an intervention program based on improving auditory sequencing. That same child, when viewed within a linguistic model, would be more likely to be seen as needing a program whose content is to improve syntactic or discourse structuring.

An information-processing model does not always answer questions about how and what to teach. For example, assume a child has multiple articulation problems and is in need of intervention. Is the child's primary problem located in the auditory-processing, phonological rule-learning, or motor-production box? These different options need to be decided upon prior to intervention, since interventions are likely to differ for each.

Information-processing models, when used to determine intervention targets, also require a decision about the direction of processing. Interventionists who see the problem as a bottom-up one, in which information at the lower levels of processing (more peripheral) flow up along a pathway to higher level processing, are likely to focus their early interventions on training auditory skills—the auditory training approach. The particular skills worked on may depend upon the child's profile on audiometric tests, or they may depend upon the program materials at hand. If the interventionist has available the bottom-up auditory training program developed by Masters, Stecker, and Katz (1998), for example, he or she will work on decoding (interpreting units of information), tolerance fading memory (storing items in short-term memory), integration (decoding plus tolerance fading memory), and organization (organizing and sequencing information).

The view of auditory processing articulated by Masters et al. is a bottom-up one because the listing of processing areas proceeds from peripheral to central. Alternatively, interventionists may cast information processing as proceeding in a top-down fashion. Therapy programs based on a top-down model are more likely to begin with language learning. For example, children's inabilities to blend sounds are treated as linguistic rather than auditory problems. Children are given metaphonological tasks and explanations to remedy their sound-blending difficulties.

Some clinicians may adopt a combined bottom-up and top-down intervention approach, working on both auditory and language skills. Chermak and Musiek (1997) recommend just such a combination, which they call "comprehensive management approaches." These authors in some instances recommend language techniques for improving auditory skills (e.g., note taking to maximize auditory summation). In other instances they use auditory methods to enhance auditory skills (e.g., training to identify brief, 1-millisecond gaps in auditory stimuli). In still other instances they recommend language tasks for improving language difficulties (e.g., recognize and explain connectives to improve listening comprehension) (Chermak & Musiek, 1997, Ch. 8).

How does one go about evaluating the different models and choosing from among them? This issue is a delicate one, since the approach used to evaluate a model also originates in one or more frames. For example, a child may improve on his ability to identify gaps in an auditory stimulus, thereby justifying the effectiveness of that approach from within a frame that sees that skill as important, but may not improve in his ability to take notes, an evaluation approach based in a different frame. More will be said about evaluation frames in the next chapter.

Summary

Language intervention goals are usually designed to fix deficits derived from diagnostic and assessment information. For this reason, they are in keeping with a medical model. Interventions goals are likely to differ depending upon the assessment instruments used. Speech–language pathologists and teachers working within different assessment frames will create different kinds of intervention goals. The models most commonly used by speech–language pathologists are linguistic ones, leading to goals formulated as language rules, and information-processing ones, leading to goals that have to do with enhancing identified areas of information processing.

There are a number of other frames from which to choose and which serve to guide the intervention approach. One way to discover an underlying frame is to examine the name of a method for what aspect of intervention it is referring to. Often intervention approaches are framed as dichotomies, as separable. Interventions combining features of each part of a dichotomy are said to be using hybrid approaches.

Interventions are carried out in an "as-if" reality frame that differs in varying degrees from the taken-for-granted reality in which everyday life is experienced. The most natural interventions are those that look like everyday activities. This naturalness metaphor is commonly used to describe features of interventions that don't look like teaching or therapy.

Another metaphor commonly used when describing intervention is a functional metaphor. The functional metaphor has a number of different applications but the primary one is to describe the everyday usefulness of an intervention.

Learning theories, as we have seen, also affect intervention approaches. Behaviorally framed interventions have tended to be highly structured and focus on imitation and correct production of identifiable stimuli. Constructivist interventions focus more on whether children have discovered a rule or a targeted pattern.

INSTRUCTION

Children with language and literacy disabilities, as well as those who are typical learners, spend much of their time in contexts of instruction. That is, they are in classrooms, participating in group activities conducted by an instructor. While the term *instruction* can be extended to mean any situation that fosters learning, its everyday use is narrower. The more constricted meaning of *instruction* conjures up a situation in which a teacher is "instructing" a small or large group of students. This specific view of teaching is at the heart of the educational model.

Instruction, like intervention, can be framed in many ways. The classroom "lesson" is a three-part teacher–student exchange in which the teacher challenges a student or class, the student or class responds, and the teacher evaluates the response. This *instructional discourse frame*, which Mehan (1979) terms an *IRE* (initiation, response, evaluation), is familiar to all who have experienced traditional classrooms.

The purpose of instruction is to impart the curriculum to students. This notion of teaching the curriculum is often couched in a merged *conduit/container metaphor*. Aspects of the curriculum are conveyed or taught by the teacher to students, who learn it. The means used to convey the curriculum is through instruction.

The way children participate in these sorts of everyday instructional activities is key to their success or failure in school. Children with language and literacy difficulties are met with double problems in these situations. They not only must learn the material that is being taught through the instructional process, they must also be able to follow the discourse and to participate in the IRE exchange structure.

The content of instruction will depend upon the dictates of the curriculum (see Chapter 7 on schools) and the frame predilections of individual teachers (see Chapter 6 on literacy). For example, a third-grade child faces different instructional challenges than a second-grade child. Also, a child whose teacher adopts a whole language approach to reading will have different instructional challenges than a child whose teacher takes a phonics approach. So instructional frames not only govern what teachers teach and the way they go about it, the frames will also alter what students need to learn in the course of their classroom experiences.

When children with disabilities have difficulties, teachers often adapt their instruction to make the curriculum accessible. Adaptations are made in instruction for children who are not able to learn under typical circumstances. For example, instructions may be repeated individually, aides may provide supplementary curriculum materials, peer coaching may be arranged, or school assignments may be shortened.

These curricular adaptations, when carried out by teachers focusing on the curriculum, are seen as part of instruction. In the educational frame, adaptation is done to achieve the goal of imparting the curriculum rather than to remediate children's disabilities. In the support frame, to be described next, these same adaptive activities are reframed within a social participation model.

SUPPORT

A third mode of teaching is an indirect one, and one that requires a major shift in thinking. It has to do with seeing one's professional responsibility in terms of support rather than in term of remedying deficits or teaching the curriculum. In a support model speech–language pathologists and classroom teachers work together with students to achieve identified goals. They assume the role of supporters rather than the role of remediators, of coaches rather than of instructors, of collaborators rather than of directors.

This support model has been dubbed various things depending upon the particular aspect of the approach being emphasized. It has been called a *sociocultural model* or frame, when the focus is on the social collaboration between participants (e.g., Foreman, Minick, & Stone, 1993; Wells & Claxton, 2002) and a *situated pragmatics model* when the focus is on the event (e.g., Duchan, 1997).

Support, like intervention and instruction, comes in a number of guises. Included are approaches that focus on supporting the child in all aspects of his or her life. One example is *person-centered planning*, in which a group of individuals, the child's support circle, sometimes called a "circle of friends," meet regularly to establish short- and longterm life goals, as well as pathways to achieve them (e.g., Holburn & Vietze, 2002). This approach is used with children who have severe communication difficulties and who are in need of considerable support so that they can achieve an enjoyable, self-fulfilling life.

Another version of the support model is offered by a teaching approach called *scaffolding* (Stone, 1993, 2002; Wood, Bruner, & Ross, 1976) or *guided participation* (Rogoff, 1995). "Scaffolding" is a metaphor that is used to describe a method by which someone offers learners contextual support just outside their conceptual reach. The learners are encouraged to carry out parts of tasks that are within their ability, and the adult "guides," "fills in," or "scaffolds" the rest. The scaffolding can be focused on different areas of learning. For example, it might involve recruiting learners' interest, reducing their choices, maintaining their goal orientation, highlighting critical aspects of the task, controlling their frustration, and demonstrating how to carry out the activity to them (Wood et al., 1976; Wood & Middleton, 1975). Scaffolding is often portrayed as a collaboration between teachers and students in which the students are invited by teachers to engage in a social learning experience designed to extend their knowledge (Stone, 1993).

Scaffolding is usually portrayed as being illustrative of a *sociocultural frame* (see examples in Forman et al., 1993). Like other frames, the sociocultural frame can be interpreted broadly, in which the "socio," or social, part of the term has to do with society, or more narrowly, in which the "socio" refers to social interaction or social participation. The "cultural" part of the term is in the name of the frame because of the emphasis on how cultural teachings are internalized by members of the culture. This emphasis on cultural aspects of scaffolding is one that draws heavily from the writings of Lev Vygotsky, whose construct of a "zone of proximal development" (ZPD) has been used as a basis for designing situated support that is within the conceptual grasp of learners (Vygotsky, 1978). The ZPD described by Vygotsky is that area of knowledge between what a learner can do *without* support and what the learner can do *with* scaffolded help.

As can be seen in the person-centered and scaffolding examples of the support model, support is appropriate for all children, regardless of their abilities. The support can arise from different aspects of the situational context, and can be of different types, such as social, emotional, functional, physical, event, and discourse (see Duchan, 1995, for more detail on each of these).

Another frame that is commonplace in providing support and one that characterizes the model is a *navigation metaphor*. Support is evaluated and provided to circumvent "barriers" to participation. Communication "ramps" are provided to allow a person with disabilities "access." The participation model forwarded by Beukelman and Mirenda (1998) exemplifies the effective use of this metaphor in designing support goals and methods.

As with the intervention model, one finds the *naturalness metaphor* applied in the support model. In this frame, however, "naturalness" has to do with the way support is provided. When support is invisible and unobtrusive, it is considered "natural." The supported child should not look as if he or she is being singled out. The worry of those advocating "natural supports" is that children and adults who require multiple supports in order to perform in their everyday life contexts will be ostracized or considered different because of the supports rather than because of their disabilities. Furthermore, if they are treated in the same ways as other children, they and others will think of them as similar to others rather than as being different. So the emphasis here differs from that of deficit-based, intervention approaches that focus on the nature of the interaction or on how intervention sessions are carried out. Instead the focus in a support frame is on the situational circumstances of supported participation—what Nisbet (1992) and others call "natural supports."

Jorgensen (1992) illustrates the provision of natural supports in her discussion of Joshua, an 11-year-old fifth grader with a severe physical and communication disability. In an analysis of Joshua's daily support system, Jorgensen found a number of natural supports provided regularly by family members, friends, and school personnel. For example, different people were involved in getting Joshua to and from school and in helping him to engage in various parts of his school day: The classroom teacher helped him with his lunch, the occupational therapist adapted a paintbrush for him, the speech–language pathologist supported him in a group activity of making an anti-drug collage, and students in other grades helped him participate in a recycling project.

A second and related way the notion of naturalism is advocated for in a support model has to do with the activity. "Natural activities" are ones that occur in the child's life. Intervention, when carried out in natural ways, takes place in the course of natural activities—what Brown and colleagues call "authentic activities" (Brown, Collins, & Duguid, 1989). Authentic activities carried out within the support model would be those in which the child is provided support during regular everyday school, home, or community events (Duchan, 1997). These activities are not framed in an "as-if" reality like the activities in the intervention model. Nor are they framed as part of the curriculum, as in the instructional model. Rather, they are part of a child's taken-for-granted reality.

A third use of naturalism under the support frame applies to efforts to obtain societal acceptance as well as to create natural learning contexts. The idea, called *normalization*, became a worldwide social reform movement in the 1970s in the field of mental retardation (Wolfensberger, 1972). The term was first used by Bank-Mikkelson (1969), a Danish public administrator who made an appeal to let the mentally retarded obtain a life as close to normal as possible. In the United States this idea was elaborated on and reframed by Wolf Wolfensberger, who argued for culturally normal ways to achieve culturally normal learnings. Wolfensberger, reflecting on the achievements of the "normalization" or "social valorization movement," as it came to be called, has identified a number of societal domains that still need to be worked on to achieve normalization for those with severe disabilities. Among those listed are the following three: (1) negative attitudes about disability, (2) low expectations for people with disabilities, and (3) dumping and abandonment (Condeluci, 2000).

COMBINATIONS OF THE INTERVENTION, INSTRUCTION, AND SUPPORT MODELS

As in the case of blended models in diagnosis and assessment, intervention models such as the deficit and situated support models often occur as blends. Clinicians can act as instructors in a classroom context, in keeping with the instruction and support models, and, at the same time, focus their coaching on a child's deficit, following the dictates of an intervention model. Intervention goals may be aimed directly at classroom participation (support model) and also contain goals that focus on the child's difficulties (deficit, intervention model). Teaching on some occasions may take place during regular instruction in the classroom, on other occasions by supporting a child to participate, and on still other days by individualized instruction in a resource or speech therapy room.

A well-disseminated model that speech–language pathologists have incorporated into their clinical practices (American Speech–Language–Hearing Association, 2001b) is one promulgated by the World Health Organization (WHO). The most recent version of the WHO model, called the International Classification of Functioning, Disability, and Health (second version), or ICF, was passed at the 2001 meeting of the WHO. The ICF is substantially different from its first incarnation, the International Classification of Impairment, Disability and Handicap (ICIDH), passed in 1980. The differences reflect a conceptual shift from an intervention to a support model. (For more details on the ICF, see World Health Organization, 2001.)

The 1980 ICIDH was built around three conceptual categories: impairment, disability, and handicap. All three were problem-focused, presupposing that a person has a physical or psychological impairment that leads to functional limitations (disability) and to societal discrimination (handicap). The 2001 ICF, on the other hand, has four conceptual categories, none of which are exclusively focused on deficits. The categories are (1) body structures and functions, (2) activities and participation, (3) environmental factors, and (4) personal factors. Figure 4.1 depicts how the American Speech–Language–Hearing Association (2001b) has formulated the WHO model. It describes the full range of possibilities from normal to abnormal for each of the dimensions thusly:

> Each component can be expressed as a continuum of function. One end of the continuum indicates intact or neutral functioning; the other indicates completely compromised function or disability . . . or participation restriction. For example, the component of Body Functions and Structures has a continuum that ranges from normal variation to complete impairment; Activity ranges from no activity limitation to complete activity limitation; and Participation ranges from no participation restriction to complete participation restriction. (pp. I-27)

The recent rendition of the WHO model is much more grounded in the support model than in the deficit or intervention model. The activity and participation components have to do with whether individuals are able to engage and participate in life situations, a focus that looks away from their deficits and toward whether individuals are provided opportunities to engage in everyday life situations.

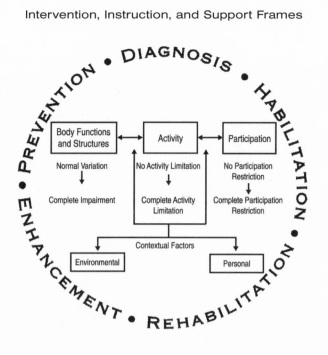

Figure 4.1. ASHA's version of the WHO model. From American Speech–Language–Hearing Association (2001b, p. 27). Copyright 2001 by the American Speech–Language–Hearing Association. Reprinted by permission.

SUMMARY

Approaches used to alter, instruct, or support the communication of children with language or literacy disabilities are governed by a multitude of different interpretive frames. (See Table 4.4 for a summary of those select few discussed in this chapter.)

Researchers, teachers, and speech–language pathologists often classify approaches into two opposing types based on a selected subset of contrasting features. This dichotomous thinking allows professionals to describe their methods and contrast them with other approaches. Commonly used subclasses are didactic versus naturalistic, adult-directed versus child-centered, and wholistic versus phonic. But, when the features of a particular method are examined in detail, it may be found to have characteristics of both types of the contrasted methods. A whole language approach to reading may contain within it phonic prompting, for example.

Table 4.4. A Summary of Frames and Associated Models of Intervention, Instruction, and Support for Children with Language and Literacy Disabilities

Frame type	Approaches
Overriding models and associated approaches	
Medical model	Intervention approaches are based on child's diagnosis. Aim is to remediate the child's identified deficits.
Educational model	Instructional approaches are based on curriculum goals.
Sociocultural and participation/access models	Support approaches are based on whether the child is being provided social and informational access to life situations. Two examples are personal futures planning and scaffolding.[a]
Metaphors associated with intervention, instruction, and support approaches	
Intervention approach	The naturalness metaphor. Most natural intervention = commonly occurring daily activities (nondidactic), carried out by family members at home, and involving natural interactions with uninterrupted flow and reciprocal emotional exchange.
	The functional metaphor. Focus on functional communicative acts (as tools), and on learning that "works" in natural communicative contexts.
Instruction approach	Curricular and classroom discourse frames.
Support approach	The naturalness metaphor. Natural supports, authentic activities, normalization.
Learning models	
What is learned (content)	Linguistic model. Information-processing model.
How it is learned (process)	Behavioral depiction of learning. Constructivist depiction of learning.

[a]The adult demonstrates the activity, which the child is invited to participate in. The child then performs parts of the activity in keeping with the demonstration.

These mixed approaches have been described by Fey (1986) as "hybrid." In the terms of this book, hybrid approaches involve a blending of models or interpretive frames.

Three frames that govern teaching practices have been described: intervention, instruction, and support. Each of these three frames is itself comprised of models and metaphors. An intervention approach may be based on an information-processing or a linguistic model, and it may presume that learning takes place according to behaviorial or constructivist learning principles. An instructional frame is governed by curricular and classroom discourse frames. Curricula are now being adapted to fit the particular needs of children with disabilities, thereby incorporating features of an intervention frame. A support approach may contain metaphors of naturalness and functionality. Methods arising from a support approach may be cast in a sociocultural frame that draws from Vygotsky or on a person-centered planning frame that is based more on a life participation model.

Frames governing teaching and clinical approaches are, in turn, based on larger paradigmatic and reality frames. For example, the intervention frame is based on assumptions of the medical model and assumes an "as-if" reality. The aim is to make therapy as natural and functional as possible, making it look as if it were part of a taken-for-granted reality.

The instructional frame comes from an educational model. Teachers instruct, children learn. The curriculum is the focus and the goal is to impart the curriculum to all children in the class. The curriculum is adapted for children who are not successful using typical instructional approaches.

The support frame is grounded in the situation. The problem underlying a child's apparent poor performance is seen as being due to a situational or social barrier blocking the child's access to information or preventing him or her from being able to show his or her competence or to engage fully in what is going on.

One can find many examples of blended approaches in which intervention, instruction, and support models are used together. A classic example of such a blend is the World Health Organization's newest ICF model which renders physical aspects of disability as individual deficiencies that are in need of interventions, and activity and participation aspects of disability as situated terms in need of environmental support.

FIVE

Framing Progress of Students and Professionals

Using a clock to measure time defines a model for time as proceeding at a consistent pace, in a single direction and brings with it a taxonomy that includes seconds, minutes, hours, days, years.

—Byock (1999, p. 89)

Using clock time as a measure of time seems to be an obvious, uncontestable measure of external reality. However, it does not capture a person's experience of time's passage. Instead, it portrays a notion of time as something that only exists in the objective world apart from people's experience of it. There are many changes in children's development that are well served by using objective measures, like that of clock time, as an evaluation instrument, but for some purposes experience measures might best meet their needs. For example, a listing of a mother's ideas about her child's history would give more information were it to focus on what she sees as significant meanings and milestones rather than on the objective dates of onset (e.g., "He stopped talking just after we moved to our new house" vs. "He stopped talking when he was 3"). Capturing the subjective or experiential side of language disability fits into another frame, one that has been called a *phenomenological approach* (Dreyfus, 1990; Husserl, 1913/1931; Merleau-Ponty, 1962) or a *life world* approach (Mishler, 1986).

Most efforts to measure the outcomes of clinical and education interventions try to eliminate measurement biases that come from the experiences of the evaluators or the people being evaluated. Efforts to maintain objectivity derive from an objective reality frame in which the real world is taken to reside outside people's experience of it. I will be calling this worldview an *objective reality frame*.

Its opposite is a view that assumes that reality is constructed, and that this construction takes place in people's inner lives such as thoughts, feelings, and beliefs. This *subjective reality frame* takes a phenomenological, life world approach. It leads to outcome measures that include the subjective experience of those whose progress is being measured.

The contrast of objective and subjective reality frames provides an example of frames that are different from the models and metaphors I have been talking about in previous chapters. Reality frames are more pervasive and influential than models or metaphors in that they have to do with the broad conceptual stance an evaluator takes toward what is being evaluated. The reality frame selected is likely to limit or influence other models or metaphors used in evaluation. For example, an objective perspective will exclude the use of a model of evaluation that examines the personal experiences of those receiving intervention.

THE OBJECTIVE REALITY FRAME

An evaluator working within an objective reality frame tries to be a neutral data gatherer. The presumption is that, given the proper controls, an evaluator can eliminate the influence of his or her own subjective distortions about what is being observed by carefully controlling for *experimenter bias*. The assumption underlying this goal of keeping evaluations objective is that data being used to ascertain intervention or instructional effects are in the "real world," and that they, like time measured with a clock, have the status of unassailable facts that are discoverable whenever biases are controlled for.

Under this objective view, the evaluator looks for well-defined ways of measuring changes, ways that are not subject to distortions from the evaluator or those being evaluated. Achieving this neutrality requires that the aspect of reality being examined, one that demonstrates the effect of the intervention, be measured in objective ways, preferably numerically. Furthermore, extraneous factors need to be kept constant or, when this is not possible, need to be taken into consideration when interpreting the findings.

Sometimes evaluation is done by designing an experimental study in which the thing being measured is regarded as the dependent variable and the treatment as the independent variable. This *experimental research paradigm* includes within it a *causal metaphor.* The aim of evaluation is to discover whether an independent variable causes changes in a dependent variable. The observer tests this relationship by manipulating the independent variable and measuring changes in the dependent variable. Or the observers may compare objective conditions, when different variables are present, or he or she may compare conditions with and without a causal variable. *Independent variables* (i.e., the elements causing change), like *dependent variables* (i.e., the elements that are affected by change), should be identifiable, isolable from other variables, and quantifiable.

A primary test for the believability of objective studies done within the experimental research paradigm is that the data collected and the measures taken are *replicable.* That is, evaluation techniques are judged successful when they achieve the same results over and over again, regardless of who is doing the evaluation. The data are regarded as objective truths, as facts that are discoverable and stable.

The experimental research paradigm is thought of as *the* scientific method. Doing social science, in the eyes of many of today's researchers who study the effect of intervention on children's language and literacy improvement, requires the testing of well-formed causal hypotheses. The hypotheses are based on a notion of direct causality, in which the factor or variable being manipulated—the treatment—is seen as causing significant changes in the children being tested. This approach, hypothesis testing, is regarded as what one must do to be a bona fide scientist. It is also the research basis that practitioners are typically asked to provide to justify their selection of teaching or therapy approaches.

Evaluators using the objective scientific method must select models that yield measurable outcomes that are relevant to the therapies chosen. If their measures concern the effects of a therapy or teaching method on a child's memory, attention, or auditory or language processing, evaluators are likely to use an evaluation system that is based on an information-processing model. Similarly, if the therapy is based on a linguistic rule model, evaluators are likely to look for objective measures of linguistic rule acquisition.

Evaluators working within an objective reality frame also must select a way to collect their data. They have available a variety of measurement techniques ranging from direct observation to the use of well-designed and highly controlled experiments. A randomized clinical (or controlled) trial is a kind of experiment, considered by those who take the objective perspective as the ultimate standard for determining the worthiness of an intervention (e.g., Friel Patti, 2001). Some call this a "gold standard," using the metaphor of a difficult-to-attain precious metal to describe the high regard with which the randomized controlled trial is held.

Under a randomized controlled trial (RCT) approach, evaluators assign children randomly to an experimental group and to a control group. Children in the experimental group receive an intervention. The children in the control group (or groups) receive another equally valued intervention, a placebo intervention, or no intervention at all. In order to avoid ethical concerns about excluding children from receiving a preferred approach, there should be uncertainty within the expert community about the comparative merits of the various interventions (Catt, 1999; Freedman, 1987). Treatments for both the experimental and the control groups are administered in a carefully controlled way. Effort is made to treat every participant in the group the same. Testing is also carefully controlled, often through the use of standardized tests.

To avoid bias, the participants in the study are sometimes not told what group they are in. This type of condition is called a "blind experiment," using a metaphor having to do with vision. Even the experimenter may not know what group a particular subject is assigned to (this is called a "double-blind experiment"). Tests are given before and after the treatment. Statistically significant differences between the performance of the children in the comparison groups are viewed as solid evidence that the experimental treatment caused changes in the children's performance. Improvements in scores of children in the experimental group that go beyond any improvements due to developmental maturation are interpreted as being caused by the treatment condition, the independent variable. These positive results allow the researchers and clinicians to claim that a treatment is efficacious—that it had a significant impact on the participants under these carefully controlled conditions.

Ironically, one problem with the highly controlled condition based on an objective perspective is that the conditions of the experiment are different from real-life conditions. The worry is that the results from the experiment are not results that would be obtained in naturally occurring contexts. They are not ecologically or socially valid (Lincoln, Onslow, & Reed, 1997). This is a concern having to do with naturalness and based on a *naturalness metaphor.*

So another way for discovering whether a treatment is making or has made a difference is to measure changes thought to be the result of therapy or instruction carried out in uncontrolled situations. This is done by comparing a child's performance in naturally occurring situations before, during, and after the treatment condition takes place. The uncontrolled method is more credible when comparisons are made in similar contexts and if they are quantified. For example, language sampling may be done during a particular natural activity, say a conversation with a friend. The child's production of a targeted structure such as a phonological rule or a morphological inflection is analyzed later, during the same activity, for changes over time (Ingram, 1976; Miller, 1981).

Measuring Change Objectively

There are a variety of other ways to measure something objectively. Some involve fewer resources than those needed for randomized controlled trials. Administering standardized tests, for example, is a popular way to obtain objective scores. Test scores can be used to measure an individual's performance broadly (e.g., language ability, educational aptitude) as well as in specific areas (e.g., morphology, memory span, spelling skills).

Normative Frames

Tests scores are often required by regulating agencies because they offer quick and easy comparisons of children's performance before and after a treatment regimen. The tests are built upon a *normative model* in that they evaluate the performance of individuals in relation to the preformance of others in a comparison group or in relation to their own previous performance. The measures are seen as objective because they are usually administered in a prescribed, uniform way, thereby eliminating the naturally occurring variables that would affect performance and render scores unreliable or invalid. Standardized tests, when used to evaluate the outcomes of an intervention or educational method, are usually administered at least twice, once before and once after the intervention. The degree of impact of the method is revealed in the difference between scores on the pre- and post-measures.

The *linguistic model*, used to discover changes in a child's production of linguistic rules, is often combined with a normative model. For example, clinicians may trace a child's use of inflectional morphology using Miller's (1981) data analysis method to see if the child is progressing through expected stages of normal language development. The combination involves analyzing a child's language for linguistic structures and then comparing those with developmental norms (e.g., Gerrard, 1991; Miller, 1981).

Functional Frames

Functional frames that conjure up questions about how well communication serves life purposes have also had a strong influence on the conceptualization and design of objective measures to evaluate therapy outcomes. For example, a taskforce of the the American Speech–Language–Hearing Association (ASHA) is collecting data on an instrument for objectively measuring whether a child's communication has become more functional (i.e., useful) as a result of language intervention (ASHA, 1996a). The functional communication measures used by the taskforce were designed to evaluate outcomes in 14 domains, among which are pragmatic precursors, cognitive play, pragmatics, cognitive orientation, attachment, interaction (of caregiver), prespeech sound production, articulation/intelligibility, language comprehension, and language production.

Each item in the taskforce's instrument is associated with seven levels of functional performance. The child's performance is classified both before and after the treatment into one of the functional levels on the scales that fit with the child's goals. Table 5.1 exhibits an ASHA taskforce example for the domain of pragmatic precursors (ASHA, 1996a). The levels of competence from Level 1 (least functional) to Level 7 (most functional) are shown for vocalization, social interaction, vocal interaction, symbolic strategies, and communication.

Another scale in the ASHA taskforce's functional communication measuring system is one involving a teacher's ratings. The teacher is asked to rate a student's communication on each of 18 status items in order to ascertain how the child's therapies have affected his or her functioning in the classroom. For each item the teacher identifies a level, choosing from among seven possibilities

Table 5.1. Levels of Functional Performance in the Domain of Pragmatic Precursors[a] to Language Development

	Noncrying vocalization	Social interactions	Vocal interactions	Presymbolic/symbolic strategies	Communication
Level 1	No noncrying or nonvegetative sound making	Cries when uncomfortable or hungry	Limited vocal sound making		
Level 2	Gains attention when hungry/uncomfortable	Lacks attention to people in environment	Random vocalizations		No initiation or response
Level 3	Gains social attention	Directed gaze associated with smiling or vocalizing	Responds inconsistently to social attention—changes facial expression/vocalization	No reciprocal interactions	No initiation
Level 4	Gains attention and responds	Responsive and reciprocal to social interaction	Increased vocalization, facial expression, or body movement in response to social interaction	May engage in reciprocal interactions	No initiation
Level 5	Gains attention and conveys general ideas			Engages in reciprocal interactions	Limited repertoire of strategies
Level 6		Imitates adult's body movements and vocal patterns	Age-appropriate	Readily engages in presymbolic strategies	Inconsistently imitates interaction using symbolic strategies, in limited contexts
Level 7		Engages with both peers and adults in variety of social contexts	Age-appropriate		Consistently initiates and responds

Note. From American Speech–Language–Hearing Association (1996a, p. 47). Copyright 1996 by the American Speech–Language–Hearing Association. Reprinted by permission.

[a]*Definition:* Child's ability to use vocal interactions, play, or laughter to communicate with a variety of peers and adults in a variety of social contexts. *Intended audience:* Infant/child who is at the prespeech, preverbal, or presymbolic level of development

that range from Level 1 (child does not perform the task identified) to Level 7 (child performs the task independently).

Table 5.2 identifies the 18 status items in the ASHA taskforce's teacher rating scale. The items qualify as "functional" because nearly all have to do with how well a child is able to function in activities that take place in the classroom (items c, e, h), or in a specified educational event, such as an oral presentation (item k), giving or following directions (items l, m), responding to classroom questions (item b), listening to and recalling educationally based information (items n, o, q), or making oneself understood (item a).

In sum, evaluators often presuppose an objective reality frame when evaluating therapy or educational outcomes. They are doing this regardless of what sort of measure is selected, whether a rating scale or some other standardized measure. They are also doing this using different frames, such as a normative or a functional one. This objective stance is expressed by Rao, Blosser, and Huffman (1998) when they describe a speech–language pathologist who "views each intervention as a mini experiment—proposing and testing hypotheses, learning from the results of the testing, and then revising one's behavioral strategies to achieve even better results" (p. 91). Rao et al. conclude: "Without measurement, the effectiveness of these 'mini experiments' is left to subjective impression" (p. 91)—a fate that they would have us take great pains to avoid.

THE SUBJECTIVE REALITY FRAME

The perceived dangers of relying on subjective impressions as expressed by Rao et al. (1998) evolve from a view that one can successfully separate the objective from the subjective experience of reality. Achievement of this separation is not possible when viewing reality from a subjective perspective. This subjective frame goes by different names: an experiential perspective (Biklen & Duchan, 1994), an interpretive approach (Geertz, 1973), social constructivism (Hacking, 1999), a phenomenological approach (Segal, 1995), a life world approach (Mishler, 1986), or the one I will be using, a *subjective reality frame*. Within this subjective reality perspective, clinicians' and teachers' attempts to separate an objective reality from their own subjective view is seen as an impossible and fruitless task. The notion of a world containing discoverable factual information existing outside the experience or interpretation of individuals is itself seen as a conceptual construction. So-called facts and truths depend

Table 5.2. Functional Status Measures from the National Treatment Outcomes Measurement System: Speech–Language Pathology Services for Children in Educational Settings

Status measures: For each statement please mark the response that indicates how well the student functions in each of these areas within the educational environment. (Choices: 0 = no basis for rating; 1 = does not do; 2 = does with maximal assistance; 3 = does with moderate to maximal assistance; 4 = does with moderate assistance; 5 = does with minimal to moderate assistance; 6 = does with minimal assistance; 7 = does.)

a. The student's speech is understood

b. The student responds to questions regarding everyday and classroom activities

c. The student produces appropriate phrases and sentences in response to classroom activities

d. The student communicates wants, needs, ideas, and concepts to others either verbally or by use of an augmentative/alternative communication system

e. The student uses appropriate vocabulary to function within the classroom

f. The student describes familiar objects and events

g. The student knows and uses age-appropriate interactions with peers and staff

h. The student initiates, maintains, and concludes conversations with peers and staff within classroom environments

i. The student initiates, maintains, and concludes conversations with peers and staff in non-classroom settings

j. The student indicates when messages are not understood

k. The student completes oral presentations

l. The student demonstrates the ability to give directions

m. The student demonstrates the ability to follow directions

n. The student demonstrates the ability to recall written information presented in the educational environment

o. The student demonstrates the ability to recall auditory information presented in the educational environment

p. The student demonstrates the ability to use verbal language to solve problems

q. The student demonstrates appropriate listening skills within the educational environment

r. The student recognizes and demonstrates comprehension of nonverbal communication

(continued)

Table 5.2. continued

Other measures: Please respond to the following items using the scale rating from strongly agree to strongly disagree or not applicable

 a. The student speaks easily without frustration

 b. The student's speech does not call attention to itself

 c. The student speaks loudly enough for small group and cooperative learning

 d. The student demonstrates improved social and education skills due to intervention by the audiologist

 e. The student demonstrates improved social and educational skills due to intervention by the speech-language pathologist

 f. The student's successful progression through the education process was positively affected by speech-language pathology and audiology intervention

Note. From American Speech–Language–Hearing Association (1996a, Appendix C). Copyright 1996 by the American–Speech–Language Hearing Association. Reprinted by permission.

upon one's worldview and upon the models and the metaphors that one uses to create what one takes to be objective realities.

This view that one's sense of reality depends upon one's personal experience or conceptual take on the world has permeated our U.S. culture in recent years. Michael Pollan (2001), a reporter commenting on the acquisition of an organic food company by General Mills, noted on the philosophy of the company:

> At General Mills . . . the whole notion of objective truth has been replaced by a kind of value-neutral consumer constructivism, in which each sovereign shopper constructs his own reality: "Taste You Can Believe In." (p. 30)

The subjective stance not only applies to the personal biases of the evaluator, it also raises questions about how those being evaluated experience their therapy or educational or support programs. In order to judge the success of programs, one must access the thinking and experiences of the students or clients. The most obvious way to tap into the subjectivity of students or clients is to borrow from the techniques of anthropologists who aim to discover the various ways people from different cultures experience their worlds. Ethnographic methods designed for this purpose include doing detailed interviews with members of the culture, writing field notes about what goes on in the culture from differing points of view, and engaging with members of the culture as they carry out their every-day lives (Spradley, 1980). Along the way, the author might collect and examine artifacts, such as written records and objects, in the search for clues about how members of a culture experience their practices.

Researchers and practitioners may then study and analyze the information gathered, looking for themes and patterns in the data. Some delve even deeper, looking for meanings that reside under more surface themes and patterns. For instance, Clifford Geertz (1973) uses a viscosity metaphor, "thick description," to interpret the cultural significance of events such as a Balinese cockfight for the Balinese.

There is a relatively plentiful literature in the field of education devoted to uncovering children's subjectivities. Vivian Paley, an author and former kindergarten teacher, has spent many years searching for life-relevant meanings about school and life con-veyed by children as young as 2 years. Paley uses two methods to find out what children think. The first is talking with children about issues relevant to their lives. In her book *You Can't Say You Can't Play* (Paley, 1992), she reports the reactions of kindergarten and elementary school children to imposing a rule about whether they can exclude someone from their social play.

Paley's second method for discovering children's inner lives is by listening to and analyzing their oral stories. In her books about the children in her kindergarten classroom, she has analyzed the underlying personal, social, and moral significance of the oral sto-ries they tell her and their classmates (Paley, 1981, 1990, 2001). This use of students' stories (Engel, 1995; O'Connor, 1996), diary entries (Freedom Writers & Gruwell, 1999), and samples of their drawing and writing (Bissex, 1980) provide intriguing insights into children's subjective lives.

While one can easily find examples of children's subjective ex-periences in the education literature, they are hard to find in the literature written by those in speech–language pathology. One gets little direct sense from the professional literature on children with communication disorders about what the children are thinking or feeling. Furthermore, except for self-generated biographies, there are few renderings of student outcomes on the lives of their rela-tives and friends.

Student files, for example, a place where one would go to look for documentation of progress, have no natural way for housing the personal expressions of students or their associates. Unlike ethnographic records that are replete with quotes, transcripts, and other documents revealing the experienced reality of the informants or study participants, clinical files are purged of documents that are considered too subjective or impressionistic to deserve a place in the "official record" (Duchan, 1999; Hegde, 1994; Pannbacker, 1975).

But there are indications that the single-minded commitment in the clinical literature to collecting only verifiable, objective truths of students may finally be changing. In recent years there has been a growing appreciation for the importance of how students are experiencing their lives and their disabilities. This appreciation is congruent with an intellectual trend in the social sciences in the United States toward the study of the *personal narratives* of both adults (Becker, 1997; Crossley, 2000; Polanyi, 1989) and children (Heath, 1983; Peterson & McCabe, 1983). This cultural trend toward the use of narratives in the social sciences has been called a "narrative turn" (Riessman, 1993).

In keeping with the narrative turn, clinical interviews are used now not only to discover factual information about a person's medical and developmental history, but also to discover how the person goes about portraying his or her life history (Jefferson, 1979; Polanyi, 1989). Included in this endeavor are many metaphors. For example one often finds in a person's life stories *journey metaphors* (traveling along life pathways) and *navigation metaphors* (portrayal of problems as barriers and of disability as lack of access). (See Mastergeorge, 1999, for many more metaphors found in the life stories of parents whose children have communication disabilities.)

Clinical reports might not only include the clinician's test results about a person's deficits, but also information about how those deficits impact the person's life, as expressed in his or her life stories (see, e.g., Becker, 1997). Case studies can and have included a person's life stories (e.g., Sacks, 1996). Finally, and most relevant to my purposes in this chapter, is the possibility that outcome measures can be designed to include oral reports from students or older clients who are asked to talk how their therapies or educational experiences have impacted them in their daily lives (Parr, Byng, & Gilpin, 1997; Pound, Parr, & Duchan, 2001).

There is another way a subjective rendering of a person's life experiences can be revealed—one that is different from listening to and analyzing his or her life stories. This method also comes from the educational literature (e.g., Grace & Shores, 1991; Herbert, 2001; Murphy & Smith, 1991). It involves the use of *portfolios* to collect materials over the course of an intervention or educational program. Portfolios, a personal kind of record keeping, contrast dramatically with the typical school or clinical records kept on a child. Whereas typical records have traditionally excluded personal materials or personal profiles, portfolios can emphasize the personal. They provide clinicians, teachers, and students a place to archive personal effects. Portfolios have been used as a way for those with disabilities to express their personal identity and to reflect on their achievements (Pound, Parr, Lindsay, & Woolf, 2000). They have also been used as way for clinicians and teachers to assess and evaluate a child's progress (Kratcoski, 1998).

The subjective reality frame has the distinct advantage over objective approaches for bringing a client's or student's lived experience into view. This perspective has eye-opening reframing potential for all areas of clinical and educational practice. (See Table 5.3 for examples of how to elicit and collect experience-based evaluations.)

The subjective frame has been shown to be relevant for evaluating any aspect of clinical or educational practice. It is particularly relevant when evaluating how interventions have impacted the lives of those with language and literacy disabilities. Outcomes indicators designed from within the subjective frame raise new and interesting issues for clinicians and teachers, ones that are invisible when working within the objective frame. These include concerns about authenticity and authorship, and about privacy and power.

Table 5.3. Examples of Ways to Elicit Information about a Student's Personal Experiences of Different Areas of Clinical Endeavor

Diagnosis: Interview of family members or students about the impact of their diagnosis on their lives (e.g., Galasso, in press).

Assessment: Use of approaches that work from client's or student's experiences such as personal futures planning (Mount, 1994), needs assessments (Jorgensen, 1994), and student-centered Individualized Educational Programs (Cheng, 1990).

Intervention: Use of personal narratives (Paley, 1981, 1990), development of personalized portfolios displaying accomplishments, involvement of students in the selection of their intervention goals, and evaluation of their progress.

Outcomes assessment: Interviews with parents or student about changes in a student's quality of life resulting from interventions or support programs; use of consumer evaluation surveys; evaluation of portfolios; analysis of personal narratives.

Authenticity

Authenticity, as it is most often portrayed, describes the degree to which a clinical or educational method resembles a "real-life" situation. Kohonen (2002), when arguing for authentic assessment of language and literacy abilities, defines it thusly: "Authentic language assessment refers to the procedures for evaluating learner performance using activities and tasks that represent classroom goals, curricula and instruction in as realistic conditions of language use as possible" (section 2.1). The authenticity metaphor, like the naturalness metaphor (see Chapter 4), treats clinical or educational approaches in an *"as-if" reality frame*, and bases the degree of authenticity on how much the happenings in that reality frame resemble those in the taken-for-granted world.

The issue of whether a method is authentic is often raised in relation to standardized tests. For instance, Schraeder, Quinn, Stockman, and Miller (1999) have argued against the exclusive use of standardized tests because test results do not examine the impact of "variables such as the interaction partner(s), conversational and discourse parameters, materials, setting, task, and information processing" (p. 196). To include such objective variables, Shraeder et al. contend, makes assessment results more authentic.

The advantages and goals of authentic assessment expressed above are framed within an objective reality frame. In this frame, "authenticity" refers to the degree to which clinical and educational methods simulate the objective conditions of real-life situations. "Authentic evaluation" is taken to mean that measurement situations should contain variables that are also present in familiar life situations (e.g., familiar interactants and commonly occurring discourse and event contexts).

A different concern about authenticity is raised within the subjective reality frame. In this frame, teachers and clinicians worry about whether they are being true to the client's or student's subjective experience and understandings. Evaluation is regarded as authentic when the rendering of change is consistent with what the person being evaluated thinks. For example, Maxwell (1990), when describing authenticity in ethnographic research, wonders whether the ethnographer's findings about people's experiences are consistent with how the people represent that experience to themselves. Methods have been devised by ethnographers to find multiple ways to access people's experience on a particular subject of concern so as to assure that what the ethnographers report is authentic—that is, is true to the experience and conceptualization of the people they are studying.

Authorship

Concerns about subjective authenticity also raise an issue of *client or student authorship*. Researchers and practitioners working from within the objective frame try to eliminate the child's perspective to avoid subjective bias. This is not the case for those working within a subjective frame. Those operating within a subjective, experiential frame try to gain access to a person's subjectivity. For example, they may elicit the student's perspective during various phases and types of interactions and alter their practice depending upon what the student says or feels.

An issue of authorship is raised in relation to student self-reports because there is a high potential for speech–language pathologists and teachers to put their own words and ideas into students' reported responses, especially for those students who have severe communication difficulties (Antaki & Rapley, 1996). Evaluators using subjective methods need to take extra precautions to minimize their own influence on what the student is conveying (Duchan, Calculator, Sonnenmeier, Diehl, & Cumley, 2001). Cheng (1990), for example, offers a set of suggestions for creating an unbiased subjective approach to assessment. Among them is the following recommendation to prevent bias:

> Interact with the students, being sensitive to their needs to create meaning based on what they perceive, their frame of reference, and their experiences. This is necessary in order to understand the students' perspective. When conversing with them, allow these students the freedom to explore, digress, explain, and expand on their feelings and topics of discussion. During these interactions, allow them to struggle, succeed, or fail with their interactions. Don't second guess their words or complete their thoughts for them. Allow them to interact from their perspective even if it is communicatively difficult. (p. 117)

Privacy

Another significant issue raised within the experiential approach has to do with clinicians or teachers invading a student's *privacy*. Professionals exploring the intimate, subjective lives of children have a considerable obligation to respect those children's rights to have their private lives remain private. Privacy issues have been raised in particular in relation to quality-of-life assessments designed to obtain judgments from students or clients about their emotional well-being, interpersonal relations, material well-being, personal development, physical well-being, self-determination, social inclusion, and rights (Hatton, 1998). Hatton worries that "quality of life assessments, with their emphasis on subjective as well as objective indicators of all aspects of a person's life, can be construed as extending the range and power of services to exact surveillance on the person with mental retardation, counter to notions of privacy and independence" (p. 110).

Power

Finally, the subjective perspective can offer the opportunity for students to evaluate their teachers, thereby reversing the usual *power relations* between professionals and students (Stiegler, in press). While teachers or speech–language pathologists do not usually consider their relations with their students as ones of power wielding, the uses and abuses of such power are made apparent on certain occasions. For example, detailed studies of who decides what to do and say during most professional–student interactions reveal the overwhelming control exerted by professionals. Professionals typically choose the activity or topic, they decide whose turn it is in an activity and when to stop, and they evaluate whether the activity was effective (e.g., Prutting, Bagshaw, Goldstein, Juskowitz, & Umen, 1978). Even very young children are aware of their subservient roles evidenced by their reenactments of therapy interactions (Ripich & Panagos, 1985). These nonegalitarian roles are also evident in popular culture's rendition of speech and language therapy indicated by media depictions of domineering and misguided speech–language pathologists working with victimized clients (Pound, Parr, & Byng, 1999).

There are a few occasions wherein power relations are reflected upon by clients and clinicians or by students and teachers. David Sedaris (2000) still chafes when recollecting as an adult his elementary school interactions with his all-powerful speech–language pathologist. Sedaris dubs his clinician "Agent Samson" and describes his experience of her power abuses thusly:

> Sometimes I'd spend the half hour parroting whatever Agent Samson had to say. We'd occasionally pass the time examining charts on tongue position or reading childish s-laden texts recounting the adventures of seals or settlers named Sassy or Samuel. On the worst of

days she'd haul out a tape recorder and show me just how much progress I was failing to make. (p. 8)

The focus so far has been on ways of eliciting a student's or a client's subjective experience and the issues these approaches raise. Among the concerns have been those related to authenticity and authorship of the data collected, protection of a student's or a client's privacy, and protection from the authoritarian and all-powerful professional. The subjective perspective, when applied to evaluation, leads one to examine ways students feel about their teaching and therapy experiences.

Evaluation of Clinicians and Teachers

Students who are enrolled in preprofessional curricula in the fields of speech–language pathology or elementary school teaching or special education need to learn the conceptual bases and practices of their professions. For students enrolled in departments of communication disorders, the conceptual bases are taught in classrooms in courses involving different areas of disability, such as voice, fluency, phonology, motor speech, swallowing, and child and adult language. Students enrolled in elementary or special education curricula learn their conceptual frameworks in methods courses related to various aspects of the curriculum such as reading, mathematics, and social studies.

The information contained in educational and clinical conceptual models is often presented as a set of nonnegotiable truths, as canons and facts that need to be mastered before the student is allowed to implement them in practice teaching situations. Acquisition of knowledge taught in this objective frame is, not surprisingly, measured objectively. Teachers evaluating student learning in these classroom contexts usually do so by giving group tests. Students' mastery of the material is evaluated by examining their test scores.

Once college students in either educational or clinical curricula have passed the prerequisite courses, showing that they have learned the fundamentals of their professions' knowledge base, they are enrolled in a student-teaching practicum. Practice teaching, whether it be in a school or a clinic setting, unlike classroom learning, usually involves individualized supervision in which each student's performance is evaluated. During planning and evaluation meetings students are often asked to engage in reflective practices in which they present and evaluate their rationales and performance (See Table 5.4 for quotes from students in an educa-

**Table 5.4. Quotes from Students Showing Their Appreciation
of Supervisors Who Allow Self-Reflection**

"I do appreciate my supervisor. . . . She always asks me what I think before
she gives me her view. She always has something concrete to back up what
she is saying" (p. 77).

"I've really gotten into the competencies and self reflection" (p. 89).

"She has been good. At first I didn't know what to think of the journals we
had to keep. It's really made me think about the way I do therapy" (p. 89).

"As soon as I start to say something, Mr. Elton interrupts and then tells me
what he thinks I should do. It makes me feel like an idiot" (p. 120).

Note. Quoted in Dowling (2001).

tion curriculum about how they favor supervisors who engage
them in self-reflective practices.)

Many seasoned professionals also engage in reflective practices
on a regular basis in order to evaluate the services they are delivering. Their reflections may be done as part of quality improvement
approaches, wherein clinicians and teachers examine their own
competencies and report on their perceived strengths and weak-
nesses in areas identified by the quality improvement tools.

There are several procedural approaches for engaging professionals in reflective practices in the course of an evaluation process. One, developed as part of a quality improvement approach
used in industry (Deming, 1986, 1994; Langley, Nolan, & Nolan,
1992), has been adapted for use in improving health care (Leebov
& Ersoz, 1991). The approach, named for its activity, has been
called the "plan, do, study, act cycle" (PDSA) or the "Deming cycle" after W. Edwards Deming, its originator (Deming, 1986). It has
recently been recommended for improving the performance of
speech–language pathologists working in hospital settings (Dowling & Bruce, 1996; Frattali, 1998, pp. 179–181).

The aim of the PDSA approach is to objectify impressions of
improvement through a four-step cycle of planning and evaluation. Those engaged in the procedure first identify an area for improvement and then (1) design a *plan* for altering a current
approach; (2) *do* the plan, carrying it out and collecting data on it;
(3) *study* the data, comparing recent performance with original performance; and (4) *act* on the findings by adopting the approach
that produced the best results.

The PDSA approach has been recommended as a process
model for quality improvement by professionals because "the col-

lection and use of data help to overcome the subjectivities inherent in observation, provide more objective evidence with which to make clinical decisions, and can lead to better patient outcomes" (Frattali, 1998, p. 179). While the approach was designed to make subjective reflection more objective through data collection and analysis, it aims to capture the subjective perspective of professionals. That is, the approach requires professionals to engage in a subjective, self-reflective process to evaluate and improve their otherwise taken-for-granted practices.

Another model for evaluating professional progress and performance lays out a set of *procedural protocols* for use in identifying and solving specific professional teaching problems (Dowd, Jorgensen, & Weir, 2001). The protocols identify the players in a group interaction, specify who talks when and for how long, and provide general suggestions about the nature of the talk. For example, a consultancy protocol involves "helping an individual or a small group of people think more expansively about a particular concrete problem or dilemma" (Dowd et al., 2001).

A third model that leads professionals through a process of self- and group-reflection is *action research*, a method for identifying and solving problems and improving performance in the workplace (Elliott, 1991; Hart & Bond, 1995). The approach involves critical reflection with an eye toward discovering and implementing change. The method is a multistep reiterative approach including steps such as (1) identifying an idea or area in need of improvement; (2) collecting information about the area and analyzing it; (3) creating an action plan; (4) implementing the action plan and monitoring its effects; (5) evaluating the results of the action plan; (6) creating a new action plan based on the results of the first one; (7) implementing the second action plan and monitoring its effects; (8) continuing with new action plans data collection and evaluation (steps 3, 4, 5) for three or four cycles; and then, when a path for creating change has been arrived at, (9) writing up results and implementing them. (See Elliott, 1991; Hamilton & Knill-Greisser, 2001; and Hart & Bond, 1995, for case examples.)

The three models used to improve health care and educational practices all engage participants in a process whereby they reflect on their professional experiences. The Deming cycle requires participants to identify and reflect on the nature of a problem and then institute a sequence of activities (plan, do, study, act) to solve it. The protocol approach scripts activities for a group to engage in as they respond to a member's reflections. Action research involves an iterative set of actions for researching a way to change problem practices. While these models differ in details, they resemble one another in their overall conceptualization, goals, and procedures. They are all designed to solve a problem, they all offer a means for brainstorming solutions and trying them out, and they all go about doing these things through a process of self-reflection. The three apparently different approaches thereby can be reduced to one, a more general model that involves steps in *problem solving.*

WORLD HEALTH ORGANIZATION'S ICF MODEL: BLENDING THE MEDICAL AND SOCIAL MODELS

Like other domains of educational and clinical practice, evaluation approaches can involve blendings of different models. One highly visible example of such blending is the model recently developed by the World Health Organization (WHO). That model, called the International Classification of Functioning, Disability, and Health, or ICF model, was designed to be used as a "framework to code a wide range of information about health" (WHO, 2001). It is offered as a guide for clinicians and potentially teachers to carry out outcome evaluation (WHO, 2001).

As I noted in Chapter 4, the ICF framework provides classification and rating of health information in different areas, including a physical domain, involving body function (physiological and psychological systems) and body structure (anatomical processes); and an activity/participation domain rating a person's ability to perform a task and engage in everyday life situations. Health conditions in the different domains range from normal to abnormal, or what is cryptically termed in ICF language "functioning" (normal) and "disability" (abnormal).

The ICF contains classification codes (e.g., b16811, problem with expression of written language). Problems of a child's body structure or function domains can be ranked for level of severity (0 = no problem, 4 = severe problem), and the body structure domain allows for a further qualification indicating the degree to which the condition has changed.

The activity/participation categories in the ICF provide a mechanism for judging the degree of severity of a person's condition (0 = least severe, 4 = most severe) under two sets of circumstances. Conditions termed *capacity conditions* are ones that are controlled, context-stripped, standardized conditions, and those termed *performance conditions* have to do with the familiar contexts of everyday life.

To confine the use of the ICF only to those who have disabilities, as is exemplified by the examples above, is actually to misuse it. "There is a widely held misunderstanding that ICF is only about people with disabilities; in fact, it is about all people" (WHO, 2001, p. 7). One can see how the category system might be used when collecting health data for an entire population, a purpose that might be the goal of an epidemiologist. But when used as a guide for developing outcome measures, the frame of its use shifts from the whole population to those who are diseased or disabled, and from an epidemiological goal of gathering information about large groups of people to a medical one having to do with the provision of services to individuals with specifiable impairments.

The medical focus of the ICF has been adapted for use in the field of speech–language pathology by Threats (2001), who has provided codes of clinical categories from the ICF category system that are likely to present difficulties for those with communication disorders (Threats, 2001). For example, under the *body structure codes* are ones having to do with problems of soft palate (s32021) and vocal folds (s3400); under *body function codes,* he identifies sustaining attention (b1400) and expression of written language (b16811); and under *activity/participation codes,* he lists solving simple problems (d1750), communication with spoken messages-receiving (d310), and speaking (d330).

But the ICF doesn't stop there. The model also includes a second section, termed Part 2 of the model. Included here are "contextual influences" on health, including what the WHO authors call "environmental factors" that are part of an individual's social and situational context and "personal factors" that make up the person's psychological and social constitution (see Table 5.5 for the exact wording from WHO, 2001, on these two types of factors).

These environmental and personal factors are not of the same ilk as the physiological, psychological, and functional factors in the rest of the ICF model as it applies to those with disabilities. These factors do not have to do with a person's impairment or functional limitations. Rather, they pertain to the opportunities and support provided them, as well as to their personal background that is not part of their diagnosed condition. This discrepancy between the two sections of the model was recognized by the developers of the ICF, as shown in their description of the difference between the medical and social models. Table 5.6 indicates that these two previously incompatible models are brought together in the ICF. It is not surprising, however,

Table 5.5. Contextual Factors Indicated in the ICF

Environmental factors make up the physical, social and attitudinal environment in which people live and conduct their lives. These factors are external to individuals and can have a positive or negative influence on the individual's performance as a member of society, on the individual's capacity to execute actions or tasks, or on the individual's body function or structure.

Personal factors are the particular background of an individual's life and living, and comprise features of the individual that are not part of a health condition or health states. The factors may include gender, race, age, other health conditions, fitness, lifestyle, habits, upbringing, coping styles, social background, education, profession, past and current experience (past life events and concurrent events), overall behaviour pattern and character style, individual psychological assets and other characteristics, all or any of which may play a role in disability at any level. Personal factors are not classified in ICF.

Note. From World Health Organization (2001, pp. 16–17). Copyright 2001 by the World Health Organization. Reprinted by permission.

that the medical and social models are in separate "parts" and not comfortably embedded in one another.

The measures selected for use from within the ICF model will differ depending upon whether assessors are focusing on the medical or the social models within it. If their approach to measurement is from within the medical model, their measurements are likely to be based on a question about whether the skills of the person with the diagnosis have improved. Has the person's impairment decreased in severity? Has the impact of the impairment on the person's performance in everyday activities lessened? They might answer these questions by comparing test performance before and after intervention or by having relevant parties fill out functional rating scales.

If assessors take Part 2 of the ICF, the social model component, as their focus, they are more apt to use outcomes measures to get at the personal, experiential, subjective impact of the treatments. They might, for example, interview children in the classroom about the changes instituted, or collect narratives from the target child or members of the child's family to ascertain the child's perceptions of increased opportunities. Or, if the changes were brought about through reflective practice, they might examine the evaluation component or summary of the chosen procedure to determine its impact.

Table 5.6. International Classification of Functioning, Disability, and Health of the World Health Organization

A variety of conceptual models has been proposed to understand and explain disability and functioning. These may be expressed in a dialectic of "medical model" versus "social model." The medical model views disability as a problem of the person, directly caused by disease, trauma or other health condition, which requires medical care provided in the form of individual treatment by professionals. Management of the disability is aimed at cure or the individual's adjustment and behavior change. Medical care is viewed as the main issue, and at the political level the principal response is that of modifying or reforming health care policy. The social model of disability, on the other hand, sees the issue mainly as a socially created problem, and principally as a matter of the full integration of individuals into society. Disability is not an attribute of an individual, but rather a complex collection of conditions, many of which are created by the social environment. Hence the management of the problem requires social action, and it is the collective responsibility of society at large to make the environmental modifications necessary for the full participation of people with disabilities in all areas of social life. The issue is therefore an attitudinal or ideological one requiring social change, which at the political level becomes a question of human rights. For this model disability is a political issue.

ICF is based on an integration of these two opposing models. In order to capture the integration of the various perspectives of functioning, a "biopsychosocial" approach is used. Thus, ICF attempts to achieve a synthesis, in order to provide a coherent view of different perspectives of health from a biological, individual and social perspective.

Note. From World Health Organization (2001, Section 5.2, p. 20). Copyright 2001 by the World Health Organization. Reprinted by permission.

SUMMARY

The approaches for evaluating clinical and educational outcomes employ many different types of conceptual frames. I have considered two of the most obvious: those arising from an objective reality frame that lead to objective measures and those growing out of a subjective reality frame leading to subjective evaluation approaches. Table 5.7 presents some criteria used by each of these two reality frames for determining whether an evaluation is valid.

I have also discussed the importance of models and metaphors when determining what outcomes need evaluating and how to measure them. These included a number of the same models and metaphors that govern the diagnostic, assessment, and intervention approaches described in previous chapters: normative, linguistic, functional, and information processing. Finally, I showed how

Table 5.7. A Summary of Frames and Associated Measures Used to Evaluate Clinical and Educational Progress

Frame type	Measures
	Reality frames
Objective (factual)	Experiments containing randomized controlled trials ("the scientific method")
	Standardized tests
	Rating scales
Subjective (experiential)	Written or oral biographies
	Interviews
	Portfolios
	Personal futures planning procedures
	Professional's reflections (PDSA, procedural protocols, action research—all involving a problem-solving model)
	Criteria for judging the quality and validity of evaluation approaches made from objective and subjective perspectives
Objective perspective	Replicability, ecological validity
Subjective perspective	Authenticity, authorship, privacy, power relationships
	Conceptual models
Normative	Standardized tests
	Developmental stage assessments
Linguistic	Language sample analysis
Functional	Assessments of a student's functioning in various domains (e.g., motor, speech, language, social communication)
Information processing	Tests and documentation of a student's performance in various areas of information processing (e.g., memory/retrieval, attention, phonological awareness)
World Health Organization's blend of medical and social models	Rating of body structure and function, student's engagement and participation in activities, and environmental and personal factors affecting life participation

two other models, a medical and social one, have been blended together to create the increasingly popular evaluation framework developed by the WHO (2001).

In conclusion, all outcome measures, no matter how objective they strive to be, are based on a set of assumptions derived from underlying frames and models that are subjectively held by the individual selecting the measures. Different measures focus on different aspects of intervention, and should be chosen with an awareness of not only what they take to be significant, but also what they omit from their purview. I will explore this topic further in Chapter 8, but before we get there, I need to examine the frames underlying the practices involved in school literacy, to which I now turn.

SIX

Framing Literacy

"Reading" and "writing" are abstractions, convenient abbreviations enabling us to refer to certain kinds of human activities. These terms can also lead us to believe that what they refer to has a concrete existence. For example, we are told the "reading" level of various groups of children, although *groups* do not read. Only individuals read. We are not told what these individuals have been asked to read or under what conditions, nor are we reminded that "reading" tests can only indirectly measure "reading." Unless we keep reminding ourselves that "reading" and "writing" are abstractions and abbreviations, we may come to believe—or just as dangerously, to act as though we believed—in their disembodied existence.

—BISSEX (1980, p. ix)

Bissex is arguing that reading and writing are complex constructs that are not directly observable. Her insight illustrates why reading is portrayed differently depending upon the nature of the particular frame being used to understand it. This interpretive view of reading is evident when examining the recent literature on how the growth of a new paradigm in literacy changed previously held ideas of what reading is.

Under a traditional interpretation, reading typically begins around age 5, about the time children enter school. However, be-

fore they actually read, children need to master a variety of prerequisite skills, such as recognizing the letters of the alphabet, learning
correspondences between speech sounds and letters (i.e., the alphabetic principle), and learning to match colors and shapes. They
also need to master understandings of concepts such as "same" and
"different," or the concept of time progression across a sequence of
pictures. These "readiness" activities may be carried out in
preschools, kindergarten, or at home. This idea of needing to be
"readied" for reading is what has been called a "reading readiness
paradigm," since it presumes that children should be not taught to
read until they have the requisite prereading skills (McCormick &
Mason, 1986; Parker, 1990; Pearson, 1998; Smith, 1990).

Reading readiness materials that have been recommended for
parents to use as they "ready" their child for reading have included
materials for teaching same and different concepts, opposites, sequencing, analogies, picture matching, eye–hand coordination,
and rhyming words (see website of School Zone Publishing Company, 2002).

A counterview to reading readiness, one that has come to be
called *emergent reading* or the *emergent literacy frame,* regards children's development of reading in a much different way. In this second paradigm, there is no readiness stage. What is treated as
prerequisite to reading in the reading readiness view becomes part
of reading in the emergent literacy view. "Learning literacy is seen
as a continuous process, beginning in infancy with exposure to
oral language, written language, books, and stories beginning in
the home and extending to other environments" (Morrow &
Smith, 1990, p. 1).

Reading, as seen from within the emergent literacy frame, begins when children are first exposed to print, for example, via familiar brand names and logos, or printed words in storybooks that
are read to them (Clay, 1984; Erickson, 2000; Goodman, 1986).
Through their interactions with picture books, children not only
develop insights about print, but also gain other essential knowledge that is involved in reading. For example, understanding pictures in books gives children a way of contemplating things in the
world, instead of just acting on them directly (Snow & Ninio, 1986,
p. 119). Being read to offers children a way of separating language
from the immediate contexts of the here-and-now (Snow & Ninio,
1986, p. 199). Experiences with picture-book stories provide children a means for entering into imaginary worlds, separated from
the world they experience in their own everyday reality, but closely
tied to it (Snow & Ninio, 1986, p. 135).

The reading readiness and emergent literacy views of reading deserve to be classified as paradigms, a type of model, because each is a large structure containing smaller frames. I describe each in turn, before moving on to discuss other frames used when defining, assessing, and teaching literacy to children.

THE READING READINESS FRAME

The reading readiness frame contains a *decoding metaphor* for depicting reading. The metaphor of "decoding" conjures up a message conveyed in a code that needs to be deciphered to be understood. When applied to reading, this decoding task requires the child to identify letters and their associated sounds and to synthesize these elemental language components into words. Reading is seen as building from the smallest elements (letters/sounds) to the largest units (discourse), often in step-like progressions (letters, syllables, words, phrases, sentences, discourse).

When using a decoding metaphor to determine a child's ability to read, one would examine such things as the child's ability to identify letters, to associate letters and sounds, and to recognize written words. These abilities have been generically referred to as "phonics skills" and "word recognition skills." Other skills closely associated with phonics and word recognition are those that have come to be called "phonological awareness skills." These skills in-

Table 6.1. Examples of Instruments for Assessing Decoding and Phonological Awareness

- Comprehensive Test of Phonological Processing (Wagner, Torgesen, & Rashotte, 1999)
- Woodcock Reading Mastery Tests—Revised (Woodcock, 1998)
- Test of Word Reading Efficiency (Torgesen, Wagner, & Rashotte, 1997)
- Comprehensive Test of Phonological Processes in Reading (Wagner, Torgesen, & Rashotte, 1997)
- Lindamood Auditory Conceptualization Test (Lindamood & Lindamood, 1979)
- Phonological Awareness Test (Robertson & Salter, 1995)
- Rosner Test of Auditory Analysis (Rosner, 1975)
- Test of Phonological Awareness (Torgensen & Bryant, 1998)
- Yopp–Singer Test of Phoneme Segmentation (Yopp, 1995)

clude finding words that begin with the same sound, rhyming words, and segmenting words into phonemes (Blachman, 2000). (See Table 6.1 for tests that have been designed to measure children's decoding and phonological awareness abilities.)

As for assessment, most reading readiness teaching programs are based on a decoding model. The aim of the programs is to expose children to the letters of the alphabet and their associated sounds so that they can eventually sound out and interpret written words. (See Table 6.2 for examples of sound decoding and phonological awareness teaching programs.)

Another frame that is associated with the decoding metaphor is an information-processing one. The emphasis of this second frame is not just focused on decoding letters but on the various stages through which the information gleaned from those letters passes as it moves through the learner's mind on its way to inter-

Table 6.2. Decoding and Phonological (Phonemic) Awareness Approaches for Teaching Reading and Their Commercial Web Addresses

Orton–Gillingham	*http://www.ortongillingham.com*
Earobics	*http://www.cogcon.com/products/step1.stm*
Wilson Reading System	*http://www.wilsonlanguage.com/about.html*
Lindamood–Bell Sensory Cognitive Programs	*http://www.learningstrategies.org/ lindamoodbell.html*
Lindamood Phoneme Sequencing Program	*http://www.commlearn.com/s_programs/ lindamnd.html*
Phonemic Awareness Kit	*http://www.linguisystems.com/ itemdetail.php?id=354*
Phonemic Awareness in Young Children: A Classroom Curriculum	*http://www.pbrookes.com/store/books/adams-3211/ index.htm*
The Road to the Code	*http://www.pbrookes.com/store/books/blachman-4382/*
Seeing Stars	*http://www.lindamoodbell.com/ symbolimagery.html*

pretation (for more details, see Catts & Kamhi, 1999, pp. 5–6, and the more detailed discussion below).

The information-processing model is not only used to trace how information gets from the page to its interpreted version, it is also used to find out what might be causing a reading problem—if there is one. In this context, a causal frame is added to the information-processing one. Problems with processing at earlier stages in the processing model are seen as causing problems in later stages of processing. For example, a child's specific problem with sound–letter correspondence causes that child's particular problems with word recognition, which in turn causes the child's particular problems with meaning interpretation. Some have used a broad version of this *causal metaphor* to attribute overall reading and spelling problems to general difficulties with the phonological aspects of language (Ehri, 2000; Scarborough, 2001; Silliman et al., 2002).

In sum, a reading readiness paradigm has embedded within it other frames, such as decoding and causal metaphors and an information processing model. These frames favor a view of reading that is analytic, in which sounds on the page are seen as elements that are recognized, synthesized, and eventually converted into meaning. They have been used by researchers, clinicians, and educators alike to assess and treat children with literacy learning difficulties.

THE EMERGENT LITERACY FRAME

The emergent literacy paradigm contains a *life experience* or *event model* that emphasizes the significance of the everyday experiences in literacy. Learning to read, in this view, is based on a variety of event-based understandings such as the power and responsibilities of those involved in the event and what participants do when they engage in commonly occurring activities.

The understandings of events are sometimes portrayed as requiring a complex concept, or *schema*. The schema depicts and organizes information having to do with a type of event, such as a birthday party or eating at a restaurant (Duchan, 1991, in press; Nelson, 1986; Nelson & Gruendel, 1981; Schank & Abelson, 1977). Event schemas, called *generalized event representations* (GERs) by Nelson and Gruendel (1981), are like clinical and teaching models in that they are a complex and abstract mental representation. They are called "schemas" when they are related to events. These frames allow children (and adults) to recognize an example of the event when it occurs, to know what to do and think during a particular occurrence of an event, to understand the relationships of the elements of the event to the whole, and to remember experiences related to occurrences of a specific event type (e.g., a particular birthday party).

Clinicians, teachers, or reading researchers working from within a life experience paradigm have depicted reading as an activity that takes place in the course of everyday life events. The first stages of reading involve recognizing words such as "stop" written on a stop sign or "McDonald's" written on a fast food restaurant, which are a part of event schemas related to car rides and eating in restaurants. Reading specialists have dubbed this type of everyday life reading as "functional reading," and they use functional reading tasks as a way to assess a child's level of reading competence (Scribner, 1988).

Picture-book activities with preliterate children are events that have been especially focused upon by researchers, clinicians, and teachers. The picture-book event is regarded by all as key to later reading abilities (Commission on Reading, 1985; Scarborough & Dobrich, 1994). Aspects of picture-book interactions that have been studied and assessed include children's early understandings of how books are held, how pages are turned (Clay, 1991), and how joint attention is achieved between those engaged in naming pictures or talking about story events (Snow & Goldfield, 1981). There also have been many studies on the nature of the discourse between those engaged together in the reading of picture books (e.g., Snow & Ninio, 1986). Finally, some researchers have examined the contents of picture books as a way for children to come to understand things about their world (Butler, 1987).

From their life experiences, such as engaging with an adult in a picture-book activity, children develop early notions of what print is and how it functions (Purcell-Gates, 1998). These ideas about print have been assessed informally by observing what the surrounding context provides children (Smith & Dickinson, 2002) and by assessing children's ideas of print (e.g., Purcell Gates, 1998).

In sum, an emergent literacy approach to beginning reading is often based on evaluating children's life experiences, with special attention paid to picture books and everyday life events. The life experience approach can also be used to assess children at later stages in their reading or writing development (see Table 6.3 for some examples).

As in the case of the reading readiness paradigm, the emergent literacy paradigm makes use of an *information-processing frame*. But

Table 6.3. Life Experience Approaches for Assessing Literacy of School-Age Children

Approaches	An example of how the approach can be used to assess a child's personal experiences	Sources from the literature
Portfolio approaches	Collections are made of children's responses to what they have read and samples of their writing. The samples are collected in folders *(portfolios)* over a period of time. During an evaluation meeting, the teacher and student get together to talk about how the child felt about the work in the portfolio.	Murphy and Smith (1991); Salinger and Chittenden (1994); Tierny, Carter, and Desai (1991)
Curriculum-embedded assessment	The literacy requirements of the curriculum are identified and compared with the student's competencies. Plans are developed for modifying the language arts curriculum to make it accessible to the student.	Hoffman et al. (1996)
Event- or script-based assessment approaches	Students, families, and teachers are interviewed about everyday events. Students are observed in their classrooms for how they manage various scripted events.	Donahue (2002)
Readers workshop approach	Student-based group approach where students select what they read and talk about what they have read in literature circles. Students assess their own accomplishments in accord with specific assessment instructions.	Keene and Zimmerman (1997); Stuart (2002)
Early Language and Literacy Classroom Observation (ELLCO)	Three observational tools for gathering data about what is going on in classrooms (preschool through third grade): (1) Literacy Environment Checklist, (2) Classroom Observation and Teacher Interview, and (3) Literacy Activities Rating Scale	Smith and Dickinson (2002)

the information-processing frame is used differently in the two paradigms. Discussions of emergent literacy typically focus on what has been called *top-down processing*. In contrast to the bottom-up view of the reading readiness approach, which proceeds from real-world perception of letters to their interpretation, top-down views hold that reading processing begins early in a child's life with synthetic conceptual schemas or wholistic constructs and proceeds to analytic ones at around the time they enter school. Children learn to read by recognizing whole words as part of everyday situations—stop signs, McDonald's logos—and later begin to decode the particular elements of words. Reading is seen as a contextualized guessing game at first. The top-down metaphor refers to the child's progression in development from the top of a processing model—the region that contains wholistic meaningful concepts—to the bottom of a processing model, in which processing focuses on elemental, letter-by-letter analysis of words.

In short, there are major differences between the reading readiness and the emergent literacy paradigms that govern practices in early literacy acquisition. These two paradigms are ones that have been used to understand children who are beginning to dip their toes into the literacy waters. They can be regarded as paradigms because they are large conceptual systems that contain other frames within them. The reading readiness paradigm contains the decoding metaphor and bottom-up processing models. In contrast, the emergent literacy paradigm contains a life experience reality frame, an event schema, and a top-down processing model.

CONTRASTING FRAMES IN LATER LITERACY

So far in this chapter I have concentrated on frames that have been employed to represent what is going on with children who are in the beginning stages of reading. Some of these same preliteracy frames are also used to make sense of later developing reading. Indeed, the contrast between the reading readiness and emergent literacy views has its parallels in later learning, although the terminology is different. For example, two differing frames for depicting later literacy, the phonics and the whole language approaches, and the teacher-centered and the student-centered approaches, have their traces in the reading readiness and emergent literacy models for preliteracy.

These later approaches, like the early ones, qualify as models, since they each contain a number of other frames.

When comparing the phonics and whole language models of reading, most would emphasize their contrasts. The decoding versus experiential camps found in designers of preschool curricula continue into the early school years. Phonics teachers regard reading as needing to begin with sound–letter associations, that is, with the alphabetic principle. Whole language teachers emphasize life experiences as fundamental. Members of each group view one another as negligent in providing children with the essential fundamentals, since their paradigms lead them to different conclusions about what is fundamental.

Another two approaches that have been placed in opposition to one another are a skills-based model and a comprehension- or meaning-based one. In this contrast "skills" tend to refer to what one does, rather than to what one knows. A *skill* is an observable indicator of a person's literacy knowledge. Skill is to knowledge as performance is to competence (see Chomsky, 1965, for the competence–performance distinction).

Sometimes a skills portrayal of reading is done with the aim of distinguishing skills involving reading *decoding* from those involving reading *comprehension*. Assessing children's decoding skills has included such things as analyzing their performance on tasks requiring sound–letter associations and sound blending, whereas assessing a child's reading comprehension skills has focused on the child's ability to identify main ideas and to infer information from what is provided in the text.

On occasion, the term *skills* is used more narrowly to distinguish a decoding view of reading from a comprehension (whole language) view. For example, Coles (1998) has argued against a "skills-based" focus on phonics teaching and in favor of a "meaning-based" approach for introducing young readers to the wonders of stories. Similarly, Wilhelm (1995) fears that too much emphasis on beginning readers' skills development will lead them to miss the point of reading: the excitement of living in the world of the story and seeing it through the eyes of the characters. In Wilhelm's view, stories are subjective experiences requiring a subjective reality frame.

A third contrast made using frames is that involving teacher-centered instruction and student-centered instruction. These two models of instruction lead to different views about what should be learned in school, attitudes toward individual differences, and attitudes toward the use of textbooks and other teaching materials

Table 6.4. Excerpts from Chall's Depiction of the Differences between Teacher-Centered and Student-Centered Approaches to Literacy

Teacher-centered instruction	Student-centered instruction
What should be learned in school?	
Knowledge from the past, present, and foreseeable future; skills important for the individual and society. A core curriculum based on the traditional disciplines of reading, writing, literature, mathematics, science, social studies, and art—arranged in an increasing order of difficulty.	School learning should be based on the learner's interests and needs. Theoretically there is **no** required core curriculum that is arranged hierarchically. Subject matter is **not** structured. The emphasis is on the learning process and on a variety of subjects that are integrated to make them more meaningful.
Attitudes toward individual differences	
All students are expected to learn the basic skills and the traditional content subjects as their aptitude permits. While individual differences in ability are recognized, all who attend school are expected to reach at least some minimal standards in knowledge and skills.	Student learning is expected to vary by interests, motivation, and ability. Therefore, **not** all are held to the same standards. Also, because of the knowledge explosion, students **cannot** be expected to learn all there might be to learn. Therefore they should learn **not** subjects, but how to learn, think, and solve problems; and they should know how to find what they need when they need it.
Attitudes toward the use of textbooks and other teaching materials	
Textbooks are important to assure minimal coverage of content. Additional materials are recommended as well, for example, encyclopedias and other reference works, books, newspapers, magazines, and more recently computer programs.	Original sources—for example, children's literature, novels, historical works, original documents, and more recently computers—are preferred to textbooks. Textbooks are **not** preferred because they are considered dull and not geared to the individual needs and interests of students. For science, hands-on experiences are preferred to reading materials.

Note. From Chall (2000, pp. 187, 189–190). Bolded items are added to the original to emphasize the negative stance Chall takes toward student-centered instruction. Copyright 2000 by Jeanne S. Chall. Reprinted by permission of The Guilford Press.

(Chall, 2000). When evaluating the approach from one frame, the other frame seems to be lacking. This negatively framed stance toward methods arising from other frames is evidenced in Jean Chall's (2000) description of the "student-centered" approach. Much of what she describes for student-centered classrooms focuses on what the teachers are not doing. She compares these things to what teachers are doing in teacher-centered approaches. (See the highlighted negatives in column 2 in Table 6.4 that Chall uses to describe the insufficiencies of student-centered approaches.)

While these dichotomous frames are most often portrayed as conflicting and incompatible, there are occasions in which they are blended in interesting ways. For example, a group of first-grade whole language teachers studied by Dahl, Scharer, and Lawson (1999) embedded phonics teachings within their whole language approach. One of the teachers conducted a literature class in which she selected high-quality children's literature to read aloud to the class. As part of the discussion that ensued she and the class talked about what phonetic devices the author used to get her ideas across (e.g., rhyming words and alliteration).

FRAMES ASSOCIATED WITH LITERACY DIFFICULTIES OR DISABILITIES

Not all frames in literacy come in pairs. Some exist on their own, and are chosen for use depending upon the needs of the particular situation. For example, if a child is having difficulty with literacy, there is a need to explain the cause and to figure out what to do about it. This is a ripe context for using a medical model, often in combination with other models such as a linguistic model, an information-processing model, and a cognitive model.

The Medical Model

Children with literacy problems are sometimes seen as having difficulties in particular domains, for example, struggling readers, or as children with spelling or writing difficulties. On other occasions children with literacy difficulties are placed in a diagnostic category—an indication that the problem is more serious and worthy of special attention from professionals.

Diagnostic terms such as *dyslexia*, *reading disorder*, and *writing* or *spelling disability* have been used not only to describe literacy problems, but also to explain them and to figure out how to remediate them: the diagnostic frame is thereby in keeping with the type of thinking that fits with a *medical model*. The diagnostic and medical frames point to the importance of diagnosing the cause of the child's difficulty so that one can design a therapy to fit the diagnosis. Catts and Kamhi (1999), for instance, differentiate three diagnostic subcategories in order to provide professionals with a set of constructs for creating a remediation plan:

> In our classification scheme, children with dyslexia are defined as having word recognition problems and normal listening comprehension abilities whereas children with a language learning disability are defined as having deficits in both word recognition and listening comprehension. A third group of children, those with hyperlexia, have normal word recognition abilities with deficient listening comprehension abilities. We think that this classification system will allow practitioners to provide more appropriate intervention for children with reading disabilities. (p. x)

Diagnosticians working within the medical model, as I noted in Chapter 2, favor biological diagnoses over psychological ones. This view leads some to ask what is going on in the brain, nervous system, or genetic makeup of children that might be causing the reading or writing disabilities. Answers to this question call for a neurobiological model (also referred to as "physiological" or "neurological"), one that is adopted by those who are looking for the physical causes of literacy difficulties (e.g., Duane & Gray, 1991; Pennington, 1999).

One biological approach to reading disabilities has been to merge the *information-processing model* with a biological, brain-based one. For example, some reading specialists have used an information-processing model, but see different parts of the brain as specializing in different kinds of information processing. Reading problems in different information-processing domains (boxes in information-processing diagrams) are then depicted in biological terms (e.g., Shaywitz, 1996). If a child is found to have a problem processing rapid auditory signals, for example, this problem is depicted as a weakness or lesion in the area of the brain in which that sort of processing takes place. Therapy done from this point of view is not only seen as improving information processing, but as improving brain function (Tallal et al., 1996).

Another biological approach that has been used to account for literacy difficulties is a genetic one. Genetic explanations for why children have reading disorders have been highlighted lately because of recent breakthroughs in identifying genetic codes associated with dyslexia (e.g., Grigorenko, Wood, Meyer, & Pauls, 2000).

The Linguistic Model

Linguistic categories and levels have been a focus of assessment and instruction of students' literacy. A classic example of the use of a linguistic model to assess reading is *miscue analysis*, developed by Yetta Goodman and Ken Goodman. Miscue analysis involves a detailed linguistic analysis of students' reading errors to see what type of linguistic knowledge they violate (K. Goodman, 1965; Y. Goodman, 1986).

Some reading texts have been organized from within a linguistic frame so as to elicit and teach children the linguistic rules inherent in word patterns (i.e., they use linguistic readers). Invented spelling has been analyzed for its linguistic patterns in order to see what rules children are using when the first engage in writing (Read, 1971; Treiman & Bourassa, 2000). The linguistic structuring of teachers' discourse during classroom reading sessions, as well as the discourse organization of books that children read, has also been analyzed. The aim of these discourse analyses has been to determine what knowledge of discourse children need in order to understand what is going on in literacy activities (Blank, 2002).

Linguistic variation among U.S. dialects has also been studied in relation to literacy acquisition and performance (Craig, Washington, & Thompson-Porter, 1998; Silliman, Badr, Wilkinson, & Turner, 2002). The concern has been whether dialect differences place children at a disadvantage for learning to read and write in a code that is closely tied to standard English dialect.

Finally, linguistics has recently been applied to children's acquisition of spelling in which the patterns underlying invented spellings of children are examined for linguistic regularities. Gentry (1982) describes five stages in children's development of spelling (Table 6.5). The stages reflect a linguistic sensibility. Children, for example, rely at first on sounds and letter names and later progress to learning the rules of the English orthographic system.

The Information-Processing Model

A *bottom-up* version of the information-processing model has influenced the diagnosis and teaching of children with reading difficulties. Similarly, but in reverse, writing is portrayed as progressing in a *top-down* direction from ideas to the creation of text. Spelling, being an expressive modality, also has been portrayed as top-down pro-

Table 6.5. Stages in the Development of Spelling

In the *precommunicative stage,* the child uses symbols from the alphabet but shows no knowledge of letter–sound correspondences. The child may also lack knowledge of the entire alphabet, the distinction between upper- and lowercase letters, and the left-to-right direction of English orthography.

In the *semiphonetic stage,* the child begins to understand letter-sound correspondence—that sounds are assigned to letters. At this stage, the child often employs rudimentary logic, using single letters, for example, to represent words, sounds, and syllables (e.g., "U" for "you").

Children at the *phonetic stage* use a letter or group of letters to represent every speech sound that they hear in a word. Although some of their choices do not conform to conventional English spelling, they are systematic and easily understood. Examples are "KOM" for "come "and "EN" for "in."

During the *transitional stage,* the speller begins to assimilate the conventional alternative for representing sounds, moving from a dependence on phonology (sound) for representing words to a reliance on visual representation and an understanding of the structure of words. Some examples are "EGUL" for "eagle" and "HIGHEKED" for "hiked."

In the *correct stage,* the speller knows the English orthographic system and its basic rules. The correct speller fundamentally understands how to deal with such things as prefixes and suffixes, silent consonants, alternative spellings, and irregular spellings. A large number of learned words are accumulated, and the speller recognizes incorrect forms. The child's generalizations about spelling and knowledge of exceptions are usually correct.

Note. From Gentry (1982, pp. 199–200). Copyright 1982 by the International Reading Association. Reprinted by permission.

cessing model that proceeds from the meaningful word, through a set of rules governing sound–letter correspondences, to the selection and formation of letters as the word is written out. Catts and Kamhi (1999) describe both bottom-up and top-down models in relation to different aspects of oral and written language processing:

> Bottom-up models view spoken and written language comprehension as a step-by-step process that begins with the initial detection of an auditory or visual stimulus. The initial input goes through a series of stages in which it is "chunked" in progressively larger and more meaningful units. Top-down models, in contrast, emphasize the importance of scripts, schemata, and inferences that allow one to make hypotheses and predictions about the information being processed. Familiarity with the content, structure, and function of the different kinds of spoken and written discourse enables the listener and reader to be less de-

pendent on low-level perceptual information to construct meanings. (pp. 4–5)

Top-down and bottom-up processing models are often depicted in the form of box-and-arrow diagrams. The direction of the arrows shows whether the frame is a bottom-up or a top-down depiction of processing. In top-down processing, the arrows go from meaning or knowledge to external signals, either perceptual or motor. For example, Figure 6.1 offers a picture associated with the stages of reading and listening comprehension. In this picture, the authors Catts and Kamhi (1999, p. 6) depict most of the arrows going from left (bottom) to right (top). (Catts & Kamhi, 1999, p. 6). This model interprets listening comprehension as beginning with a perceptual analysis of the input (auditory or visual) and ending with a comprehension of that signal.

Also associated with the processing frame is the metaphor of *resource allocation*. This is a frame that examines processing in terms of the psychological resources required. The question is whether the child makes the most of the limited processing resources at his or her disposal. This resource allocation frame is discussed often in relation to one particular level of processing, that

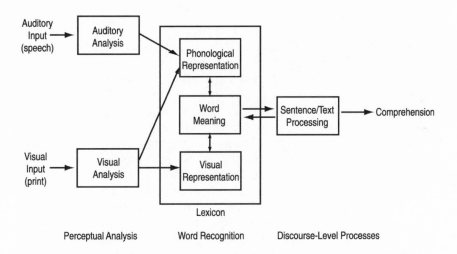

Figure 6.1. A bottom-up rendering of reading and listening comprehension. From Catts and Kamhi (1999, p. 6). Copyright 1999. Published by Allyn & Bacon. Copyright 1999 by Pearson Education. Reprinted by permission of the publisher.

involving "working memory" (Baddeley, 1998). At this level, there needs to be a quick and efficient analysis of information before it is passed on to long-term memory for further analysis and storage.

Once the processing resources have been used up, the processor is in a position of "information overload" or "processing overload," and processing is in jeopardy of breaking down. The person engaged in a literacy task must allocate limited resources wisely, in order to avoid processing overload or breakdown (Sinatra, Brown, & Reynolds, 2001).

As seen above, bottom-up and top-down views of information processing are often used to distinguish literacy modalities of reading and writing. In an information-processing model, reading is typically depicted as proceeding from perception to cognition (bottom-up) and writing is typically depicted as proceeding from cognition to motor performance (top-down). When these two processing views are applied to the same modality, frame clashes are likely to occur. This is exemplified by the phonics versus whole language views of reading. The phonics model treats processing as progressing in a bottom-up direction, going from the letters on the page to meanings, and the whole language model has a more top-down emphasis, proceeding from meanings to decoding.

The Cognitive Model

Another model that is commonly drawn upon to understand literacy in normal and atypical learners is a cognitive one. This model has been more associated with logic and meanings underpinning reading and writing than it has with decoding or encoding messages. Readers and writers are depicted as needing to use a conceptual model in order to make sense of the written word. They also need to engage in problem solving, a cognitive activity, in the course of figuring out how to express their own meanings when writing or to interpret others' meanings when reading.

The notion of a conceptual model or *schema* is a frame-based notion that ascribes to children complex cognitive structures. Schemas, are abstract organized conceptualizations that are used to understand and produce discourse, events, or metaphors, for example. One version of a schema is a *story grammar* (Stein & Glenn, 1979).[1] Included in story grammars are settings, initiating events

---

[1] See Chapter 3 for a linguistic rendition of a story grammar schema. A story grammar is a good example of merged models: in this case, linguistic and cognitive. In the linguistic model, the constituents of the story and their tree-structure, grammatical relations are emphasized. In the cognitive model, the conceptual logic of the story is the focus.

that set up a problem for the story, internal responses of a character to the problem set up in the initiating event, an attempt by the protagonist to solve the problem, and the result of the protagonist's attempts. Story grammars have been used by teachers and clinicians to help children understand and remember the parts of a story and to understand the relationships of the parts to the whole (see Duchan, in press, for a review). Other schemas that have been used to analyze and teach children stories are high points (Labov & Waletsky, 1967); time, space, and character perspectives (Duchan, Bruder, & Hewitt, 1995); story themes (Williams, 2002); and story stanzas (Gee, 1999).

Everyday events have also been studied and taught from within a schema frame (Nelson, 1986; Nelson & Gruendel, 1981). In order for children to understand the ideas being depicted in written language, they need to understand how the events taking place are ordinarily enacted—who does what, where, when, how. As I mentioned early in this chapter in relation to life experience frames, Nelson's name for these schemas are *generalized event representations*.

Strategies are another sort of cognitive frame associated with literacy assessment and intervention. Students are taught to adopt a strategic, metacognitive stance toward the text and toward what they must do to understand it. Some of the strategies are carried out in response to a teacher's guiding questions (e.g., Kamhi, 1997; Kamhi & Catts, 2002); others involve following prescribed strategic steps themselves (e.g., Graham & Harris, 1999; Singer & Bashir, 1999); and still others are carried out in peer action situations where students work in groups to help one another glean meaning from their reading (Klingner & Vaughn, 1999). (See Table 6.6 for a listing of a few reading comprehension programs and their associated strategies.)

OBJECTIVE AND SUBJECTIVE REALITY FRAMES

Until recently, therapies and teaching approaches have favored an objective, text-based frame over a subjective reality frame. In an objective reality frame, texts are treated as informational sources rather than as experiential ones. Wilhelm, a middle-school teacher turned academic, describes the text-based approach thusly:

> Teachers influenced by this approach may emphasize knowing and recognizing literary devices, getting at the "internal logic" of a text's

Table 6.6. A Few Comprehension Programs for Teaching Children to Understand What They Read

Collaborative strategic reading (CSR; Klingner & Vaughn, 1999)	The method includes four strategies: preview, monitor comprehension during reading, get the gist, wrap-up. Strategies are first modeled by the teacher and then carried out by students in small reading groups.
Concept-oriented reading instruction (CORI; Guthrie, et al., 1998; Guthrie & Ozgungor, 2002)	Reading is organized to achieve a knowledge goal. Instruction has students (1) observe and personalize, (2) activate background knowledge, (3) comprehend and integrate information, and (4) communicate it to others.
Students achieving independent learning (SAIL; Pressley et al., 1994)	Teachers talk about particular strategies and their usefulness to the children, and model them using a "think-aloud" procedure. Children employ the strategies differently depending upon what the situation calls for.
Theme–scheme (Williams, 2002)	A a step-by-step program for extracting thematic meanings from narratives: (1) prereading discussion, (2) teacher reads story aloud to students and class discusses story, (3) teacher and students answer questions about story themes and events, and (4) theme is identified using "'should' statements" (main character "should" have . . .).

construction by studying various patterns and codes, and relating a work's central "organic" meaning to how this meaning was expressed. There may be an emphasis on "rightness" of literary interpretation. Interpretive questions about the text will be answered after reading; thesis essays assigned; and discussions mediated by the teacher, who acts as the authority on the text. The text is what is studied, and it is an artifact regarded with something rivaling reverence. (p. 14)

Wilhelm advocates instead for a more reader-centered, subjective approach in which "the reader [is] an active meaning-maker, one who connects personally to what is read, who spends pleasurable and stirring time with stories, and who might judge or resist the text and its author" (p. 15).

Reading specialists have begun to shift their frame for thinking about reading from an objective to a subjective one. They are trying to find out what readers and writers think as they engage with texts. Bruner (1986), in an oft-cited distinction, talks about being able to understand the plot and what happened as one level of understanding a narrative, one he calls the "landscape of action," and being able to experience the text as the characters do as a second level of understanding narrative. This second level, a subjective one, he calls the "landscape of consciousness." Within the landscape of consciousness, a reader experiences the intentionality, feelings, and motivations of the characters. McKeough (1998) offers a concrete illustration of Bruner's distinction:

> The story my mother told me offered an excellent model of intentionality. My grandfather's actions were motivated by his intention to immigrate to Australia, and the thwarting of this intention was what gave the story its "punch." Such models are essential to literacy development since young children typically describe the landscape of action in their stories long before they successfully integrate the landscape of consciousness.

Other subjectively framed reading approaches include (1) one that involves the students in thinking aloud about what they are reading (Trabasso & Magliano, 1996); (2) one that focuses on their experience of the text rather than on the information contained in the text (Paley, 1981); and (3) one that is concerned with encouraging students' engagement with the material they read (Guthrie & Ozgungor, 2002).

The subjective frame brings with it new concerns about how well things are going for readers and writers and about their subjective readings of the characters in the texts they read. For example, a subjective frame leads to a concern about voices in a text—from whose point of view is the text written? Issues are also raised concerning the authenticity of the text—about whether it contains an accurate and convincing depiction of characters' feelings. Also at issue in a subjectively framed reading assessment is whether the reader has understood the emotional states and motivations driving the story (Gernsbacher, Hallada, & Robertson, 1998; Hewitt, 1994).

SUMMARY

We have traversed the literature and practices related to literacy and discovered a number of frames along the way. My focus in this chapter has been on how a set of frames have been used to think about and work with children who have difficulties reading and writing.

The first group of frames described here were contrasting ones, in which they are pitted against one another in frame clashes. These included reading readiness versus emergent literacy paradigms, phonics versus whole language paradigms, and skills-based versus comprehension models. When the frames are treated as opposing, one is often cast negatively in constrast with the other and both are identified in terms of their contrasting features. But contrasting frames need not be opposing. In some cases they can be combined as was shown by Dahl et al. (1999) in their example of a first-grade teacher who combined frames that are usually depicted as contrastive.

A second group of frames were talked about in relation to children with literacy disabilities. They included the medical model, the linguistic model, the information-processing model, and the cognitive model. These models are often used to guide diagnosis and remediation of children with reading or writing difficulties. They focus on what is wrong with the child and on how to fix it, in keeping with a medical model.

Lastly, it was pointed out that most frames used in relation to literacy and literacy disabilities are ones that describe the world of the child in objective terms. What needs further exploring are what the child is thinking and feeling about what he or she reads and writes—a subjective reality frame.

There are many other frames that affect how teachers and speech–language pathologists regard literacy—frames that haven't been mentioned in this chapter. They include ones emanating from school organizations (institutional structures), cultural politics (liberal versus conservative views), and a critical theory stance. These are discussed in detail in the next chapter on school frames.

SEVEN

School Frames

Schools have their own ways of doing things, and those ways can be thought of as being based on conceptual frames. Frames influence how teachers and school speech–language pathologists conduct themselves and how they think about their roles and activities. In this chapter I examine some currently used frames associated with public school practices in the United States.

Let's begin by imagining two speech–language pathologists who, having taken the same classes, graduate the same year from the same university program in the United States. One takes a job in a hospital and adopts a strict medical model for carrying out services. She will see and work with patients using the medical model that regards communication disorders as part of a disease or syndrome complex. The second takes a job in a public school. Unlike her hospital counterpart, whose work is defined by the medical model, this school clinician is likely to adopt aspects of the educational model. In the school context, diagnoses serve as entitlements to specialized services and as a means for determining special class assignments. There will be many other differences between the hospital- and the school-based speech–language pathologists, as is suggested by the different terminology used. Therapy plans of care associated with a medical setting become Individual-ized Education Programs (IEP) in school settings, patients become students, clinicians become educators, and clinical services are seen as related services. Included in the job of the school clinician are school-based tasks involving team meetings for carrying out curriculum-based assessment, for planning and executing IEPs, and for facilitating children's social, intellectual, communicative, and social inclusion in regular education classrooms.

In this chapter I discuss various frames used by teachers and cli-nicians who work in educational settings with children who have language and literacy disabilities. In the first section I discuss some frames that directly tie to the everyday practices of schoolteachers and clinicians. Included will be frames underlying their (1) service delivery, (2) their creation and carrying out of IEPs, and (3) their ideas about the curriculum. Later in the chapter I describe some more behind-the-scenes frames. These have to do with the political, edu-cational, and legal structures governing school practices.

SERVICE DELIVERY FRAMES

Schools now require that their teachers and speech–language pa-thologists elect an approach for working together to deliver services to children with communication disabilities. The service delivery choices made by the professionals have been conceived in terms of a frame that focuses on the social relationships between professionals, job sharing, and the differential responsibilities of professionals in the school setting. For example, the American Speech–Language–Hearing Association (1991) has distinguished three service delivery models that govern professional team practices: transdisciplinary, interdisciplinary, and multidisciplinary.

Types of Models

The Transdisciplinary Model

In this service delivery model, also called a "collaborative service de-livery," knowledge, information, and duties are shared among team members. Disciplinary boundaries are not seen as fixed. Rather, pro-fessionals negotiate their professional duties, sharing responsibili-ties with one another. Their professional roles are based not only on disciplinary expertise, but also on what jobs need doing by team members. One person on the service team may serve as the coordinator, another as a group leader, and another may assume the primary responsibility for tracking a student's progress toward a specified goal. Roles may be rotated to assure that power relationships between members are egalitarian.

The Interdisciplinary Model

Team members using an interdisciplinary model of service delivery work separately, each carrying out jobs that are in keeping with their specialized discipline. Once they have gathered information, they share it with others on the team for purposes of establishing related goals, coordinating therapies, and writing common reports.

The Multidisciplinary Model

In a multidisciplinary model, professionals work independently, reporting their findings or intervention accomplishments to the team. Professionals develop their own goals, and work within their own area of expertise.

The trans-, inter-, and multidisciplinary models are so named because they emphasize the ways professionals work together. This places them within a more general *social participation model*. The three models differ in the way they construe power relationships, define their roles, and allocate amounts of social contact among team members. In the collaborative, transdisciplinary model, power relations between professionals are nonhierarchical, roles are assigned and rotated, and members are in regular contact with one another. In the interdisciplinary and multidisciplinary models, traditional hierarchical relationships among the different professions are preserved: roles and responsibilities are based on one's professional identity. The interdisciplinary and multidisciplinary models differ in the degree of social interaction and communication among their team members, with the interdisciplinary model involving more interaction than the multidisciplinary one. (See Table 7.1 for more distinctions that have been made between the three versions of the social participation model.)

Push-In and Pull-Out Metaphors

Another frame that has been used to distinguish models of service delivery in speech–language pathology has to do with where the speech–language pathologists carry out their therapies. Clinicians can elect to work with children in their classrooms, or they can "pull them out" of their classrooms to work with them individually or in

Table 7.1. Social Models of Professional Interaction

Model	Assessment	IEP objectives	Intervention	Therapy location	Social interaction between professionals
Transdisciplinary	Assessment done to determine student's performance in different aspects of the curriculum (curriculum-based assessment)	Authentic and functional objectives related to classroom expectations	Shared instruction in the classroom	Classrooms	Role sharing, complementary instruction
Multidisciplinary	Standardized tests and descriptive assessment done by the speech–language pathologist evaluating performance related to classroom expectations	Objectives reflect curriculum goals	Activities to classroom needs	Combination of classroom and speech room	Communication and cooperation between the speech–language pathologist and the teacher
Interdisciplinary	Standardized tests and descriptive assessment to discover student's communication deficits	Objectives focus on deficits with the hope that the learning will generalize to classroom performance	Deficit-based, often unrelated to classroom needs	Pull out to a separate setting	Minimal contact between speech–language pathologists and teacher

small groups in a separate location ("the speech room"). These two approaches have been called the *push-in* and *pull-out* approaches to service delivery. The "in" and "out" are spatial metaphors, describing the physical location of the speech–language pathologists in relation to the classroom.[1]

While the spatial language related to push-in and pull-out approaches emphasizes the different models in terms of the location of the therapy, their impact has also been described using socially based terms. In "push-in" therapy, clinicians are more likely to work with the classroom teacher when conducting curriculum-based assessment, creating IEPs, and carrying out therapy goals. Speech–language pathologists working in the classroom might teach lessons to the whole class or strategize with the classroom teacher for how best to meet a particular child's communication goals during regular classroom activities. These collaborative activities are less likely to occur between teachers and clinicians when clinicians work in separate quarters (DiMeo, Merritt, & Culatta, 1998).

FRAMING INDIVIDUALIZED EDUCATION PROGRAMS

One central activity of a school speech–language pathologist's practice is to work with a team of individuals to develop an IEP for children with speech or language disabilities. This is a written statement outlining an annual educational plan for a particular child. The plan or program is developed, reviewed, and revised regularly during meetings of an IEP team.

Federal legislation enacted in 1997 indicates what information an IEP must include in it (Individuals with Disabilities Education Act [IDEA], 1997). Among the required ingredients are (1) identifying information about the child, (2) his or her present levels of educational performance, (3) annual goals and short-term objectives for achieving them, (4) an indication of needed special education and related services, and (5) how the child's progress toward the goals will be measured. The team must also justify exclusion of a child from regular class activities or school- or state-mandated assessments, as well as any changes in how assessments are carried out. Finally, the IEP report needs to indicate how the child's par-

---

[1]The verb associated with classroom-based services varies. Paul uses "sit in" (2001, p. 485), and DiMeo, Merritt, and Cullata use "pull in" (1998, p. 176). What is consistent is the use of the word "in," thereby indicating its basis in a spatial metaphor.

ents will be informed about their child's progress. (See Table 7.2 for the federal wording and more details about what must go into an IEP.)

An examination of the details of the IEP requirements reveals several assumed frames. One is a *growth metaphor* with the added twist that what takes place at one period of time doesn't just happen but was caused by what happened previously. This *causality metaphor* associated with development is assumed in the requirement that the IEP contain statements describing how a child's disability has interfered with (i.e., caused problems for) the child's participation in activities or progress in the curriculum (items 1i and 1ii). Also tied to the growth/causality frame is the notion that services and supplementary aids will lead to (i.e., cause) progress in the general curriculum and toward the attainment of long-term goals (items 3i, 3ii, 3iii).

Interestingly, the child's difficulties are not described as "deficits", as would be the case when using a medical model. Rather, they are described using *growth/causality metaphors* as "needs resulting from [i.e., caused by] a disability" (item 2i). And the solutions to the child's difficulties, rather than being described within the "rehabilitation" frame of a medical model, are rendered as one of "meeting the needs of the child," which will then enable (i.e., allow/cause) the child to be involved in and progress both curricular (item 2i) and extracurricular activities (item 3ii).

Another manifestation of the growth metaphor built into the IEP is the notion of interim steps along the way to larger goals. These short-term objectives, or benchmarks, imply a growth path moving in a linear direction to an identified ultimate destination. The aim of the IEP is to aid the child in advancing appropriately toward attaining annual goals (item 3i). Other path-like images are associated with the child making "progress" in the general curriculum (item 3ii) and in school activities (item 2i). The path and destination notions are associated with what has been referred to as a *journey metaphor* (Lingual Links, 2002).

The IEP format also includes language that calls for a *social participation model*. This event-based frame is revealed in the vocabulary related to participation in activities (item 2i) and with other children (item 3iii). Another manifestation of this participation frame is the considerable effort to avoid the child's exclusion from regular activities, including assessments (items 4, 5i, 5ii).

One core feature of the IDEA legislation is its expectation that children with disabilities should be educated in a "least restrictive environment." This expectation is described as follows:

Table 7.2. IEP Requirements

(a) **General.** The IEP for each child with a disability must include—

(1) A statement of the child's present levels of educational performance, including—

    (i) How the child's disability affects the child's involvement and progress in the general curriculum (i.e., the same curriculum as for nondisabled children); or

    (ii) For preschool children, as appropriate, how the disability affects the child's participation in appropriate activities;

(2) A statement of measurable annual goals, including benchmarks or short-term objectives, related to—

    (i) Meeting the child's needs that result from the child's disability to enable the child to be involved in and progress in the general curriculum (i.e., the same curriculum as for nondisabled children), or for preschool children, as appropriate, to participate in appropriate activities; and

    (ii) Meeting each of the child's other educational needs that result from the child's disability;

(3) A statement of the special education and related services and supplementary aids and services to be provided to the child, or on behalf of the child, and a statement of the program modifications or supports for school personnel that will be provided for the child—

    (i) To advance appropriately toward attaining the annual goals;

    (ii) To be involved and progress in the general curriculum in accordance with paragraph (a)(1) of this section and to participate in extracurricular and other nonacademic activities; and

    (iii) To be educated and participate with other children with disabilities and nondisabled children in the activities described in this section;

(4) An explanation of the extent, if any, to which the child will not participate with nondisabled children in the regular class and in the activities described in paragraph (a)(3) of this section;

(5)

    (i) A statement of any individual modifications in the administration of State or district-wide assessments of student achievement that are needed in order for the child to participate in the assessment; and

    (ii) If the IEP team determines that the child will not participate in a particular State or district-wide assessment of student achievement (or part of an assessment), a statement of—

        (A) Why that assessment is not appropriate for the child; and

        (B) How the child will be assessed;

(6) The projected date for the beginning of the services and modifications described in paragraph (a)(3) of this section, and the anticipated frequency, location, and duration of those services and modifications; and

(continued)

Table 7.2. continued

(7) A statement of—

(i) How the child's progress toward the annual goals described in paragraph (a)(2) of this section will be measured; and

(ii) How the child's parents will be regularly informed (through such means as periodic report cards), at least as often as parents are informed of their nondisabled children's progress, of—

(A) Their child's progress toward the annual goals; and

(B) The extent to which that progress is sufficient to enable the child to achieve the goals by the end of the year.

Note. From Individual with Disabilities Education Act (1997, Subpart—Services, Individualized Education Programs §300.347, Content of IEP).

To the maximum extent appropriate, children with disabilities, including children in public or private institutions or other care facilities, are educated with children who are not disabled, and special classes, separate schooling, or other removal of children with disabilities from the regular educational environment occurs only when the nature or severity of the disability of a child is such that education in regular classes with the use of supplementary aids and services cannot be achieved satisfactorily. (IDEA, 1997, Part C)

This judgment about environments being more or less restrictive moves the problem focus from inside the child to outside the child. The frame thereby shifts from an *impairment* or *deficit model* to a *social participation model* in which environments are seen as contributing to or blocking a child's potential growth.

Two metaphors are frequently used in conjunction with the social participation model. One is a *container metaphor*. The event, activity, or classroom is construed as a container that includes or excludes children with disabilities. Also used with a social participation model is a *navigation metaphor*. This portrays contexts as having the potential of exerting "barriers" that "block" the child's participation or progress. Blocking forward progression brings with it a notion of open "access." Contexts are judged accessible or not accessible, and, if not, the intervention or support goal is to make them more accessible.

In a recent report of a presidential panel, recommendations were made that are likely to result in changes in the requirements and format of IEPs for school children with disabilities. In its final report of July 2002, the President's Commission on Excellence in Special Education recommended, among other things, that children be evaluated in terms of what they do in classrooms rather than on their inherent inabilities. The report recommends that services to all children become more "results-oriented," and that a program be evaluated in terms of the "opportunities it provides and the outcomes achieved by each child." The panel also recommended that there be one system of education, general education, within which all services, both special education and regular education, be provided (U.S. Department of Education Office of Special Education and Rehabilitative Services, 2002).

A reauthorization of IDEA based on these recommendations is likely to move services further toward the social participation model. Children with disabilities will be assessed to determine their participation (inclusion) in the regular education curriculum, and IEPs will be designed to provide children with the support needed to access and participate in that curriculum.

The social participation frame that renders the context metaphorically as an avenue with barriers or open access is a fundamental part of a subfield of speech–language pathology: augmentative alternative communication (AAC). Augmentative communication systems—for example, computers or picture boards—are seen as ways to access a communication context such as a classroom lesson, and interventions are designed to reduce barriers and promote participation in that event (Beukelman & Mirenda, 1998; Tashie et al., 1993).

CURRICULAR FRAMES

Everyone would agree that schools have *curricula*, but not all would agree on the meaning of the term. Some would be referring to the information taught within subject areas ("the social studies curriculum" or "the language arts curriculum"). Some may see it as an overall course of study, progressing from basic to advanced information. These different construals of the curriculum arise from different frames.

The frames used to understand what a curriculum is will also influence how the curriculum is organized and executed. For example, the goals of a curriculum might differ, depending upon how it is framed. Some curricula may be based on how to encourage critical thinking ("the critical thinking curriculum"), and others may be preparing children for their roles in the outside world ("the vocational curriculum," "learning by doing," "the professional curriculum"). Each of these angles on a curriculum emerges from a different frame—one that matters when doing curricular-based assessment, teaching, or intervention. Let's look at a few prominent ones in today's educational and clinical literatures.

Curriculum as Subject Matter

The most common way of framing a curriculum is in terms of its subject matter. In this frame, the curriculum is the subject matter to be taught in a state, a school, or covered in a particular grade or by a particular teacher. A third-grade curriculum in U.S. schools is likely to include language arts (reading, writing, literature), social studies, mathematics, and science. Other subjects such as art, music, or physical education are usually considered "extracurricular."

Once a curriculum is selected, it is "taught" to children in classrooms. Teachers teach the curriculum, often according to a predetermined grade-specific time schedule. Students are seen as recipients of the curriculum. This model of the curriculum portrays information in the curriculum as being passed through an invisible conduit to the student, whereupon the student stores it for future use. An educated student is one who has received and stored the subject matter associated with the curriculum. Friere (1970) calls this view of the curriculum a *banking metaphor*. It treats the curriculum from within both a *conduit metaphor* (the transfer or transmission of information from one locale to another) and a *container metaphor* (the deposit and storage of information).

The *subject matter curricular model* along with its conduit/container metaphors is considered to be politically neutral (Apple, 2001). History teaches us that Columbus discovered American in 1492. Children in U.S. schools need to know this fact, and they learn it somewhere in their exposure to their elementary school's curriculum.

Yet another aspect to the conduit/container rendering of a curriculum is to assess how well it has been learned by students. Schools, teachers, and students are evaluated for what the students know about the curriculum. Achievement tests in different subject areas provide an index for measuring the teaching success of schools and teachers in teaching the curriculum, and for measuring the success of children in learning the curriculum. Standards and benchmarks for curricular learning at different grade levels have been created by each state in the U.S. and used throughout the school year to evaluate how well students are progressing in learning the curriculum. These are grounded in a *normative model*, where children's performance levels are compared with a normal standard. Smith and Dickinson (2002) have called this focus a "product model." The curriculum becomes closely associated with its outcomes. Teachers "teach to the test," and children compete for grades. Some educators are concerned about the overemphasis on the curricular product because it gets in the way of a student's intellectual curiosity about the curriculum (Pope, 2001).

The part of the conduit/container metaphor that is in focus in this product model of the curriculum is what has been learned (stored) by children after they have been taught the curriculum and what they can retrieve (from the container) when their knowledge is being tested. Teachers and clinicians have called this general approach to viewing the curriculum as "curriculum-based assessment" (Nelson, 1998). The special focus on children's formal test performance has been dubbed the "standards move-ment" in education. In its extreme form, children's performance is judged by one or two scores on a standardized test. This ap-proach to judging children's educational competence in a partic-ular subject matter has come to be called "high-stakes testing" since the results of the tests are used to make educational judg-ments about the quality of schools or the competence of teachers or children.

Speech–language pathologists carry out their own version of curriculum-based assessment. Their goal is to determine how chil-dren are able to process the language that is used to transmit the subject matter of the curriculum. It is the children's handling of the language requirements of the curriculum that is assessed rather than their knowledge of the subject matter itself (Nelson, 1998). This specialized version of curriculum-based assessment, one that has been referred to as "curriculum-based communication assess-ment" (CBCA), is in keeping with the conduit/container meta-phors. The focus in this case is on the ability of the child to place subject matter communicated in classrooms in mental storage. (See Table 7.3 for an example of guiding questions proposed by Nelson, 2001, for conducting CBCA.) In order to understand the subject matter, children also must process it, calling forth a model of information processing. The conduit/container metaphors are thereby embedded in a communication-processing model. These two sets of frames, like those applied to other areas of communica-tion, form the fundamental frames for carrying out curriculum-based assessments.

Two of the questions in CBCA as shown in Table 7.3 also per-tain to intervention. Curriculum-based communication interven-tion has involved translating information in the curriculum to

Table 7.3. Questions Guiding Curriculum-Based Communication Assessment

1. What communication skills are needed for successful participation in this part of the curriculum?
2. What does the student usually do when attempting this curricular task?
3. What communication skills and strategies might the student acquire to become more successful?
4. How should the curricular task be modified?

children who don't understand it in its standard presentation. In this way of thinking, like for CBCA, the curriculum is treated as subject matter that needs to be translated and then transmitted to them. It therefore fits with the conduit/container metaphor.

Table 7.4 contains a few examples of the conduit/container view of the subject matter curriculum as expressed by speech–language pathologists and teachers. For example, the curriculum is described as what needs to be learned (acquired, stored) by children or speech–language pathologists, as something that is taught (transmitted), as something that can incorporate (contain) speech and language goals, and as something that, once stored, can be assessed to determine further instructional needs.

The Functional Curriculum

In the final analysis, a school curriculum is seen by educators as a means for children to become educated and socialized into mainstream society. In this sense, a curriculum is regarded as a tool that functions to achieve certain end goals: (1) for individuals to obtain the skills and knowledge necessary for being productive in society and (2) for society to maintain itself. Thinking in this vein has resulted in a *functional metaphor* being combined with the conduit/ container metaphor. Speech–language pathologists also construe the curriculum as functional. They see it as a vehicle for achieving communication goals on a child's IEP.

Some curricula are made more explicitly functional than others. Functionally organized curricula are sometimes referred to as "training programs" and are epitomized by vocational or professional schools in which the curricula are skill-based, teaching students what they need to know to carry out certain jobs. Learning is called "work" and students' learning behaviors are judged as being "on task" or "off task." This curricular view contrasts with other,

Table 7.4. Language of Professionals Reflecting Their Idea of Curriculum as a Container of Subject Matter to Be Taught (Transmitted) to Children

Montgomery (1992)	Speech–language pathologists attended regular school in-services to "learn the curriculum" (p. 363).
Roller, Rodriquez, Warner, and Lindahl, (1992)	"We modify and adapt the curriculum as needed to ensure that IEP goals are met" (p. 386).
Borsch and Oaks (1992)	"Implementation of these goals in the classroom curriculum may vary" (p. 367).
Brandel (1992)	"We explored alternative ways to teach language arts collaboratively and decided to teach groups of children in separate classrooms" (p. 369).
Ferguson (1992)	"Beginning with one idea and one science topic, and planning activities that reinforce specific goals and objectives, I eventually found myself comfortable incorporating speech and language goals into content areas [of the curriculum]" (p. 371).
Moore-Brown and Montgomery (2001)	An obstacle to successful collaborative practices is the "extension of language goals into the classroom curriculum" (p. 154).
Tucker (1985)	"Curriculum based assessment includes any procedure that directly assesses student performance within the course content for the purpose of determining that student's instructional needs" (p. 200).

less functional views in which educators see themselves as "educating" rather than "training" their students.

School speech–language therapists may work with teachers and students within these functionally based curricula to aid students in the communication aspects of tasks associated with work. For example, they may aid the student in managing the discourse of classroom lessons or the discourse of job interviews (e.g., Prelock, 2002).

The Hidden Curriculum

When rendered through a conduit/container metaphor, the curriculum emphasizes the explicit teaching of subject matter. However, teachers know that there are other less explicit things that children need to learn in schools. For instance, children need to learn how to participate in classroom events and school discourse. They also need to find out which behaviors are considered appropriate or inappropriate and how they are expected to conduct themselves socially in different social subcultures and at different school events. They are expected not only to cooperate with others in the school environment, but also to compete with them (Gatto, 1991; Reeves, 2001).

These contextual aspects of the curriculum have been talked about by teachers as a "hidden" or "pragmatic" curriculum (e.g., Anyon, 1980; Kanpol, 1999), and more pejoratively as "the feel-good curriculum" (Stout, 2000). Whereas the subject matter components of the explicit, official curriculum are regarded by all as "school work," the content of the hidden curriculum is not officially recognized. There is no time allocated for teaching it, nor are teachers or students given official recognition for improvements in their behavioral, social, or discourse arenas associated with the school's context.

These different views of the curriculum can be held by the same individual, depending upon the circumstances in which the curriculum is being discussed. And there are other views of the curriculum that reveal themselves upon reflection. For example, a critical or political view of curriculum content would focus more on the cultural and political agendas underlying curricular choices (see Chapter 8 for more on this topic).

The alternative views of the curriculum will lead practitioners to different clinical and teaching practices. So when teachers and clinicians engage in curricular planning, they need to be clear about what they mean by "curriculum" in the first place. (See Table 7.5 for a summary of different curricular frames.)

OTHER FRAMES USED IN SCHOOL PRACTICES

The Political Reality Frame and Its Associated Metaphors

Another way that public school practices have been talked about is from within various political metaphors. Schools are seen, for in-

Table 7.5. Different Versions of the Curriculum as Seen from Different Curricular Frames

The model	Example of the model	The assumptions
Curriculum as subject matter	Children need to know about circumstances surrounding Christopher Columbus's discovery of America	The subject matter view of the curriculum is built upon a conduit and container frame of information transmission and storage. It is based on established cultural canons about what an educated child needs to know and assumes that such knowledge is value-free (neutral).
The functional curriculum	Why should the teacher spend time teaching kids about Christopher Columbus when they don't even know how to tie their shoes?	The curriculum is an instrument for teaching children how to operate in the everyday contexts of the real world. A vocational curriculum is an example.
The hidden (pragmatic) curriculum	How do I get the teacher to call on me so I can answer the question about Christopher Columbus?	The hidden or pragmatic curriculum emphasizes the rules of classroom discourse and the participation structure of classroom events.

stance, as institutions designed to socialize children into fixed cultural roles with particular status rankings (Cornbleth, 2000; Freire, 1970; Macedo, 2000). Unlike the conduit metaphor that portrays the educational endeavor as value-free, the political view of education focuses on how the curriculum, both explicit and hidden, teaches children U.S. values. Teachers knowingly or unknowingly prepare children for carrying out their eventual roles in a politically defined, stratified society. This broad use of a political point of view might best be seen as a broad-based *political reality frame* in which all things are seen in political terms.

A political view often divides the world into political subtypes such as conservative and liberal (e.g., Lakoff, 2002), with the occasional addition of radical (e.g., Engel, 2001). Subscribers to the different political camps see education from within their specifiable political reality frame. Conservatives, who support the socio-cultural status quo, see the job of educators as one of socializing children to believe in, understand, and abide by U.S. values. Children need to learn the cultural canons that will allow them to become good citizens. Conservatives may lobby against court rulings that prohibit the recitation of the Pledge of Allegiance in the classroom. For example, Republican senators in the U.S. Congress have recently protested a court ruling that the Pledge of Allegiance be banned from school classrooms.

Liberals, assuming a different political reality frame, have focused their attention on the preservation of multicultural differences among U.S. citizens. They lobby schools to offer multicultural perspectives, to emphasize civil rights, and to celebrate the differences of all Americans. Radicals, on the other hand, take a critical perspective on the United States. They see education as a form of indoctrination and proselytizing in which the values and power of the political elite are maintained. Noam Chomsky, the linguist and political theorist, criticizes the U.S. educational system for failing to encourage independent and critical thought: "It is the obligation of any teacher to help students discover the truth and not to suppress information and insights that may be embarrassing to the wealthy and powerful people who create, design, and make policies about schools" (Chomsky, quoted in Macedo, 2002, p. 21).

State departments of education, school administrators, and teachers act on their own particular political views by requiring children to read and interpret select materials in certain ways (Anyon, 1980). Textbooks are selected to reflect politically differentiable points of view, standards and benchmarks measure children's progress in achieving predetermined politically oriented goals, curricular decisions are made to provide children with what the developers consider to be "proper" knowledge, and children are taught to behave in politically and morally correct ways.

Heroes in one political reality frame are villains in another, facts become fiction, irrelevant details become main points, all depending upon the political orientation of those doing the administering and teaching. The "fact" that Christopher Columbus discovered America in 1492, for example, may be treated by political liberals or radicals as biased toward a Eurocentric perspective. Columbus was the first European to discover America, but to say that he discovered it first without this qualification appears as an arrogant fiction for anyone who takes a Native American point of view.

But where do these political frames originate? Lakoff (2002) has proposed that U.S. conservatives and liberals are working from two distinct metaphoric conceptual systems. The conservative system is drawn from a metaphor of strict parenting in which a parent (or the government) has the responsibility for the well-being of the family. One parent, typically the father, serves as the family patriarch, taking on an authoritarian role. The patriarch makes the rules, enforces them, and assumes ultimate responsibility for the other family members. Lakoff calls this a *strict father metaphor.*

The liberal system casts parents and the government in a more nurturing role, in which all family members are treated as having their own points of view and as needing to take on their own responsibilities. The family is governed in a committee style, with family members taking care of one another. The power relationships are not authoritarian, as in the conservative metaphor, but rather, egalitarian. Lakoff calls this the *nurturant parent metaphor.*

Lakoff examined how both the strict father and the nurturant parent metaphors guide the thinking of conservatives and liberals on different moral and political issues. His analysis might well be extended to the ways teachers construct their roles and teaching approaches.

The strict father metaphor contains ideas that underlie didactic approaches in which the teacher plays the role of strict father. The school authorities, teachers, and speech–language pathologists working in this frame decide what children need to learn, and deliver the teachings in a directive, didactic manner. The school discourse format that lends itself well to this orientation is a lesson or drill session during which teachers provide a prompt (e.g., a sentence to be imitated, a question to be answered), children respond, and teachers evaluate their responses (Mehan, 1979).

School personnel using the nurturant parent metaphor conduct themselves in more egalitarian ways. Their approaches are designed to encourage critical and reflecting thinking. Teaching methods are child-centered, nondirective, and discovery-based. Teachers or speech–language pathologists might place children in a dilemma that they need to resolve in order for them to learn through problem solving. Dynamic approaches are used where information is provided within the child's educational grasp (Vygotksy's [1981] "zone of proximal development").

According to the authoritarian, strict father metaphor, children need to be punished when they misbehave. The behavioral approach, consistent with this family metaphor, provides a systematic means for rewarding good behaviors and punishing undesirable behaviors. A child who hits himself is placed in a program in which his hitting is ignored or punished.

These same undesirable behaviors, viewed within the nurturant or egalitarian metaphor, are treated in their motivational context. Teachers using a nurturant frame might try to reason with children who hit themselves to get them to stop, or they might ask the children how best to help them control themselves.

The Economic Reality Frames

When the finances associated with education are brought into focus, a new broad-based reality frame comes into being, one based on economics (Coulson, 1999; Kozol, 1992). Schools are examined in terms of financial costs and benefits. Using this economic frame, school administrators make decisions about what services and resources are affordable and how to allocate their limited funds. Any growth or change in personnel, services, or programs must be justified in terms of whether they will be "cost-effective." Those in control of school budgets must decide what is affordable, and in so doing they decide which services are provided and how much to pay for them.

School budgets in the United States are heavily dependent upon local property taxes. Kozol (1992), in his poignant book describing the appalling educational conditions among U.S. inner-city schools, noted: "A typical wealthy suburb in which homes are often worth more than $400,000 draws upon a larger tax base in proportion to its student population than a city occupied by thousands of poor people" (pp. 54–55). The result of this inequality, along with many others, is the creation of what Kozol has called a "savage inequality" in U.S. schools. Educational resources, including numbers of teachers, state of the school building, and quantity of school books and other educational materials, are much more plentiful in suburban schools than in inner-city schools.

Recently, efforts have been made to offer families a choice of schools for their children. For example, school voucher systems have been instituted which offer the family the option of "buying" access to the school of their choice for a particular child. Private charter schools have also been organized to allow parents a choice of education for their children outside the public school system.

Arguments in favor of school choice have come from both liberals and conservatives. In the 2001 presidential election, both Gore and Bush advocated programs to enable families to choose their child's school. If one were to apply Lakoff's strict father and nurturant parent metaphors to account for this unusual agreement, it becomes apparent that the two political perspectives argue for school choice for different reasons. An argument for school choice from the strict father, or conservative, frame is based on a view in which power is provided to families, allowing them the authority to make their own educational decisions. An argument for school choice from the nurturant parent, or liberal, frame has to do with creating a more egalitarian society.

The impact of the June 27, 2002, Supreme Court decision to allow parents to use vouchers to pay for their children's private school education has yet to play out. If the states implementing the decision take a conservative stance, they may opt for a profit-making goal for private schools. For example, Florida's private schools are now permitted to charge families fees beyond the amount of the voucher. Rothstein (2002) has used an economic frame to analyze the impact of the voucher program on a particular private school in West Palm Beach, Florida. The school was bought by a private company, the Educational Services of America. Rothstein comments:

> The Progressive School took vouchers as full payment this year. But it can no longer afford to do so, and will add fees in September. Although its costs are low—its top teacher salary is $38,000, compared with the $56,000 in nearby public schools—special needs cannot be met with a $4,500 voucher. Next year, parents of children with mild disabilities will pay an extra $2,500, parents of those with greater disabilities more. (p. 7)

Another type of study carried out using an economically based analysis of public schools is how the economics of a child's community influences what the child learns in school. Bowles and Gintis (1976), for example, argued from their informal observations that students from working-class backgrounds are rewarded in schools for their obedience, while those from middle- and upper-class backgrounds are rewarded for their initiative and assertiveness.

In 1980, Anyon carried out an ethnographic study that provided strong support for Bowles and Gintis's informal observation. In a now-classic article on the economically motivated hidden curriculum of schools, Anyon studied five schools. Two were working class, with most parents having blue-collar jobs. A middle-class school included children whose parents were skilled workers, white-collar workers, or held middle-management jobs. A fourth school, an affluent professional school, had a parent population with upper-income-level salaries. In the fifth school, the executive elite school, many of the families had a member, usually the father, who was a top executive in a corporation.

Anyon's findings showed dramatic differences in the teaching and learning for the different schools. Schools with working-class students used authoritarian teaching practices. Fifth-grade children in these working-class communities learned to follow rules and answer questions, without being told what they were about, and they were required to carry out school tasks that bore little relevance to their lives or their interests. The schools were organized along the lines of a "strict father" in which obedience and subservience were emphasized.

Children from the middle, professional, and executive classes were treated by their teachers in more egalitarian, less authoritarian ways. They were taught to work independently and to judge for themselves whether rules made sense. Differences between these three other schools progressed along a continuum of student independence, egalitarianism, and encouragement of creativity.

The Legal Reality Frames

Services in school that are provided to children with communication disabilities are required to be consistent with federal legislation. Such legislation offers yet another unique frame governing school practices. This frame is quite broad in scope, applying to an entire worldview. It includes a variety of other conceptual frames. Because of its breadth and encompassing nature, it qualifies as a reality frame.

Legislative Acts

Public Law 105-17, commonly referred to as the IDEA, specifies which children are covered by the act by outlining a group of diagnostic categories. The diagnoses, arising from a medical frame (see Chapter 1) include (1) mental retardation, (2) hearing impairment (including deafness), (3) speech or language impairment, (4) visual impairment (including blindness), (5) serious emotional disturbance, (6) orthopedic impairments, (7) autism, (8) traumatic brain injury, (9) other health impairments, and (10) specific learning disabilities (PL 105-17, section 602A).

Individual Rights

The foundational frame for legislative acts and their implementation is one based on the protection and *guarantee of individual rights*. The most general statement identifying the particular rights that are being protected originated in 1975 with Public Law 94-142, or the Education for All Handicapped Children Act. The act mandates that a child with a disability has the right to a free appropriate public education (FAPE). FAPE guarantees that the child's education will be paid for by the public school system (it is free) and that the education fits (it is appropriate for) the child's individual needs and abilities (PL 94-142, PL 99-457, PL 105-17).

Other rights that are guaranteed through federal legislation include the right to information, to due process, to equality (nondiscrimination), and to access. All these together are described as making up a person's educational rights. More particularly, federal laws provide individuals with the following legal rights:

1. The parent or guardian's right to be informed about services rendered to her or his child. (PL 94-142, PL 99-457).
2. The parent or guardian's right to be involved in creating her or his child's educational and therapeutic goals (PL 94-142, PL 99-457).
3. The parent or guardian's right to be informed about her or his child's educational progress (PL 94-142, PL 99-457).
4. The parent or guardian's right to have access to her or his child's educational and clinical records (PL 94-142, PL 99-457).
5. The parent or guardian's right to due process. She or he can appeal decisions made by schools about her or his child's educational program (PL 99-142, PL 99-457).
6. The child's right to being educated with nondisabled children in a least restrictive environment (PL 94-142, PL 99-457).

7. The child's right to nondiscriminatory assessment and educational approaches (PL 93-112, PL 94-142, PL 99-457, PL 101-336, PL 105-17).
8. The child's right not to be expelled from school for disciplinary reasons if the disruptive behaviors are related to the child's disability (PL 015-17).

The Precious Gem Metaphor

If one were to examine the language of the laws or the government's descriptions and explanations of the laws, one would see that rights have been cast in the metaphor of a precious gem that is owned by someone and that needs to be: "protected," "guaranteed," and "safeguarded." Sometimes the precious commodity is described as not yet obtained. In these cases, language is used that would allow one to attain or have access to the precious right. Rights should "not be denied," one should be given "opportunities" to attain rights, or one should be provided with a "least restrictive context" for obtaining the right.

Adverse Effects

Different renderings of the wording of the IDEA has resulted in a denial of speech therapy services to children with speech and language diagnoses who are doing well academically. The problem results from a narrowly framed interpretation of "adverse effects of a speech and language disorder" on a child's academic progress. ASHA's response to this narrow interpretation has been to argue that speech and language performance is part of academic performance and should be counted as part of the curriculum (Dublinski, 2002). Further arguments have been made having to do with broadening the scope of practice of speech–language pathologists to include literacy. This also has to do with framing—in this case, the frame is related to language and communication.

A second frame underlying the dialogue on adverse effects is the "causality metaphor." The "adverse effects" idea is one that requires the use of a causal chain frame wherein an academic problem is seen as caused by a disability.

School Standards and Benchmarks

Also relevant to the legal frame are the recent federal, state, and locally legislated approaches designed to evaluate the performance of schools and teachers. These school standards and benchmarks have grown out of a long-standing interest of Americans in obtaining objective and standardized measures of almost anything and everything (Hanson, 1993; Sacks, 1999; Zenderland, 1998). It is based in the objectivist frame that treats the real world as made up of observable and measurable facts (see Chapter 5, on the differences between objective and subjective reality frames).

In order to measure whether a school system or child has met the subject matter standards and benchmarks for a particular curriculum, teachers have children take achievement tests. The notion of standards and benchmarks is build upon a *spatial metaphor*, usually a straight-up line, with the highest standard at the top and benchmarks along the way up. The line can become a *path* or a *journey* when time is added. A curriculum or a child's learning of it is depicted as beginning at the bottom of the path and achieving the various knowledge benchmarks as it progresses to the top.

Assessment methods have been designed to measure performance along this vertical standard. There are two basic types: (1) standardized or objective tests, and (2) performance or authentic tasks. The standardized tests are designed to obtain comparison scores of children's growth by using norm referencing. The *growth metaphor* involves a normative comparison between the person or group taking the test and a standard group. The comparison may be of a child with his or her classmates, a classroom of children with other classrooms, a school with other schools, or an entire school system with other systems. Since the items on the standardized tests are designed to yield an objective measure of the child's knowledge, the answers need to be right or wrong, with nothing in between. Items in the test are often decontextualized—that is, they are unrelated to one another and unrelated to the particular experiential understandings from which the items are drawn. Understanding that Christopher Columbus discovered America in 1492 is hoped to be part of a much fuller understanding of who Columbus was, why he sailed, where he sailed from, where he landed, the dangers he and his crews faced, the historical period when all this happened, and so on. Standardized tests focus on an isolated "fact" that is hoped to be part of this fuller understanding. In order to get the right answers, children must either be able to extract isolated facts from their fuller understanding, or they must be able to retrieve memorized, isolated facts—or, if the item on the test offers a choice of answers, they must be good guessers.

Performance tasks, unlike standardized tests, are grounded more in an *experiential frame*. The knowledge and abilities of children are assessed by having them carry out projects, write essays, or perform tasks involving the use of particular information. Performance tests are commonly described as authentic because they are contextualized and experienced. These tests are also judged against a standard, but the standard is an experiential, situated one. Children can judge their performance in the context of their past performance and in the context of other children in the class. Teachers can judge the performance of individual children in relation to how they did in the past, whether they are progressing toward their individualized goals, or how they compare with other children in their own or other classes.

Performance assessment tasks have also been called authentic because they have "face validity." That is to say, those taking them and those administering them know what the test is for, and see the relevance of the test to their school lives. A performance assessment is more like everyday tasks than a specialized test situation with its own specialized rules and regulations.

FRAME CLASHES IN SCHOOLS

Sometimes frames governing school practices lead to disagreements *among* professionals in schools and *between* professionals and school administrators. These clashes have to do with (1) different ideas about professional responsibilities, (2) different conceptual frames adopted by different professionals, (3) different criteria used to allocate resources, (4) and different political and legal views about the education of children with disabilities.

Scope of Practice Clashes

One bread-and-butter conflict among frames for professionals working in schools has to do with how responsibilities among professionals are distributed. This issue is described using the visually oriented metaphor "scope of practice." An illustration of the politically based framing of professional practices are the skirmishes among special educators, regular educators, and speech–language pathologists about who should be primarily responsible for the evaluation and remediation of children with language and literacy disabilities.

A recent domain in which speech–language pathologists have expanded their practices is that of literacy (American Speech–Language–Hearing Association, 2001). Expansion and clarification of the scope of practice in relation to literacy is reflected in a 2001 position statement forwarded by ASHA. The statement outlines the roles and responsibilities of speech–language pathologists to include (1) preventing written language problems by fostering language acquisition and emergent literacy; (2) identifying children at risk for reading and writing problems; (3) assessing reading and writing; (4) providing intervention and documenting outcomes for reading and writing; (5) assuming other roles, such as providing assistance to general education teachers, parents, and students, and advocating for effective literacy practices; and (6) advancing the knowledge base (American Speech–Language–Hearing Association, 2001).

These responsibilities include many that regular or special education teachers could regard as an infringement on their assigned territory. The scope-of-practice negotiations often involve a *war metaphor* depicting the disagreements as battles over territories. The warring parties in these cases are depicted as fighting to secure their territories or to expand their territorial boundaries. The set of recommendations from the President's Commission on Excellence in Special Education (2002) is likely to result in further scope-of-practice battles between classroom teachers, special educators, and speech–language pathologists. (As discussed in Chapter 6, these changes require an increase in collaboration between professionals in carrying out a child's IEP.)

Clashes between Disciplinary Frames

Another source for frame clashes in schools has to do with differences in disciplinary frames and practices between professionals. These frame differences may be between professionals in the same discipline as well as between professionals from different disciplines.

Speech–language pathologists in different institutional settings, for example, often work within different professional frames. Those working in hospitals are likely to adhere more closely to the medical model than those working in schools. These two groups of professionals, though trained in the same methodologies having to do with diagnoses, assessment, therapy, and evaluation of progress, will interpret and carry out these methods differently depending upon their settings. The professional in the medical setting will focus more on the physical causes and remedies of disabilities, working within a biologically based way of thinking. Educationally based speech–language specialists, especially those who are aiming toward school inclusion, are more likely to work with an education frame that calls for a professional team to integrate the child into the school's social and academic activities.

These frame differences are also apparent across professional disciplines. Classroom teachers are responsible for the curriculum and for working with children to achieve the standards and benchmarks associated with the curriculum. Classroom teachers focus on the whole class and carrying out the daily activities. Because of staffing concerns and responsibilities for class progress, classroom teachers are likely to prefer group instruction for a child with disabilities over individual instruction, and inclusion goals over individually based intervention goals. They also have more time with children and so can make the best use of child-centered, constructivist teachings. This is all in keeping with an educational model with a constructivist thrust.

School speech–language pathologists, on the other hand, are only responsible for individuals who have been identified as having disabilities. Their focus, therefore, is on the IEP goals for individual children, that is, on getting them up to speed in the specific areas in which they have identified communication deficits. Their instruction is often regarded as therapeutic rather than educational. They are likely to prefer individual over group instruction, and individually based intervention goals over ones having to do with curricular goals. Despite their efforts to move away from the medical model, their institutional responsibilities still require them to subscribe to its dictates. They are the ones who need to assess and remediate children's communication deficits—a responsibility that calls for a deficit focus. Also, because they see the child for short periods of time, for reasons of expediency, they may be drawn to remedial approaches that favor adult- over child-centered methods.

Recent and upcoming school reforms are likely to force speech–language pathologists to shift more to an educational model. Speech–language pathologists are now required, by federal legislation, to ground their intervention goals in the curriculum and to support children with communication disabilities to achieve curricular benchmarks and standards. Now they are also responsible for working on written literacy. These new responsibilities may lead them to provide more of their services in the classroom alongside the classroom teacher.

Clashes Based on Limited Economic Resources

The cost–benefit rendition of school practices that arises from an economic frame is at odds with other frames, especially those that take as their focus the provision of additional support for individual students with language and literacy disabilities. When a teacher's time is cast as an economic resource, extra time spent to provide individualized instruction can be regarded as overspending. The additional costs used to design special programs or to hire extra personnel to support students' individual needs have been seen as extravagant under a model in which economizing is uppermost in the hierarchy of values.

What proponents of specialized programs sometimes do when justifying the economic worthiness of their programs is to argue that the benefits are worth the costs. They can do this from within the economic frame by talking about the greater overall costs to society if the person being supported were to become a dropout, a criminal, or a ward of the state.

Legal and Political Clashes

Other frames have also been used to make the case for providing specialized services to students with language and literacy disabilities. For example, the legal frame brings to the table the argument that all students have a right to a free appropriate public education, and the costs of this education should be viewed as a secondary concern, thereby resulting in a frame clash—a difference of opinion resulting from a viewpoint created within different frames.

Finally, clashes arising from political differences are legion in public education. Hardly a day goes by that one can't find a newspaper article or letter to the editor arguing from one political position or another about school practices. These political clashes are often between proponents of conservative versus liberal frames. They also might be between a more radical critical frame and that represented by the more conservative school establishment.

Whatever the source of the frame clash, I would argue that those engaged in the clash can better take the perspective of their opponent if they can reflect "where the person is coming from"—that is, what sorts of frames or positions they are basing their arguments in.

Table 7.6. A Chapter Summary of Seven Areas of Public School Practices and Frames Associated with Each

Service delivery frames

> Transdisciplinary frame
> Interdisciplinary frame
> Multidisciplinary frame
> Push-in and pull-out services

IEP frames

> Growth frame
> Causality frame
> Journey and pathway frame
> Social participation frame (least restrictive environments)

Curricular frames

> Subject matter frame (along with conduit and container metaphors)
> Functional frame
> Pragmatic frame (the hidden curriculum)

School inclusion frames

> Social participation frame

Frames of school politics

> Political frame
> Strict father and nurturant parent metaphors
> Scope of practice domains

Legal frames

> Individual rights (precious gem metaphor)
> Adverse effects (causality and curricular frames)
> Standards and benchmarks (spatial, journey, and growth metaphors, objective and subjective reality frames)

Instructional frames

> Didactic (container/banking metaphors)
> Critical thinking (problem-solving frame)
> Constructivist (child as creator metaphor)

SUMMARY

This chapter has examined various aspects of public school practices as conducted by both speech–language pathologists and classroom teachers, with a particular emphasis on practices related to children with communication disabilities. Frames were described in various areas of school practice with special reference to (1) service delivery frames, (2) the IEP, (3) the notion of least restrictive environments, (4) different meanings of a curriculum, (5) depictions of school inclusion, (6) aspects of political practices framing education, (7) aspects of economic practices impacting on schools, and (8) legal frames. Included in each were a variety of other frames, as is shown in Table 7.6.

School personnel working within different frames are likely to have many differences in their preferred practices. Some of these differences were discussed in the section on frame clashes.

The various frames in this chapter and others can be seen as a set of choices for clinicians and teachers as they work with children who have communication disabilities. However, there has been little discussion yet of how to choose from among the many frames available. That is the subject of the next and last chapter.

EIGHT

Reflecting Frames

The first seven chapters of this book have examined frames affecting what educational practitioners do in the course of their clinical or educational practice. My emphasis has been on the practices of classroom teachers and speech–language pathologists. This examination has involved stepping outside our everyday sensibilities and reflecting on what goes into those sensibilities. This examination has been called *reflection on action* (Schön, 1983). This chapter calls for yet another level of analysis in order to compare available frames and decide among them. This level I will call *reflection on frames*.

There are different levels available for thinking about frames. Reflection on action, the one that has been used throughout this book, involves meta-analysis, a cover term that involves both metalinguistic analysis (analysis of language) and metacognitive analysis (analysis of thought). Earlier chapters in this book have used meta-analysis to find frames in the language and thought of practitioners and authors as they discuss assessment, diagnosis, intervention, and teaching of children with speech and language disabilities. Meta-analysis of clinical and educational activities has yielded a rich and diverse picture of models and metaphors to choose from when carrying out clinical and educational work.

The multiplicity of frames revealed by the meta-analysis is likely to raise certain questions and frustrations for practitioners who are searching for best practices. The main concern is how to choose from or merge the ones available. Answering this question involves *reflecting on frames*, that is, doing a meta-meta-analysis. That is what clinicians and teachers sometimes do when they select from familiar frames, when they create new frames, and when they evaluate the impact of what they have been doing by examining their assumptions arising from frames.

Reflecting on frames differs from evaluating framed practices. Evaluation, as described in Chapter 5, focuses on the success or failure of an intervention or an educational approach. The evaluation there involved a consideration of whether framed intervention or instructional approaches served their intended purposes, or whether approaches from different frames yielded different results. The emphasis there was not on comparing or evaluating the frames themselves.

This final chapter borrows from reflective practices used in education, as well as those used in other disciplines and in other professional contexts. My aim is to offer ways of coming to terms with the question of how to select the most appropriate frame to use when supporting schoolage children with language and literacy difficulties.

A REFLECTION ON THEORY
VERSUS PRACTICE

There is experience, and there is theory. Many want to keep these two domains separate. While practice and theory are seen as related to one another, they are mostly treated as qualitatively different. The treatment of frames in this book breaks down that dichotomy. Throughout this book, I have made the case that practitioners and classroom teachers must make decisions in the course of practice and that those decisions are based on conceptual frames. If one were to classify such frames as being either practice or theory, it would probably seem most fitting to put them in the theory category. However, the conceptual frames we have been talking about, while theoretical and abstract in nature, are part and parcel of everyday practices. Practitioners, even the ones who are suspicious of theories and think of them as divorced from practice, are theorists in disguise.

Ritchie and Wilson (2000) have described numerous problems associated with separating theory from practice. They bemoan the fact that analysis of individual teaching experiences is treated by teachers and researchers alike as irrelevant to theory. Most prople incorrectly regard everyday practices as personal and unique to particular teachers and students, and therefore not generalizable for the purpose of theorizing. Or, when moving from theory to practice, practitioners and researchers often treat theories as unrelated to issues raised in their personal everyday experience.

Ritchie and Wilson's (2000) solution to this great divide between theory and practice is to suggest that we need to do a better job when theorizing practice. These authors asked teachers to narrate their lives and their teaching experiences in order to reflect on them and thereby to theorize about them:

> The problem is that experience is often left untheorized. Without the opportunity for critical analysis of experience, teachers and students have no way to see how their experience is itself constructed in and through language and through institutional and cultural ideologies . . . Teachers need theoretical language to help them see the competing and conflicting narratives of learning and teaching. (p. 15)

Ritchie and Wilson (2000), drawing from their interviews of college students who were training to be teachers, show that students are well aware of different educational practices, but that they tend not to reflect on the conceptual frames or learning implications of these differences. Rather, the students discuss the particular methods used by their teachers in relation to how they themselves plan to conduct their classes when they become teachers. The students' depictions are personalized, and they see their decisions about how to teach as having to do with their own personal styles. Here is an example from one of Ritchie and Wilson's interviewees, who is studying to be a high school English teacher:

> I have two literature courses this semester, and just from having the two very opposite-end teachers, it's really made me realize what literature study is about and what form I would rather take. . . . In one course, we're tested over, you know, the themes and things like that, and that's all. In my other course, the twentieth century women writers course, we learn about the literature through group discussions and everybody can say what they feel, and also we write journals on the literature and discover the themes on our own, and then maybe she writes back a comment. . . . I prefer the one-on-one type of relationships with the teacher. There's a real big difference there I think, and so I'd like to have an emphasis on group discussion and critical thinking

so that it was teacher/student, student/teacher feedback and not just teacher to student feedback. (p. 65)

In this example, the two teachers are operating from different frameworks—one involving a container view of education, or what Freire (1970/1993) calls a "banking view of education." In this view knowledge is transferred or deposited into students' minds. The students are tested over the material to assure that the transfer or deposit was successful—that they have received the information and stored it.

The second teacher, the one whose methods are preferred by the student, is working from a framework that Ritchie and Wilson (and others, such as Apple, 1982; Giroux, 1983; hooks, 1994; and Illich, 1975) call a *critical theory framework*. In this reality frame, learning takes place through dialogue. Teachers invite students to reflect critically on what they read and to report on their personal reactions as they come to understand the author's intent. In so doing, students transform how they see themselves, which is the aim of the educational endeavor for teachers working within a critical theory framework.

Reflective practices, such as those carried out in the narratives of Ritchie and Wilson's college students can offer a way of uncovering and comparing the frames that lie beneath the surface of everyday teaching and clinical experience.

REFLECTIVE PRACTICES

Reflective practices are not new to U.S. education or clinical practice. John Dewey was perhaps the first educator to emphasize the importance of reflective practices in education. In his 1933 book, *How We Think*, he portrayed reflection as an activity that arises naturally from problems that occur in everyday experience. Dewey outlined steps for coming to grips with problems: (1) find the problem; (2) define the problem; (3) create a hypothesis for solving the problem; (4) engage in logical reasoning about the problem and methods of solution; (5) act on the hypothesis and implement the solution (Dewey, 1933/1997).

Paulo Freire furthered the popularity of reflective practices in education with his program of radical literacy teaching for impoverished adults in Brazil. His best-known text, *Pedagogy of the Oppressed* (Freire, 1970/1993), contains a set of principles and practices for carrying out reflective thinking in the course of teaching literacy. A central notion of the Freire approach to teaching literacy is *conscientization*, or what he describes as a critical awareness of the world, including aspects of everyday reality. Another conceptual principle forwarded by Freire, one that is closely related to conscientization, is *praxis* (Freire, 1970/1993). Praxis involves simultaneous reflection and action, with the goal of transforming the learner's construction of reality. (In the terms used in this book, the student goes through a reality-frame shift.)

Yet another influential figure in the field of reflective practices is Donald Schön. He, along with his colleague Chris Argyris, forwarded a vocabulary for thinking, talking about, and carrying out reflective practices. For example, they differentiate *single-loop reflection*, reflection that takes the current frame as given, from *double-loop reflection*, reflection that challenges the assumptions of the frame being reflected upon (Argyris & Schön, 1978).

Reflective practices were the mainstay of feminist consciousness-raising groups in the 1970s. The emphasis within those groups was on having participants reflect on their societal and personal situation as women. The life-altering experiences of many women who participated in consciousness-raising groups demonstrated and validated what Paolo Freire meant by conscientization. That is, through reflection many of the women in these groups were able to alter their realities and to develop a new sense of how their lives as women were influenced by social, political, and historical circumstances.

Feminists' depiction of consciousness raising and Freire's conceptualization of conscientization borrow from a *psychoanalytic frame* originating with Freud's (1927/1961) ideas about false consciousness. In that frame a person is unable to see his or her true circumstances because he or she holds onto a belief, idea, or ideology that interferes with it. Consciousness raising and conscientization are reflective practices designed to change or deepen one's view of oneself and to see one's previous view as originating in false beliefs. Psychoanalysis as well as other types of psychotherapy are grounded in self-reflection. Clients are guided by the expert, a psychologist or social worker, as they reflect on, reinterpret, and hopefully gain insight into various aspects of their lives.

So reflection is not a new idea. It is an established practice in a number of areas of our contemporary society. The current practices have evolved from past contributions by such thinkers as John Dewey, Paulo Friere, Donald Schön, and Sigmund Freud. They all involve examining and reframing the taken-for-granted world.

Professional implementation of reflective practices has become an integral part of the discourse for a number of professional groups, including educators (Mezirow & Associates, 2000; Paley & Delpit, 2000), nurses (Burns & Bulman, 2000; Johns, 2000), physicians (Davis-Floyd & St. John, 1998), and occupational therapists (Sinclair & Tse, 2001). The practices are used differently depending upon the profession and upon the particular focus of those creating the practices. For example, Paley and Delpit (2000) have recommended that elementary classroom teachers ask themselves, "Am I a racist?," and in so doing deal with their attitudes and teaching practices related to race. Mezirow, working in the area of adult education, has studied the transformative potential of adult learning (Mezirow & Associates, 2000). Nurses have used reflective practices to examine their individual values and career choices, and to resolve conflict. They recommend reflective practices to reveal different theoretical frames (Atkins, 2000) and to envision new ways to practice (Johns, 2000). (See Table 8.1 for specifics of an approach by Atkins, 2000.)

One interesting area of research involving reflective methods has analyzed the thinking of professionals who have experienced a sea change in how they do things. For example, Davis-Floyd and St. John (1998) carried out reflective interviews with physicians who had shifted from traditional to nontraditional practices. Through the information gained from the doctors' reflections, the authors were able to clarify a group of features that distinguished the frames underlying the different practices (see Table 8.2).

Everyday decisions made by clinicians and teachers are often done without reflection. Why is this? The most immediate answer is that there is little time for reflection in a busy day filled with teaching and providing services. Another is that there are few organizational structures designed to foster reflection, such as mentors or meetings devoted to reflective practices. A third may be that professionals are not accustomed to thinking of themselves as having choices, or as being able to evaluate the choices they have made.

CRITICAL REFLECTION: A REALITY FRAME

In order to engage in reflective practices, one must assume a perspective for evaluating and interpreting what typically goes on or what happened on a particular occasion—that is, one must move into a metareality frame. One aim of reflection is to remember and

Table 8.1. Reflective Practices for Nurses to Identify and Clarify Personal Values and to Create Life Plans

Atkins (2000) recommends three types of exercises for practicing nurses and those in training: ones done alone, ones done with a partner, and ones done with a group. The exercises with groups should be done with trained facilitators. They are aimed at developing awareness in different domains.

1. Exercises for *clarifying ones' own values* might include:

Reflecting alone: A personal value can be described by a statement that says what is important and significant to you as an individual.
Describe three of your own values below by completing this sentence:
It is important to me that:

Reflecting with someone else: Give examples of your values. Do your values guide your actions? When have they and when have they not? How did you acquire the key values in your life?

2. Exercises aimed at *evaluating one's own career choices* involve developing pictorial life maps:

Reflecting alone: Draw a map that represents the background and history of your nursing practice or training. Include as many of the following as possible: your starting point, achievements, joys, sadnesses, important people, obstacles.

Reflecting with someone else: Explain your career map to another. When listening to your partner, pay close attention to details. Things to consider: Are there patients on your map? Why or why not? What takes up the most space? Why?

Reflecting with a group: All participants should post their "maps" on the walls of the room. Look for what is in common.

3. Exercise examining *how frames affect practices:*

Reflecting in a group: Divide into several teams. Each team should identify and represent a theory used in professional nursing practice. They should then debate the following question with other teams: "What theory provides the most value to health care providers?"

Note. Data from Atkins (2000, pp. 28–51).

get clear about what happened. This involves taking a neutral stance toward practices, examining what happened or should have happened. It presupposes that the methods and frames used were appropriate. Another aim of reflection is to discover ways of thinking outside the box. This involves taking a critical stance, rather than a neutral one.

Brechin, Brown, and Eby (2000), in their book on critical practice in health and social care, define critical reflection and practices as follows:

The term "critical" is used to conceptualise practice as an open-minded, reflexive process, built on a sound skills and knowledge base, but taking account of different perspectives, experiences, assumptions and power relations. Critical practice draws on an awareness of wider ethical dilemmas, strategic issues, policy frameworks and socio-political contexts. It acknowledges that there may be no straightforward "right" answers and that powerful, established voices will often hold sway over newer, alternative ways of seeing things. (p. xi).

A specific example of critical reflection is offered by Ritchie and Wilson (2000) as they consider the usefulness of narratives as a reflective approach:

What is the context in which the story is told? Where are the gaps, the silences, the tensions, the omissions? What narratives from other lives might contradict or complicate our own? Who is privileged by these narratives? What positions and relationships do they reinforce? (p. 21)

Applying a critical reflection frame to the areas of practice covered in this book goes beyond a consideration of what it is that we do as speech–language pathologists and teachers and why we do it. It considers also how we might change how we do things. A recycling through the frames identified in each of the previous seven chapters of this book using a critical perspective can offer avenues for improving practice that seldom make their way into the educational or clinical literature on language and literacy disabilities.

Critically Framed Diagnosis

A critical stance toward identifying and labeling students as having language and literacy impairments leads one to ask about the negative as well as the positive effects of being so labeled. While considerable attention in the speech–language pathology literature is devoted to how to diagnose or classify a child correctly, for purposes of providing needed support, there is little mention of the negative effects of a label or classification—even a correct one.

An interesting approach arising from the critical theory asks students themselves about the impact of their diagnosis on their lives. One such study was carried out with high school special education students in 1998 in the New York City Public School System (Fleischer, 2001). Fleischer met with a focus group of five high school students, exploring their ideas and feelings about being placed in a special education class. She found that the students

Table 8.2. Progressing through Paradigms on a Journey from Doctor to Healer

Technocratic model of medicine	Humanistic model of medicine	Holistic model of medicine
Mind/body separation	Mind–body connection	Oneness of body–mind–spirit
The body as machine	The body as an organism	The body as an energy system interlinked with other energy systems
The patient as object	The patient as relational subject	Healing the whole person in whole-life context
Alienation of practitioner from patient	Connection and caring between practitioner and patient	Essential unity of practitioner and client
Diagnosis and treatment from the outside in (curing disease, repairing dysfunction)	Diagnosis and healing from the outside in and from the inside out	Diagnosis and healing from the inside out
Hierarchical organization and standardization of care	Balance between the needs of the institution and the individual	Networking organizational structure that facilitates individualization of care
Authority and responsibility inherent in practitioner, not patient	Information, decision making, and responsibility shared between patient and practitioner	Authority and responsibility inherent in each individual
Supervaluation of science and technology	Science and technology counterbalanced with humanism	Science and technology placed at the service of the individual
Aggressive intervention with emphasis on short-term results	Focus on disease prevention	A long-term focus on creating and maintaining health and well-being

(continued)

Table 8.2. continued

Technocratic model of medicine	Humanistic model of medicine	Holistic model of medicine
Death as defeat	Death as an acceptable outcome	Death as a step in a process
A profit-driven system	Compassion-driven care	Healing as the focus
Intolerance of other modalities	Open-mindedness toward other modalities	Embrace multiple healing modalities

Note. From Davis-Floyd and St. John (1998, pp. 142–143). Copyright 1998 by Rutgers University Press. Reprinted by permission.

used metaphors of being in chains and of bondage to describe their feelings about their life and school experiences (See Table 8.3).

Others critical of labeling have shown how diagnoses can have a negative impact on the identity or the measured performance of a child. The label acts as a stigma, influencing the child's self-identity and influencing how others interact with the child (Rosenthal & Jacobson, 1992). A child sees him- or herself, and others see him or her as "handicapped" as a result of having a diagnosis. His or her handicapped identity, in turn, affects how the child behaves and is treated. The negative impact of labeling has been called the "Pygmalion effect" from a well-known study of children's improved performance after having been labeled "late bloomers" (Rosenthal & Jacobson, 1992).

Table 8.3. Randy's View of His Sense of Bondage and Being in Chains in His Special Education High School Experience

". . . he sees the teacher in several guises: the teacher as an Other, defined on administrative and hierarchical changes; the teacher as the Man, defined on authoritarian chains; the teacher as the White Man, defined on racial chains; and the teacher as the Enemy, defined on class-dominated chains. Randy sees his hegemonic world as contained within an intricate web of chains: a complex of discourses in a formation that do not allow him entry. In these chains and webs of distinctive formations, Randy begins to identify a hegemonic 'system' of violence comprising name-calling, blaming, reversing, and 'one downing.'"

Note. Quoted in Fleischer (2001, pp. 116–117).

This negative impact may be present even for those students who feel that being diagnosed with a disability was liberating. This feeling of relief upon being diagnosed may have arisen because of a shift in causal logic associated with the diagnosis. The problem in performance or behavior is no longer regarded as the fault of the student, but rather as being caused by the diagnosis (e.g., "He hits himself because he is autistic").

New self and social identities resulting from a diagnosis are considered to be secondary effects of that diagnosis. But these "secondary" effects can be just as damaging or even more damaging to the child's growth than the difficulties that led to the diagnosis in the first place.

A third critique of the use of diagnostic labels and classifications has been that they reflect class, race, and gender bias. Studies done from a critical frame have found (1) that poor children who are having difficulty in school are more likely to be diagnosed as disabled than children who are from the middle or upper classes (Oswald, Coutinho, Best, & Nguyen, 2001); (2) that children of color are more likely to be diagnosed as mentally retarded, emotionally disturbed, or as having a specific learning disability than white children (Chinn & Hughes, 1987; MacMillan & Reschly, 1998; Parish, 2000); and (3) that boys more are likely than girls to be diagnosed (Sadker & Sadker, 1995). All this has been dubbed the *overrepresentation problem* or *minority disproportionality* in education (Safe and Responsive Schools Project, 2000; Civil Rights Project, Harvard University, 2002). This examination of cultural bias in diagnosis has been done using a critical frame that challenges the validity of assigning diagnostic labels.

Critically Framed Assessment

Assessments are typically framed in objective terms, using carefully controlled and standardized means of data collection. Tests are given, analyses of samples of children's communication are carried out, scores are obtained and evaluated against standardized norms. This commitment to the objective "facts" of the case seldom allows room for considering how the child experiences his or her difficulties in everyday life.

Better assessments would include an individual's rendering of the difficulties he or she is experiencing. Such assessments might involve interviews with a student, asking the student to report his or her feelings in personal journals, or having the student attend and comment in IEP meetings on how things are going. Some schools offer the services of advocates, individuals who take the point of view of the family and coach them through processes such as "the special education maze" (Anderson, Chitwood, & Hayden, 1990).

Some professionals have focused their entire attention on aiding students and others with severe disabilities to reach their aspirations. Under this approach, called person-centered planning (Forest & Pearpoint, 1992; Holburn & Vietze, 2002), assessment involves working with a team, including the student and his or her family members, to figure out how the student experiences his or her life. Personal profiling methods have been developed, such as mapping out a person's achievements and difficulties, so that members of the team can develop goals and plans for achieving them (e.g., O'Brien, Mount, & O'Brien, 1990). The early sessions with the team involve assessing how the student experiences life by graphically charting things such as:

1. Who are the significant people in the student's life?
2. Where does the student spend time, and what does he or she do there?
3. What choices does the student have over his or her daily life?
4. Which strategies have worked to support the student?
5. What are the hopes and fears of the student's family and close affiliates?
6. What are the barriers and opportunities for achieving social engagement and improving the student's life experience?

Critically Framed
Intervention/Support/Curriculum

Recent approaches to language intervention with both children and adults have argued for a frame shift from impairment-focused intervention to an intervention that focuses on providing support for individuals in their daily lives (Duchan, 2001; LPAA Project Group, 2001; Pound, et al., 2000). This shift from impairment- to socially based intervention has also been depicted as an add-on, in which socially based approaches are added to an impairment-based frame (Chiat, Dipper, & McKiernan, 2001; McNeil, 2001). In this add-on approach, the impairment frame is expanded, not shifted. The socially based emphasis is talked about as another area of impairment that needs remediation.

The add-on view does not require a critique or change of previous ways of doing things. In a critical approach, a critique would be made of the impairment frame. It would show that impairment work "blames the victim" or that impairment therapies mistakenly treat socially based goals as a carryover and may never get to them, or that impairment intervention ignores the problems that arise from social access barriers. The aim of impairment-focused intervention is to make the person fit the context rather than to adjust the context to include the needs of the person. Professionals assuming this critical stance toward the impairment frame have argued that the social or participatory approach be substituted for the impairment one, rather than added to it (Calculator & Jorgensen, 1994; Duchan, 2001).

Another critical approach to the impairment frame for service provision arises from the disability rights movement. In this movement, people with disabilities are aiming toward a service delivery system that is based on a rights-to-access model rather than a needs or welfare model. Oliver and Barnes (1993), for example, have argued that the poor quality of life of people with disabilities is due to the existence of physical and psychological barriers that block their rights of access. (See Table 8.4 for Oliver and Barnes in their own voice.)

Reflecting critically on everyday clinical or teaching practices also requires a careful examination of the power relationships between professionals and their clients or students. It is commonplace for professionals to complain about students, with some being described in more derogatory terms than others. For an ex-

Table 8.4. Oliver and Barnes Arguing for a Rights (Access) over a Needs (Welfare) Model of Disability

The evidence that disabled people experience a much poorer quality of life than everyone else is so overwhelming that it is not in dispute, though the precise dimensions of such deprivation and disadvantage may be. . . . There can be only two possible explanations for this: one that disability has such a traumatic physical and psychological effect on individuals that they cannot ensure a reasonable quality of life for themselves by their own efforts; the other that the economic and social barriers that disabled people face are so pervasive that disabled people are prevented from ensuring for themselves a reasonable quality of life by their own efforts.

The former has become known as the individual model of disability and is underpinned by personal tragedy theory. It has been under severe attack in recent years from a variety of sources to the point that it is now generally recognized that it is an inadequate basis for developing a proper understanding of disability. The latter has become known as the social model of disability and has shifted the focus away from impaired individuals and on to restrictive environments and disabling barriers.

Note. From Oliver and Barnes (1993, pp. 273–274).

ample from outside the world of communication disorders, Jeffrey (1979) found that professionals in accident emergency departments referred to some of their patients (e.g., the alcoholic or drug user) as "normal rubbish." Furthermore, Jeffrey shows that that label was associated with delayed resuscitation. These prejudicial frames get played out in ways that are comparable to those involved in racism, classism, and sexism. There also exists a bias growing out of what might be called "professionalism," which involves abuses of power by professionals.

A critical frame analysis would examine the abuses of power and work toward the creation of nonabusive, egalitarian relationships between professionals and their clients or students. This would require empowering individuals so that they are permitted to assume more responsibility for their own growth.

Power exploitation in work situations also gets played out among professionals and staff in the workplace. Lee-Treweeke (1994), in her study of residential care for the elderly, found that "bedroom tasks" having to do with bodily functions were assigned to lower-paid, lower-status care assistants, whereas "qualified staff" were assigned to "cleaner tasks," such as planning schedules and managing visitors. Similarly, in schools, tasks such as playground or hall duty may be seen by teachers and speech–language pathologists as lesser tasks, ones that should be done by the professionals less skilled than themselves.

Such power relationships in educational settings are familiar to teachers and clinicians who have worked together on planning teams. Negotiations between professionals, staff, and family members of different perceived status can be hampered unless the team members take a reflective and critical stance and acknowledge their hidden assumptions about one another's potential power and status. Table 8.5 contains a set of questions that might be helpful for professionals to address as they begin to break down their power biases and work toward achieving more empowering and egalitarian relationships with their clients and fellow professionals.

Critically Framed Evaluation

Another power differential that often gets played out in negative ways is that between those who are evaluated and those who do the evaluation. Administrators typically evaluate teachers and those providing related services, while teachers and speech–language pathologists evaluate their students. A critical approach to evaluation asks whether this needs to be the case, and what would happen if

Table 8.5. Reflecting on Power Relationships between Professionals, Their Clients, and Others

- Who is privileged in the materials used?
- Whose voices and perspectives are included and excluded in the activities?
- Who is the expert? How and why?
- What are the domains of the teacher/clinician's authority?
- Do student/clients/consumers have authority? In what domains?
- Are students/clients/consumers treated as intellectually subservient?
- What are the frameworks being used and how do they establish power?
- What are the views of teachers/clinicians about the ideas of their student/client?
- How are clients/students/consumers disciplined to follow the rules/ways of therapy?
- What are clients/students disciplined for?
- How is knowledge and skill regarded (as truth or as constructed by individuals)?
- How is knowledge seen as being transmitted?
- How is the person/consumer/student/client labeled?
- Who does the labeling?
- What is the client's/student's conception of the label?

the process of evaluation were shared between those doing the evaluation and those being evaluated.

Action research offers a way in which those being evaluated can play a more central role in the evaluation. In one kind of action research, evaluators and those being evaluated meet together to assess how things went (or are going) (Horton, 1999). Problems are identified by all parties, and solutions are worked out. The group then carries out the solutions, and together the members evaluate the results. The research is seen as a cyclical process in which action, reflection, and evaluation leads to new action, reflection, and evaluation, and so on. Researchers and participants continually interact with one another throughout the process. Under this approach, those being evaluated no longer feel that they are under surveillance. Rather, they are included as participants and contributors in the evaluation process, with everyone working together to improve the service.

Action research involves participants (e.g., students) in all aspects of the research, from identifying the problem to creating and evaluating the solutions. Another way of using the input of students to evaluate teaching programs is to find out how students (or consumers) see things. This aim lends itself well to *ethnographic research approaches*. What, for example do students take "school" or "therapy" to be? In her book called *Doing School,* Pope (2001) offers a strong critique of U.S. school culture by looking at how students answer this school question. Her observations and interviews with five successful high school students led her to the conclusion that their school success is based on competitive frames that require the students to compromise their values and to cheat and lie so as to get ahead in the system.

Critically Framed Literacy

One healthy, critically framed literature on literacy practices examines the materials of literacy for their bias. Sleeter and Grant (1991), in their analysis of 47 textbooks in use in U.S. public schools (grades 1 through 8), found that the materials in the social studies, math, language arts, and science books typically contained narratives written from the point of view and value system of those in power in the United States. When people of different classes or cultures, women, or people with disabilities were represented in pictures and in the stories, they were shown in secondary roles or as contributors to the overall "whitewashed" story of how the United States became what it is today. Conflict was minimized, and, when it was talked about, it was portrayed as contributing to American progress and to the happy state of affairs in America today. In sum, "the vision of social relations that the textbooks we analyzed for the most part project is one of harmony and equal opportunity—anyone can do or become whatever he or she wants; problems among people are mainly individual in nature, and in the end are resolved" (p. 110).

A second common critique of traditional approaches to literacy is that they are often divorced from the ordinary life experiences of students (Freire, 1970/1993; Gatto, 2002). Various literacy programs have been instituted to address this problem. For example, a literacy project with teenage students who were labeled by their school as "unteachable, at risk" involved the students in drawing parallels between classic books and stories and their own lives. The students called themselves "The Freedom Writers," after the civil rights activists known as the "freedom riders." They wrote about the parallels between what they read and their own lives, and they published their writings in a book called *The Freedom Writers Diary* (Freedom Writers & Gruwell, 1999). (For an excerpt from one of the students, see Table 8.6.)

Table 8.6. An Excerpt from a Diary Entry by a High School "Freedom Writer"

"Dear Diary:

"We just finished reading Romeo and Juliet; I couldn't believe that Juliet stabbed herself over a guy that she only knew for a few days. I guess I wasn't as in love as I thought I was, because I'd never do something that crazy for my boyfriend.

"At first when we started reading this story, I compared myself with Juliet. We are both young and in love with a guy that we couldn't last a day without seeing, only Juliet fell in love at first sight and it took me two months to supposedly be in love. Running away seemed like an easy way for use to rebel against my parents' disapproval of my boyfriend. Yet it didn't come out the way we had planned.

"Juliet's parents found her dead next to her boyfriend. Unfortunately, my parents found me alive next to my boyfriend. Lucky for Juliet, she did and she didn't see the reaction of her parents, nor did she have to go through punishments. I survived, and unlike Juliet's parents, my parents didn't welcome me with tears falling down from their faces. . . . "

Note. Quoted in Freedom Writers and Gruwell (1999, pp. 34–35). Reprinted by permission of Random House, Inc.

Another approach for making literacy relevant is to have students work on exciting, engaging independent study projects. Gatto (2002) had his students work with their family members on independent study projects and engage in community service experiences and research projects. These projects took up 3 days of each week. (See Table 8.7 for a description of Gatto's curriculum by a 13-year-old student.)

Critically Framed School Practices

Critical theorists, in their evaluation of how school systems work, have differentiated *schooling* from *education* (Gatto, 2002), and *authentic learning* from *indoctrination* (Chomsky, 2000). Schooling and indoctrination are seen as authoritarian approaches to education that dull critical thinking (what some have called "dumbing-down"). Indoctrination, as described by critical theorists, involves the promotion of a particular slant on the world, failing to adequately represent the varied perspectives.

Critical theorists have, for example, viewed the proposed curricula of Allan Bloom (1997) and E. D. Hirsch (1988) as exemplify-

**Table 8.7. A 13-Year-Old Student's Letter Describing the
Philosophy and Class Activities in John Gatto's Classroom**

" . . . Each of us has one-of-a-kind identity—just as we all have one-of-a-kind fingerprints—and what education means is to develop that unique personality so that we each know who we are. Self-discovery is at the bottom of being somebody real. Most kids imitate what they see on TV and do what the teacher tells them to do, but you can't become real that way.

" . . . The way Mr. Gatto likes the Lab School to work is that every kid gets . . . different kinds of experience. First and most important is independent study, a day out of the school building alone or with a friend, going anywhere we want to go and studying anything we want to study. The best kind of independent study is when you have one big idea, for instance, you want to find all the ways that the ancient Greeks, Romans, Egyptians still influence New York City, and you break that idea into parts—architecture, law, clothing, etc.—and you hunt for answers for a whole year. That way each day builds toward something big that's all your own.

" . . . The second kind of experience is apprenticeships. I'm apprenticed to an Editor at the West Side Spirit newspaper, Nubia is apprenticed to State Senator Patterson, Tuwan is a guide at the Transit Museum. What you learn in an apprenticeship is how someone thinks when they are doing their work, how they make decisions, what they look out for.

"The third kind of experience is community service. We spend one full day a week helping others, not being a parasite—for a change. Some of our kids serve at a homeless shelter, one entertains in old people's homes. . .

"Some days we're teamed up with our own parents or somebody else's to do Family Teamwork Curriculum. Maybe I'd spend the day on my father's job, or plant flowerpots with my mother, or paint a room with my uncle, or read to my grandmother. The idea is to recognize that your family is the most important thing you'll ever be part of.

"The last kind of experience is 'class' work. . . . What [Mr. Gatto] does with classroom time is to give us practice exercises in thinking. We analyze everything and anything, and we even practice 'dialectics,' which is thinking where you just automatically assume that anything an authority tells you is dead wrong. Then you work to find out whether it is dead wrong or really right. . . . "

Note. Quoted in Gatto (2002, pp. 32–34). Reprinted by permission of Berkeley Hills Books.

ing indoctrination. Both Bloom and Hirsch have proposed that schools create a curriculum based on classical texts and ideas, which they believe express universal truths. Both authors eschew the notion of cultural relativism and support the notion that classic ideas should be what make up the core curriculum. They call for a curriculum that treats these ideas as a classical canon and as foundational knowledge standards for adequate schooling in the United States.

Aronowitz and Giroux (1991), authors writing from within the critical frame, comment on Bloom and Hirsch:

> Here we have all the elements of an elitist sensibility: Abhorrence of mass culture, a rejection of experience as the arbiter or taste and pedagogy, and a sweeping attack on what is called "cultural relativism," especially on those who want to place popular culture, ethnic and racially based cultures, and cultures grounded in sexual communities (either feminist or gay and lesbian) on a par with classical Western traditions. (p. 216)

The Aronowitz and Giroux stance taken in relation to the classical curriculum proposed by Bloom and Hirsh can be applied to all areas of practice with students who have language and literacy disabilities. The critical frame, as its name indicates, requires that the common everyday beliefs of what is good about clinical and educational practices be examined with a critical eye, one that applies strong standards of relevance and fairness. The critique, unlike that arising from the statistical approaches used for evidence-based practices, has to do with evaluating whether the methods are fair, empathic, and relevant for the children and families being served.

VALUES-BASED PRACTICES

As is clearly revealed by the various critical perspectives, teachers and speech–language pathologists cannot afford to assume that their current practices are best practices—even those that pass muster when they are subjected to evidence-based studies. Rather, they

Table 8.8. "It's Turtles All the Way Down"

In *A Brief History of Time*, Stephen Hawking (1998) described an incident in which a scientist, lecturing on astronomy, described how the earth orbits around the sun and how the sun, in turn, orbits around the galaxy. A member of the audience disagreed, asserting, "What you have told us is rubbish. The world is really a flat plate supported on the back of a giant tortoise." The scientist challenged back: "What is the tortoise standing on?" The reply from the audience: "It's turtles all the way down."

need to examine their assumptions and to identify the frames from which their practices derive.

Reflective practices, like other practices, are also subject to frame bias. Finding frames that influence reflective practices feels like the "turtles all the way down" problem that is commonly described in philosophy (Hawking, 1998; see Table 8.8). In this case, one not only needs to analyze the frames involved in educational practices but also the frames used in the analysis of frames. One possible way to avoid being trapped among the turtles is to examine the values that underpin the frames. If one points to the values underlying the choice of frames, one then has an external standard against which to examine the frames.

Examination of one's values requires that clinicians and educators make their values explicit (Byng, Cairns, & Duchan, 2002). In values-based reflection, practitioners examine their own practice values and then use those values as a basis for selecting their teaching or clinical approaches. Professionals who explicitly adopt social inclusion as a value and as a goal for working with someone who is excluded by virtue of his or her communication impairment can safely use inclusion as a primary standard for electing new approaches and frames and for evaluating the ones already in use.

A number of different professional groups have advocated for values-based practices. For example, Bishop and Scutter (2001) have proposed a values-based approach as a guide for nursing, Wolfensberger (1992) has recommended social role valorization as a special education goal for children with special needs, and Byng et al. (2002) have recommended that professionals examine their practice values to discover the sources of their professional satisfaction and dissatisfaction (see Table 8.9).

METHODS FOR REFLECTION

As seen from our walk through various tributaries of the reflection literature, the process of reflecting can be done in different ways and has been done for many different purposes. Unlike Joseph Heller's character General Peckem in *Catch-22* (1996), who "liked listening to himself talk, liked most of all listening to himself talk about himself," productive reflection is done with some nonconceited questions in mind: How did that go? Can I improve upon it? Do I understand it?

A number of techniques found in professional practices have been used to promote reflection. Some can be used individually

Table 8.9. Ways of Incorporating Values-Based Reflection and Practices in a Speech–Language and Hearing Service

- Consult with clients or students about what they want from your service. This needs to be undertaken in an open and creative way, making the process fully accessible to people with communication disabilities.

- Set up discussions with your colleagues on values, ideally involving a facilitator.

- Brainstorm your values and compare them to those of your clients or students.

- Imagine the ideal service.

- Identify the barriers to delivering those ideal values.

- Identify small steps towards practices that meet those values.

- Work out how you might implement those small steps.

- Review the values and their practical effects at regular intervals.

- Use the values as means of establishing priorities in service development or allocating resources.

Note. Adapted from Byng, Cairns, and Duchan (2002, p. 106). Copyright 2002 by Elsevier Science. Adapted by permission.

by practitioners as they reflect upon their daily experience. For example, the methods in Table 8.10 include some common reflection techniques for professionals to use on their own. The authors quoted in this table advise you to think about what you are doing as you are doing it or afterward, to write down your thoughts about your practices in stories or journals, to identify problems you are having, and then to problem-solve some possible solutions.

The last three items in the reflective practice list of Table 8.10 are frame-based. They invite you to think about what frames you are using when conducting your everyday practices. In order to do this, professionals will need to examine particular practices, such as the last day's activities or a particular part of the day—say a classroom reading lesson. To begin, one might develop some guiding questions—What were your aims? Were they achieved? What did the children learn? How do you know? How might it have gone better?

After answering these questions, the professional might want to go back and examine the assumptions he or she was making that led to the earlier answers. Are your aims skill-based (e.g., teaching a vowel rule)? Or are they based in a subjective reality frame (e.g., getting children to live the experiences of the child in

**Table 8.10. Activities for Reflecting on Your Own
Practice and Experience**

- Writing down your own stories about teaching and therapy (Ritchie &
  Wilson, 2000; Roemer, 1995).
- Keeping a journal, a diary, a log, or a portfolio (Freedom Writers, 1999;
  Pound et al., 2000).
- Doing a critical analysis of textbooks and materials you use (Zipes, 2001).
- Thinking aloud about what you are doing as you watch your practice on
  a video tape (Schön, 1987, Ch. 3).
- Reflecting on what you are doing as you are doing it ("thinking on your
  feet" and "reflection in action") (Schön, 1983).
- Reflecting on what you did after you did it ("reflection on action")
  (Schön, 1983).
- Reflecting on the frameworks or assumptions that lead you to do what
  you do (Argyris & Schön, 1978).
- Determining your values and basing clinical/educational framing deci-
  sions on them (Byng, Cairns, & Duchan, 2002; Everitt & Hardiker, 1996;
  Illich, 1975).
- Examining your sense of reality and developing your consciousness to
  transform it (conscientization) (Freire, 1970/1993).
- Casting an identified issue in a problem-solving frame and proceeding
  through problem-solving steps (Dewey, 1933/1997; Freire, 1970/1993)
- Determining what frames underlie your practices (Ritchie & Wilson,
  2000).
- Critiquing the frames and practices you are using from the point of view
  of what other frames might offer.

the story)? What frames do you use when describing children's
learning? Do you use an information-processing frame that focuses
on the information provided in the lesson? When you thought
about how it might have gone better, did you focus on the children's performance or yours? Were your suggestions ones that involved alterations from within the frame you were already working
from? If so, now consider how you might reorganize the session
from within a different frame.

The recommendations in Table 8.10 require solitary reflection.
But those same activities are likely to be even more successful if
they are done together with someone else or with a group. Indeed,
the everyday discussions and musings that go on between teachers
in the gathering places of public schools are a kind of informal reflective practice. (See Jacobson, in press, for an appeal for super-
vised group reflection groups.) Or teachers and clinicians might

Table 8.11. Various Uses for Reflective Practices

- Select an activity.
- Improve an activity.
- Select a frame/approach.
- Critique a frame/approach.
- Evaluate new frame/approach.
- Evaluate a client's or student's progress.
- Evaluate the evaluation approaches used.
- Improve service delivery.
- Identify practice values.
- Make services compatible with values.
- Determine power relationships among service provider and other service providers, clients/students, and family members.

want to keep track of the chronic issues that keep coming up and then organize a more formal reflective meeting in which they are explored.

Guiding questions for a reflection meeting could follow the problem-solving steps offered by Dewey and Freire: What is the problem here? Why is this a problem? How are those involved contributing to it? What are some possible solutions? What frames are involved in creating the solution? Which should we try?

Reflection can also be put to purposes other than solving a problem. It can be done for all of the reasons listed in Table 8.11. Each of these reasons would require a different set of guiding questions, and may require different levels or types of reflection. Table 8.12 describes four such levels that can be used for different purposes. For example, if the reflection aims to answer the question of how an activity went, Level-2 reflection on action would suffice. Among the things one would do is to name the activity type, evaluate how it went, and consider minor changes to try when carrying out the activity again. This is often the type of reflection that a student and supervisor engage in just after a session with a client or a classroom lesson. But if the reflection is about whether the best approach is being taken with a child, or whether the child's difficulties are better understood within another perspective (e.g., as in need of support vs. intervention), then Level-3 reflection is called for. Level-4 reflection is more rare, resulting in sea changes in one's worldview. Metaphorically speaking, it would change the rose-colored glasses through which

Table 8.12. Levels of Reflection Found in the Literature

- *Level 1: Reflection in action.* Reflection often takes place during basic everyday, mostly nonproblematic events. This reflection involves using a directly experienced sense of reality, even if it is veiled by a guiding frame (Freire, 1970/1993) or seen through a false consciousness (Freud, 1927/ 1961). The taken-for-granted reality remains taken-for-granted and the reflection has to do with how to best negotiate the event.

- *Level 2: Reflection on action.* This involves reflecting about an event before or after it takes place. It may involve naming the event (Freire, 1970/ 1993), considering its underlying frame (meta-analysis, Freire's "unveiling reality"), or considering whether it is appropriate for use given the child's goals. Level-2 reflection fits with single-loop learning (Arygis & Schön, 1987).

- *Level 3: Reflection on frames.* Level 3 reflection involves reflecting on a set of experiences from a neutral or critical perspective for their underlying frames, values, and evaluation standards. It requires the use of meta-meta-analysis, or what Arygis and Schön (1987) call "double-loop learning."

- *Level 4: Emancipatory reflection.* Emancipatory reflection involves dramatic shifts in thinking. The result of this analysis is to transform experience, shift from one reality to another, or to emancipate oneself from previous ways of thinking. This level is what Freire (1970/1993) means by "conscientization."

---

one's current reality is being viewed to another color, revealing a different reality.

SUMMARY

This chapter has raised a number of issues that can be approached using reflective practices. The first issue is to allow clinicians and teachers to discover the implicit frames they are working from to carry out their everyday practices. This is crucial for all areas of professional practices for a variety of reasons. It allows professionals to examine their taken-for-granted ways of doing things so that they can improve upon them. It allows those who see and do things differently to examine their differences, and, when working together, to combine or alter their frames so that they can all be "on the same page." It opens new avenues of practice, ones that derive from "thinking outside the box" or frame. It allows evaluators to understand why certain ways of measuring children's progress seem incompatible with the goals of teachers, clinicians, or students.

A second issue and another one that calls for reflection arises from analyzing practices for their frames. How does one select from among the frames? If evaluation approaches are also frame-biased, as has been argued here, what means are available to decide which practices are best? If all practices and evaluations of them are constructed from frames, are they all of equal value? One way out of this paradox is to choose the frames that best fit one's professional values.

Most authors who write about the approaches and practices of speech–language pathology and education do so from a neutral frame. Another approach that is much needed is a critical one, in which common practices are examined critically for their social and political implications. This stance was explored, using findings from our sister disciplines.

Lastly, a set of reflective practices was offered as a potential guide for recognizing how frames influence everyday ways of doing things. These reflective practices, adapted from other professions, need to be honed to fit the needs and purposes of those doing the reflecting. While most reflective practices have been designed to solve identified problems and conflict, they can also be used when examining how things are going or how things went during particular teaching–learning events. The overall aim of the reflection, as was the aim of this book, is to give us insight about what we do, so that we can do a better job of servicing and supporting children with language and literacy disabilities.

References

Akerley, M. (1985). False gods and angry prophets. In H. Turnbull & A. Turnbull (Eds.), *Parents speak out: Then and now* (pp. 23–31). Columbus, OH: Merrill.

Askhoomoff, N. (2000). Neurological underpinnings of autism. In A. Wetherby & B. Prizant (Eds.), *Autism spectrum disorders: A transactional developmental perspective* (pp. 167–190). Baltimore: Brookes.

American Speech–Language–Hearing Association. (1991). A model for collaborative service delivery for students with language-learning disorders in the public schools. *ASHA, 33*(Suppl. 5), 44–50.

American Speech–Language–Hearing Association. (1996a). *A practical guide to applying treatment outcomes and efficacy resources.* Washington, DC: Author.

American Speech–Language–Hearing Association. (1996b). Central auditory processing: Current status of research and implications for clinical practice. *Journal of Audiology, 5,* 41–54.

American Speech–Language–Hearing Association. (2001a). *Roles and responsibilities of speech–language pathologists with respect to reading and writing in children and adolescents (position statement).* Rockville, MD: Author.

American Speech–Language–Hearing Association. (2001b). *Scope of practice in speech-language pathology.* Rockville, MD: Author.

Anderson, W., Chitwood, S., & Hayden, D. (1990). *Negotiating the special education maze: A guide for parents and teachers* (2nd ed.). Rockville, MD: Woodbine House.

Antaki, C., & Rapley, M. (1996). Questions and answers to psychological assessment schedules: Hidden troubles in "quality of life" interviews. *Journal of Intellectual Disability Research, 40*, 421–437.

Anyon, J. (1980). Social class and the hidden curriculum of work. *Journal of Education, 162*, 67–92.

Apple, M. (1982). *Education and power.* New York: Routledge.

Apple, M. (2000). *Official knowledge.* New York: Routledge.

Apple, M. (2001). *Review of Noam Chomsky (2000). Chomsky on miseducation.* Available: *http://coe.asu.edu/edrev/reviews/rev109.htm.*

Aram, D., & Nation, J. (1982). *Child language disorders.* St. Louis: Mosby.

Argyris, C., & Schon, D. (1978). *Theory in practice: Increasing professional effectiveness.* San Francisco: Jossey-Bass.

Aronowitz, S., & Giroux, H. (1991). Textual authority, culture, and the politics of literacy. In M. Apple & L. Christian-Smith (Eds.), *The politics of the textbook* (pp. 218–241). New York: Routledge, Chapman & Hall.

Atkins, S. (2000). Developing underlying skills in the move towards reflective practice. In S. Burns & C. Bulman (Eds.). *Reflective practice in nursing: The growth of the professional practitioner* (2nd ed., pp. 28–51). Malden, MA: Blackwell Science.

Austin, J. (1962). *How to do things with words.* Oxford, UK: Oxford University Press.

Baddeley, A. (1998). *Human memory: Theory and practice* (rev. ed.). Boston: Allyn & Bacon.

Baddeley, A., Gathercole, S., & Papagno, C. (1998). The phonological loop as a language learning device. *Psychological Review, 105*, 158–173.

Baker, E., Croot, K., McLeod, S., & Paul, R. (2001). Psycholinguistic models of speech development and their application to clinical practice. *Journal of Speech, Language, and Hearing Research, 44*(3), 685–702.

Bank-Mikkelson, N. (1969). A metropolitan area in Denmark: Copenhagen. In R. Kugel & W. Wolfensberger (Eds.), *Changing patterns in residential services for the mentally retarded* (pp. 227–254). Washington, DC: President's Committee on Mental Retardation.

Bates, E., Camaioni, L., & Volterra, V. (1975). The acquisition of performatives prior to speech. *Merrill–Palmer Quarterly, 21*, 205–216.

Bates, E., & Dick, F. (2000). Beyond phrenology: Brain and language in the next millennium. *Brain and Language, 71*, 18–21.

Bateson, G. (1972). A theory of play and fantasy. In G. Bateson (Ed.), *Steps to an ecology of mind* (pp. 177–193). New York: Ballantine Books.

Becker, G. (1997). *Disrupted lives: How people create meaning in a chaotic world.* Berkeley and Los Angeles, CA: University of California Press.

Berko, J. (1958). The child's learning of English morphology. *Word, 14*, 50–77.

Bernstein, D., & Tiegerman-Farber, E. (2001). *Language and communication disorders in children.* Boston: Allyn & Bacon.

Berube, M. (1996). *Life as we know it.* New York: Pantheon Books.

Beukelman, D., & Mirenda, P. (1998). *Augmentative and alternative communication.* Baltimore: Brookes.

Biklen, D., & Duchan, J. (1994). "I am intelligent": The social construction of mental retardation. *Journal of the Association for Persons with Severe Handicaps, 19,* 173–184.

Bishop, A., & Scudder, J. (2001). *Nursing ethics: Holistic caring practice* (2nd ed.). Sudbury, MA: Jones & Bartlett.

Bishop, D. (1994). Grammatical errors in specific language impairment: Competence or performance limitations. *Applied Psycholinguistics, 145,* 507–550.

Bishop, D. (1997). *Uncommon understanding: Development and disorders of language comprehension in children.* East Sussex, UK: Psychology Press.

Bissex, G. (1980). *Gnys at work: A child learns to write and read.* Cambridge, MA: Harvard University Press.

Blacher, J. (1984). Sequential states of adjustment to the birth of a child with handicaps: Fact or artifact? *Mental Retardation, 22,* 55–68.

Blachman, B. (2000). Phonological awareness. In M. Kamil, P. Mosenthal, P. D. Pearson, & R. Barr (Eds.), *Handbook of reading research* (Vol. 3, pp. 483–502). Mahwah, NJ: Erlbaum.

Blank, M. (2002). Classroom discourse: A key to literacy. In K. Butler & E. Silliman (Eds.), *Speaking, reading and writing in children with language learning disabilities.* Mahwah, NJ: Erlbaum.

Bloom, A. (1987). *The closing of the American mind.* New York: Simon & Schuster.

Bloom, L. (1970). *Language development: Form and function in emerging grammars.* Cambridge, MA: MIT Press.

Bloom, L. (1973). *One word at a time.* The Hague, The Netherlands: Mouton.

Bloom, L. (1978). The integration of form, content, and use in language development. In J. Kavanaugh & W. Strange (Eds.), *Speech and language in the laboratory, school, and clinic* (pp. 210–246). Cambridge, MA: MIT Press.

Bloom, L., & Lahey, M. (1978). *Language development and language disorders.* NY: Wiley.

Borsch, J., & Oaks, R. (1992). Effective collaboration at Central Elementary School. *Language Speech and Hearing Services in Schools, 23,* 367–368.

Bowles, S., & Gintis, H. (1976). *Schooling in capitalist America: Educational reform and the contradictions of economic life.* New York: Routledge & Kegan Paul.

Brandel, D. (1992). Collaboration: Full steam ahead with no prior experience! *Language, Speech, and Hearing Services in Schools, 23,* 369–370.

Brechin, A., Brown, H., & Eby, M. (Eds.). (2000). *Critical practice in health and social care.* Thousand Oaks, CA: Open University.

Bricker, D., & Cripe, J. (1992). *An activity-based approach to early intervention.* Baltimore: Brookes.

Brown, A., & Ferrara, R. (1985). *Diagnosing zones of proximal development.* New York: Cambridge University Press.

Brown, J., Collins, A., & Duguid, P. (1989). Situated cognition and the culture of learning. *Educational Researcher, 17*(1), 32–42.

Brown, R. (1973a). Development of the first language in the human species. *American Psychologist, 28,* 97–106.

Brown, R. (1973b). *A first language: The early stages.* Cambridge, MA: Harvard University Press.

Bruner, J. (1986). *Actual minds: Possible worlds.* Cambridge, MA: Harvard University Press.

Burns, S., & Bulman, C. (2000). *Reflective practice in nursing: The growth of the professional practitioner.* London: Blackwell Science.

Butler, D. (1987). *Cushla and her books.* New York: Penguin Books.

Butler, K. (1975). *Short course on auditory perception.* Washington, DC: American Speech–Language–Hearing Association.

Butler, K. (1983). Language processing: Selective attention and mnemonic strategies. In E. Lasky & J. Katz (Eds.), *Central auditory processing disorders* (pp. 297–315). Baltimore: University Park Press.

Byng, S., Cairns, D., & Duchan, J. (2002). Values in practice and practising values. *Journal of Communication Disorders, 35,* 89–106.

Byock, I. (1999). Conceptual models and the outcomes of caring. *Journal of Pain and Symptom Management, 17*(2), 83–92.

Calculator, S., & Jorgensen, C. (1994). *Including students with severe disabilities in schools.* San Diego, CA: Singular.

Camarata, M. (1995). A rationale for naturalistic speech intelligibility intervention. In M. Fey, J. Windsor, & S. Warren (Eds.), *Language intervention: Preschool through the elementary years* (Vol. 5, pp. 63–84). Baltimore: Brookes.

Carrow, E. (1974). *Carrow Elicited Language Inventory.* Austin, TX: Learning Concepts.

Casby, M. (1992). The cognitive hypothesis and its influence on speech–language services in schools. *Language, Speech, and Hearing Services in Schools, 23,* 198–202.

Catt, J. H. (1999). *Ethics roundtable: Technical issues in randomized clinical trials.* Available: *http://professional.asha.org/publications/roundtable/research/catt.htm.*

Catts, H., Gillispie, M., Leonard, L., Kail, R., & Miller, C. (2002). The role of speed of processing, rapid naming, and phonological awareness in reading achievement. *Journal of Learning Disabilities, 35,* 509–524.

Catts, H., & Kamhi, A. (Eds.) (1999). *Language and reading disabilities.* Needham Heights, MA: Allyn & Bacon.

Chall, J. (1983). *Stages of reading development.* New York: McGraw Hill.

Chall, J. (1995). *Learning to read: The great debate* (3rd ed.). New York: McGraw Hill.

Chall, J. (2000). *The academic achievement challenge: What really works in the classroom?* New York: Guilford Press.

Chapman, R. (1981). Exploring children's communicative intents. In J. Miller (Ed.), *Assessing language production in children* (pp. 111–138). Baltimore: University Park Press.

Chapman, R., Streim, N., Crais, E., Salmon, D., Strand, E., & Negri, N. (1992). Child talk: Assumptions of a developmental process model for early language learning. In R. Chapman (Ed.), *Processes in language acquisition and disorders* (pp. 3–19). St. Louis, MO: Mosby Year Book.

Cheng, L.-R. L. (1990). The identification of communicative disorders in Asian-Pacific students. *Journal of Childhood Communicative Disorders, 13,* 113–119.

Chermak, G., & Musiek, F. (1997). *Central auditory processing disorders: New perspectives.* San Diego, CA: Singular.

Chiat, S., Dipper, L., & McKiernan, A. (2001). Redressing the balance. *Advances in Speech–Language Pathology, 3,* 63–66.

Chinn, P., & Hughes, S. (1968). Representation of minority students in special education classes. *Remedial and Special Education, 8,* 41–46.

Chomsky, N. (1965). *Aspects of the theory of syntax.* Cambridge, MA: MIT Press.

Chomsky, N. (1975). *Reflections on language.* New York: Pantheon Books.

Chomsky, N. (2000). *Chomsky on miseducation.* New York: Rowman & Littlefield.

Civil Rights Project, Harvard University. (2002). *Minority issues in special education.* Available: *http://www.law.harvard.edu/civilrights/conferences/SpecEd/moreinfo.html.*

Clay, M. (1984). Literacy at home and at school: Insights from a study of young fluent readers. In J. Goelman, A. Oberg & F. Smith (Eds.), *Awakening to literacy* (pp. 122–130). London: Heinemann.

Clay, M. (1991). *Becoming literate: The construction of inner control.* Portsmouth, NH: Heinemann.

Coats, K. (2001). The reason for disability: Causes and effects in the construction of identity in contemporary American children's books. *Bookbird: A Journal of International Children's Literature, 39,* 11–16.

Coggins, T., & Carpenter, R. (1981). The Communicative Intention Inventory. *Journal of Applied Psycholinguistics, 2,* 213–234.

Coggins, T., Friet, T., & Morgan, T. (1998). Analyzing narrative productions in older school-age children and adolescents with fetal alcohol syndrome: An experimental tool for clinical applications. *Clinical Linguistics and Phonetics, 12*(3), 221–236.

Coles, G. (1998). No end to the reading wars. *Education Week, 18,* 52–55.

Commission on Reading. (1995). *Becoming a nation of readers: The report of the Commission on Reading.* Washington, DC: National Institute of Education.

Condeluci, A. (2000). *Is this a good as it gets?* Available: *http://www.cmfoc.org/compass/issue8/issue8.htm.*

Cornbleth, C. (Ed.). (2000). *Curriculum, politics, policy, practice.* Albany: State University of New York Press.

Coulson, A. (1999). *Market education: The unknown history.* New Brunswick, NJ: Transaction.

Coulson, S. (2001). *Semantic leaps: Frame-shifting and conceptual blending in meaning construction.* New York: Cambridge University Press.

Craig, H., Washington, J., & Thompson-Porter, C. (1998). Performances of young African American children on two comprehension tasks. *Journal of Speech, Language, and Hearing Research, 41,* 445–457.

Craik, F. I., & Tulving, E. (1975). Depth of processing and the retention of words in episodic memory. *Journal of Experimental Psychology, 104*, 268–294.

Crossley, M. (2000). *Introducing narrative psychology: Self, trauma and the construction of meaning.* Buckingham, UK: Open University Press.

Dahl, K., Scharer, P., & Lawson, L. (1999). Phonics instruction and student achievement in whole language first grade classrooms. *Reading Research Quarterly, 34*, 312–341.

Davis-Floyd, R., & St. John, G. (1998). *From doctor to healer: The transformative journey.* New Brunswick, NJ: Rutgers University Press.

de Villiers, J., & de Villiers, P. (1973). A cross-sectional study of the aquisition of grammatical morphemes in child speech. *Journal of Psycholinguistic Research, 2*, 267–278.

Deming, W. (1986). *Out of crisis.* Cambridge, MA: Massachusetts Institute of Technology, Center for Advanced Engineering Study.

Deming, W. (1994). *The new economics* (2nd ed.). Cambridge, MA: MIT Press.

Dewey, J. (1933/1997). *How we think: A restatement of the relation of reflective thinking to the educative process.* Boston: Heath.

DiMeo, J. H., Merritt, D. D., & Culatta, B. (1998). Collaborative partnerships and decision making. In D. D. Merritt & B. Culatta (Eds.), *Language intervention in the classroom* (pp. 37–97). San Diego, CA: Singular.

Dollaghan, C., & Campbell, T. (1998). Nonword repetition and child language impairment. *Journal of Speech, Language, and Hearing Research, 41*, 1136–1146.

Donahue, M. (2002). "Hanging with friends": Making sense of research on peer discourse in children with language and learning disabilities. In K. Butler & E. Silliman (Eds.), *Speaking, reading, and writing in children with language-learning disabilities* (pp. 239–258). Mahwah, NJ: Erlbaum.

Donnellan, A., Mirenda, P., Mesaros, R., & Fassbender, L. (1984). Analyzing the communicative functions of aberrant behavior. *Journal of the Association for Persons with Severe Handicaps, 9*, 202–212.

Dore, J. (1973). A pragmatic description of early language development. *Journal of Psycholinguistic Research, 3*, 343–350.

Dore, J. (1975). Holophrases, speech acts, and language universals. *Journal of Child Language, 2*, 21–40.

Dowd, J., Jorgensen, C., & Weir, C. (2001). *A reflective practice toolkit for coaches.* Concord, NH: University of New Hampshire, Institute on Disability/UAP.

Dowling, S. (2001). *Supervision: Strategies for successful outcomes and productivity.* Boston: Allyn & Bacon.

Dowling, S., & Bruce, M. (1996). Improving clinical training through continuous quality improvement and critical thinking. In B. Wagner (Ed.), *Partnerships in supervision: Innovative and effective practices* (pp. 66–72). Grand Forks: University of North Dakota.

Dreyfus, H. L. (1990). *Being in the world.* Cambridge, MA: MIT Press.

Duane, D. D., & Gray, D. B. (Eds.). (1991). *The reading brain: The biological basis of dyslexia.* Parkton, MD: York Press.

Dublinski, S. (2002). "Adversely affects educational performance" policy 1980–2002: Nothing has changed. *Perspectives on School-Based Issues, American Speech–Language–Hearing Association Division 16*(3), 3–7.

Duchan, J. (1991). Everyday events: Their role in language assessment and intervention. In T. Gallagher (Ed.), *Pragmatics of language: Clinical practice issues* (pp. 43–98). San Diego, CA: Singular.

Duchan, J. (1995). *Supporting language learning in everyday life.* San Diego, CA: Singular.

Duchan, J. (1997). A situated pragmatics approach for supporting children with severe communication disorders. *Topics in Language Disorders, 17*(2), 1–18.

Duchan, J. (1999). Reports written by speech–language pathologists: The role of agenda in constructing client competence. In D. Kovarsky, J. Duchan, & M. Maxwell (Eds.), *Constructing (in)competence* (pp. 223–244). Mahwah, NJ: Erlbaum.

Duchan, J. (2001). Impairment and social views of speech–language pathology: Clinical practices re-examined. *Advances in Speech–Language Pathology, 3*(1), 37–45.

Duchan, J. (in press). The foundational role of schemas in children's language and literacy learning. In C. A. Stone, E. R. Silliman, B. J. Ehren, & K. Apel (Eds.), *Handbook of language and literacy: Development and disorders.* New York: Guilford Press.

Duchan, J., Bruder, G., & Hewitt, L. (1995). *Deixis in narrative: A cognitive science perspective.* Hillsdale, NJ: Erlbaum.

Duchan, J., Calculator, S., Sonnenmeier, R., Diehl, S., & Cumley, G. (2001). A framework for managing controversial practices. *Language, Speech, and Hearing Services in Schools, 32,* 133–141.

Duchan, J., & Katz, J. (1983). Language and auditory processing: Top down plus bottom up. In E. Lasky & J. Katz (Eds.), *Central auditory processing disorders* (pp. 31–45). San Diego, CA: College Hill Press.

Duchan, J., Meth, M., & Waltzman, D. (1992). "Then" as an indicator of deictic discontinuity in adults' descriptions of a film. *Journal of Speech and Hearing Research, 35,* 1367–1375.

Ehri, L. (2000). Learning to read and learning to spell: Two sides of a coin. *Topics in Language Disorders, 20*(3), *19–36.*

Eisenson, J. (1972). *Aphasia in children.* New York: Harper & Row.

Elliott, J. (1991). *Action research for educational change.* Buckingham, UK: Open University Press.

Ellis Weismer, S. (1996). Capacity limitations in working memory: The impact on lexical and morphological learning by children with language impairment. *Topics in Language Disorders, 17*(1), 33–44.

Ellis Weismer, S., & Hesketh, L. (1996). Lexical learning by children with specific language impairment: Effects of linguistic input presented at varying speaking rates. *Journal of Speech, Language, and Hearing Research, 39,* 177–190.

Ellis Weismer, S., Tomblin, J. B., Shang, X., Buckwalter, P. J. G., & Jones, M. (2000). Nonword repetition performance in school-age children with and without language impairment. *Journal of Speech, Language, and Hearing Research, 43,* 865–878.

Engel, M. (2001). *The struggle for control of public education: Market ideology vs. democratic values.* Philadelphia: Temple University Press.

Engel, S. (1995). *The stories children tell: Making sense of the narratives of childhood.* New York: Freeman.

Erickson, K. (2000). All children are ready to learn: An emergent versus readiness perspective in early literacy assessment. *Seminars in Speech and Language, 21*(3), 193–203.

Everitt, A., & Hardiker, P. (1996). *Evaluating for good practice.* London: Macmillan.

Fauconnier, G., & Turner, M. (2002). *The way we think: Conceptual blending and the mind's hidden complexities.* New York: Basic Books.

Ferguson, M. (1992). The transition to collaborative teaching. *Language, Speech, and Hearing Services in Schools, 23,* 371–372.

Feuerstein, R. (1979). *The dynamic assessment of retarded performers.* Baltimore: University Park Press.

Fey, M. (1986). *Language intervention with young children.* Newton, MA: Allyn & Bacon.

Fey, M., Catts, H., & Larrivee, L. (1995). Preparing preschoolers for the academic and social challenges of school. In M. Fey, J. Windsor, & S. Warren (Eds.), *Language intervention: Preschool through elementary years* (Vol. 5, pp. 30–37). Baltimore: Brookes.

Fleischer, L. E. (2001). Special education students as counter-hegemonic theorizers. In G. Hudak & P. Kihn (Eds.), *Labeling: Pedagogy and politics* (pp. 115–124). New York: RoutledgeFalmer.

Fodor, J. (1983). *The modularity of mind.* Cambridge, MA: Bradford Books.

Forest, M., & Pearpoint, J. (1992). Families, friends, and circles. In J. Nisbet (Ed.), *Natural supports in school, at work, and in the community for people with severe disabilities* (pp. 65–86). Baltimore: Brookes.

Forman, E., Minick, N. & Stone, C. A. (Eds.). (1993). *Contexts for learning: Sociocultural dynamics in children's development.* New York: Oxford University Press.

Frattali, C. (1998). Quality improvement. In C. Frattali (Ed.), *Measuring outcomes in speech–language pathology* (pp. 172–185). New York: Thieme.

Freedman, B. (1987). Equipoise and the ethics of clinical research. *New England Journal of Medicine, 317*(3), 141–145.

Freedom Writers & Gruwell, E. (1999). *The Freedom Writers diary: How a teacher and 150 teens used writing to change themselves and the world around them.* New York: Broadway Books.

Freire, P. (1970). *Cultural action for freedom.* Cambridge, MA: Harvard Educational Review and Center for the Study of Development and Social Change.

Freire, P. (1970/1993). *Pedagogy of the oppressed.* New York: Penguin Books.

Freud, S. (1927/1961). *The future of an illusion* (J. Strachey, Trans.). New York: Norton.

Friel-Patti, S. (2001). Looking ahead: An introduction to five exploratory studies of Fast ForWord. *American Journal of Speech–Language Pathology, 10*(3), 195–202.

Froeschels, E. (1918/1980). Child language and aphasia: Thoughts on aphasia based on child language development and its anomalies. In R. Reiber (Ed.), *Language development and aphasia* (pp. 91–227). New York: Academic Press.

Galasso, M. (in press). Diagnosis as an aid and a curse in dealing with others. In J. Duchan & D. Kovarsky (Eds.), *Diagnosis as cultural practice.* Hawthorne, NY: De Gruyter.

Gathercole, S., & Baddeley, A. (1990). Phonological memory deficits in language disordered children: Is there a causal connection? *Journal of Memory and Language, 29,* 336–360.

Gatto, J. T. (1991). *Dumbing us down: The hidden history of compulsory education.* Gabriola Island, BC, Canada: New Society.

Gatto, J. T. (2002). *A different kind of teacher: Solving the crisis of American schooling.* Albany, CA: Berkeley Hills Books.

Gee, J. (1999). *An introduction to discourse analysis: Theory and method.* New York: Routledge.

Geertz, C. (1973). Thick description: Toward an interpretive theory of culture. In C. Geertz (Ed.), *The interpretation of cultures* (pp. 3–30). New York: Basic Books.

Gentry, J. R. (1982). An analysis of developmental spelling in GNYS AT WRK. *Reading Teacher, 36,* 192–200.

Gerber, S. (1998). *Etiology and prevention of communication disorders* (2nd ed.). San Diego, CA: Singular.

Gernsbacher, M., Hallada, B., & Robertson, R. (1998). How automatically do readers infer fictional characters' emotional states? *Scientific Studies of Reading, 2,* 271–300.

Gerrard, K. (1991). A guide for assessing young children's expressive language skills through language sampling. *National Student Speech Language Hearing Association, 18,* 87–95.

Gilger, J., & Wise, S. (in press). Genetic correlates of language and literacy impairments. In C. A. Stone, E. R. Silliman, B. J. Ehren, & K. Apel (Eds.), *Handbook of language and literacy: Development and disorders.* New York: Guilford Press.

Giroux, H. (1983). *Theory and resistance: A pedagogy for the opposition.* South Hadley, MA: Bergin & Garvey.

Goffman, E. (1974). *Frame analysis.* New York: Harper & Row.

Goodman, K. (1965). A linguistic study of cues and miscues in reading. *Elementary English, 42,* 639–643.

Goodman, Y. (Ed.). (1986). *Children coming to know literacy.* Norwood, NJ: Ablex.

Grace, C., & Shores, E. (1991). *The portfolio and its use: Developmentally appropriate assessment of young children.* Little Rock, AR: Southern Early Childhood Association.

Graham, S., & Harris, K. R. (1999). Assessment and intervention in overcoming writing difficulties: An illustration from the Self-Regulated Strategy Development Model. *Language, Speech, and Hearing Services in Schools, 30,* 255–264.

Greenspan, S., & Wiedner, S. (1998). *The child with special needs: Encouraging intellectual and emotional growth.* Reading, MA: Addison Wesley.

Greenspan, S., & Wiedner, S. (1999). A functional developmental approach to autism spectrum disorders. *Journal of the Association for Persons with Severe Handicaps, 24,* 147–161.

Greenspan, S., & Wiedner, S. (2000). A developmental approach to difficulties in relating and communicating in autism spectrum disorders and related syndromes. In A. Wetherby & B. Prizant (Eds.), *Autism spectrum disorders: A transactional developmental perspective* (pp. 297–306). Baltimore: Brookes.

Grigorenko, E., Wood, F., Meyer, M., & Pauls, D. (2000). Chromosome 6p influences on different dyslexia-related cognitive processes: Further confirmation. *American Journal of Human Genetics, 66,* 715–723.

Guthrie, J., & Ozgungor, S. (2002). Instructional contexts for reading engagement. In C. C. Block & M. Pressley (Eds.), *Comprehension instruction: Research-based best practices* (pp. 275–288). New York: Guilford Press.

Guthrie, J., Van Meter, P., Hancock, G., McCann, A., Anderson, E., & Alao, S. (1998). Does Concept-Oriented Reading Instruction increase strategy use and conceptual learning from text? *Journal of Educational Psychology, 90,* 261–278.

Gutierrez-Clellen, V., & Pena, E. (2001). Dynamic assessment of diverse children: A tutorial. *Language, Speech, and Hearing Services in Schools, 32,* 212–223.

Hacking, I. (1999). *The social construction of what?* Cambridge, MA: Harvard University Press.

Halle, J., & Spradlin, J. (1993). Identifying stimulus control of challenging behavior. In J. Reichle & D. Wacker (Eds.), *Communicative alternatives to challenging behavior* (Vol. 3, pp. 83–109). Baltimore: Brookes.

Halliday, M. A. K. (1975). *Learning how to mean: Explorations in the development of language.* London: Arnold.

Hamilton, E., & Knill-Griesser, H. (2001). A personal inquiry into improving student writing. *Ontario Action Researcher, 4*(1),1.

Hanson, F. A. (1993). *Testing testing: Social consequences of the examined life.* Berkeley and Los Angeles, CA: University of California Press.

Hart, B., & Risley, T. (1968). Establishing the use of descriptive adjectives in the spontaneous speech of disadvantaged preschool children. *Journal of Applied Behavior Analysis, 7,* 243–256.

Hart, B., & Rogers-Warren, A. (1978). Milieu language training. In R. Schiefelbusch (Ed.), *Language intervention strategies* (Vol. 2, pp. 193–235). Baltimore: University Park Press.

Hart, E., & Bond, M. (1995). *Action research for health and social care.* Buckingham, UK: Open University Press.

Hatton, C. (1998). Whose quality of life is it anyway?: Some problems with the emerging quality of life consensus. *Mental Retardation, 36*(2), 104–115.

Hawking, S. (1998). *A brief history of time*. New York: Bantam Doubleday Dell.

Heath, S. B. (1983). *Ways with words: Language, life and work in communities and classrooms*. New York: Cambridge University Press.

Hegde, M. (1994). *A coursebook on scientific and professional writing in speech–language pathology*. San Diego, CA: Singular.

Heller, J. (1996). *Catch-22*. New York: Scribner's.

Herbert, E. (2001). *The power of portfolios: What children can teach us about learning and assessment*. San Francisco: Jossey-Bass.

Hewitt, L. (1994). Facilitating narrative comprehension: The importance of subjectivity. In J. Duchan & L. Hewitt, & R. Sonnenmeier (Eds.), *Pragmatics: From theory to practice* (pp. 88–104). Englewood Cliffs, NJ: Prentice-Hall.

Hirsch, E. D., Jr. (1988). *Cultural literacy: What every American needs to know*. New York: Vintage Books.

Hodson, B. (1980). *The assessment of phonological processes*. Danville, IL: Interstate Printers and Publishers.

Hoffman, J., Worthy, J., Roser, N., McKoll, S., Rutherford, W., & Strecker, S. (1996). Performance assessment in first-grade classrooms: The PALM model. In K. Leu, C. Kinzer, & K. Hinchman (Eds.), *Literacies for the 21st century* (pp. 100–112). Chicago: National Reading Conference.

Holburn, S., & Vietze, M. (Eds.). (2002). *Person-centered planning: Research, practice and future directions*. Baltimore: Brookes.

hooks, b. (1994). *Teaching to transgress: Education as the practice of freedom*. New York: Routledge.

Horton, S. (1999). Improving a service for dysphasia through consultation. *British Journal of Therapy and Rehabilitation, 6*, 424–429.

Husserl, E. (Ed.). (1913/1931). *Ideas: General introduction to pure phenomenology* (F. Kersten, Trans.). New York: Macmillan.

Individual with Disabilities Education Act, Part C. (1997). Available: *http://www.ideapractices.org/law/regulations/index.php*.

Illich, I. (1975). *Tools for conviviality*. London: Fontana.

Ingram, D. (1976). *Phonological disability in children*. London: Elsevier/North-Holland.

Ingram, D. (1989). *First language acquisition: Method, description and explanation*. New York: Cambridge University Press.

Itsy Bitsy Webs. (2002). *IEP for a child with a cochlear implant*. Available: *http://www.ibwebs.com/Sample%20IEPs/4.htm#Sub-area:%20Syntax%20and%20Grammar*.

Jacobson, T. (in press). *Confronting the discomfort*. Woburn, MA: Butterworth Heineman.

Jefferson, G. (1979). Sequential aspects of storytelling in conversation. In J. Schenkein (Ed.), *Studies in the organization of conversational interaction* (pp. 219–248). New York: Academic Press.

Jeffrey, R. (1979). "Normal rubbish": Deviant patients in casualty departments. *Sociology of Health and Illness, 1*, 98–107.

Johns, C. (2000). *Becoming a reflective practitioner.* Oxford, UK: Blackwell Science.

Joint Commission on Accreditation of Healthcare Organizations. (1997). *Accreditation manual for hospitals.* Oakbrook Terrace, IL.

Jorgensen, C. (1992). Natural supports in inclusive schools: Curricular and teaching strategies. In J. Nisbet (Ed.), *Natural supports in school, at work, and in the community for people with severe disabilities* (pp. 179–215). Baltimore: Brookes.

Jorgensen, C. (1994). Developing individualized inclusive educational programs. In S. Calculator & C. Jorgenson (Eds.), *Including students with severe disabilities in schools* (pp. 27–74). San Diego, CA: Singular.

Jung, J. (1989). *Genetic syndromes in communication disorders.* Boston: College Hill Press.

Kaiser, A., Yoder, P., & Keetz, A. (1992). Evaluating milieu teaching. In S. Warren & J. Reichle (Eds.), *Causes and effects in communication and language intervention* (Vol. 1, pp. 9–47). Baltimore: Brookes.

Kamhi, A. (1997). Three perspectives on comprehension: Implications for assessing and treating comprehension problems. *Topics in Language Disorders, 17*, 62–74.

Kamhi, A., & Catts, H. (2002). The language basis of reading: Implications for classification and treatment of children with reading disabilities. In K. Butler & E. Silliman (Eds.), *Speaking, reading and writing in children with language learning disabilities* (pp. 45–72). Mahwah, NJ: Erlbaum.

Kanpol, B. (1999). *Critical pedagogy: An introduction* (2nd ed.). Westport, CT: Bergin & Garvey.

Karnes, M. (1968). *Activities for developing psycholinguistic skills with preschool culturally disadvantaged children.* Washington, DC: Council for Exceptional Children.

Keene, E. O., & Zimmerman, S. (1997). *Mosaic of thought: Teaching comprehension in a reader's workshop.* Portsmouth, NH: Heinemann.

Kephart, B. (1998). *A slant of sun: One child's courage.* New York: Norton.

Killilea, M. (1952). *Karen.* New York: Prentice-Hall.

Kirk, S., & McCarthy, J. (1961). The Illinois Test of Psycholinguistic Abilities: An approach to differential diagnosis. *American Journal of Mental Deficiency, 66*, 399–412.

Kirsh, D. (2000). A few thoughts on cognitive overload. *Intellectica, 30*, 19–51.

Klingner, J., & Vaughn, S. (1999). Promoting reading comprehension, content learning, and English acquisition through Collaborative Strategic Reading (CSR). *Reading Teacher, 52*, 738–747.

Kohonen, V. (2002). *Authentic assessment as an integration of language learning, teaching, evaluation and the teacher's professional growth.* Available: http://www.uta.fi/laitokset/okl/tokl/eks/finelp/index.html.

Kovarsky, D., & Duchan, J. (1997). The interactional dimensions of language therapy. *Language Speech and Hearing Services in Schools, 28*(3), 297–307.

Kozol, J. (1992). *Savage inequalities*. New York: HarperCollins.

Kratcoski, A. M. (1998). Guidelines for using portfolios in assessment and evaluation. *Language Speech and Hearing Services in Schools, 29,* 3–10.

Kuhn, T. (1996). *The structure of scientific revolutions*. Chicago: University of Chicago Press.

Labov, W., & Waletsky, J. (1967). Narrative analysis: Oral versions of personal experience. In J. Helm (Ed.), *Essays on the verbal and visual arts* (pp. 12–44). Seattle: University of Washington Press.

Lahey, M. (1988). *Language disorders and language development*. New York: Macmillan.

Lai, C., Fisher, S., Hurst, J., Vargha-Khadem, F., & Monaco, A. (2001). A forkhead-domain gene in a severe speech and language disorder. *Nature, 413,* 519–523.

Lakoff, G. (2002). *Moral politics: How liberals and conservatives think*. Chicago: University of Chicago Press.

Lakoff, G., & Johnson, M. (1980). *Metaphors we live by*. Chicago: University of Chicago Press.

Lakoff, G., & Johnson, M. (1999). *Philosophy in the flesh: The embodied mind and its challenge to Western thought*. New York: Basic Books.

Langley, G., Nolan, K., & Nolan, T. (1992). *The foundation of improvement*. Silver Spring, MD: Associates in Process Improvement.

Leary, D. E. (Ed.). (1990). *Metaphors in the history of psychology*. New York: Cambridge University Press.

Lee, L. (1971). *Northwestern Syntax Screening Test*. Evanston, UL: Northwestern University Press.

Lee Treweeke, G. (1994). Bedroom abuse: The hidden work in a nursing home. *Generations Review, 4,* 2–4.

Leebov, W., & Ersoz, C. (1991). *The health care manager's guide to continuous quality improvement*. Chicago: American Hospital.

Leonard, L. (1981). Facilitating linguistic skills in children with specific language impairment. *Applied Psycholinguistics, 2,* 89–118.

Leonard, L. (1989). Language learnability and specific language impairment in children. *Applied Psycholinguistics, 10,* 179–202.

Leonard, L. (1998). *Children with specific language impairment*. Cambridge, MA: MIT Press.

Lincoln, M., Onslow, M., & Reed, V. (1997). Social validity of the treatment outcomes of an early intervention program for stuttering. *American Journal of Speech-Language Pathology, 6,* 77–84.

Lindamood, C. & Lindamood, P. (1979). *Lindamood Auditory Conceptualization Test*. Allen, TX: Developmental Learning Materials.

Lingual Links. (2002). Activity as journey metaphor. Retrieved December 8, 2002, at *http://www.sil.org/lingualinks/lexicon/MetaphorsInEnglish/WhatIs AnActivityAsJourneyMetap.htm*.

LPAA Project Group. (2001). Life participation approach to aphasia. In R. Chapey (Ed.), *Language intervention strategies in aphasia and related neurogenic communication disorders* (4th ed., pp. 235–245). Philadelphia: Lippincott, Williams & Wilkins.

Lund, N., & Duchan, J. (1978). *Assessing children's language in naturalistic contexts.* Englewood Cliffs, NJ: Prentice-Hall.

Lund, N., & Duchan, J. (1993). *Assessing children's language in naturalistic contexts* (3rd ed.). Englewood Cliffs, NJ: Prentice-Hall.

Macedo, D. (Ed.). (2000). *Chomsky on miseducation.* New York: Rowman & Littlefield.

MacMillan, D., & Reschly, D. (1998). Overrepresentation of minority students: The case for greater specificity or reconsiderabtion of the variables examined. *Journal of Special Education, 32,* 15–24.

Markman, E. (1990). Constraints children place on word meaning. *Cognitive Science, 14,* 57–77.

Mastergeorge, A. (1999). Revelations of family perceptions of diagnosis and disorder through metaphor. In D. Kovarsky, J. Duchan, & M. Maxwell (Eds.), *Constructing (in)competence: Evaluations in clinical and social interactions* (pp. 245–256). Mahwah, NJ: Erlbaum.

Masters, M. G., Stecker, N., & Katz, J. (1998). Central auditory processing disorders: *Mostly management.* Needham Heights, MA: Allyn & Bacon.

Matthews, P. (Ed.). (1997). *The concise Oxford dictionary of linguistics.* Oxford, UK: Oxford University Press. See also *http://www.xrefer.com/entry/571565.*

Maurice, C. (1993). *Let me hear your voice: A family's triumphs over autism.* New York: Fawcett Columbine.

Maxwell, M. (1990). The authenticity of ethnographic research. *Journal of Childhood Communication Disorders, 13,* 1–18.

McCormick, C., & Mason, J. (1986). Intervention procedures for increasing preschool children's interest in and knowledge about reading. In W. Teale & E. Sulzby (Eds.), *Emergent literacy: Writing and reading* (pp. 90–115). Norwood, NJ: Ablex.

McGregor, K., & Leonard, L. (1995). Intervention for word-finding deficits in children. In M. Fey, J. Windsor, & S. Warren (Eds.), *Language intervention: Preschool through the elementary years* (Vol. 5, pp. 85–105). Baltimore: Brookes.

McKeough, A. (1998). Story telling: A foundational pillar of literacy. *Transition Magazine, 28* [electronic magazine].

McNeil, M. (2001). Promoting paradigm change: The importance of evidence. *Advances in Speech–Language Pathology, 3,* 55–58.

Mehan, H. (1979). *Learning lessons: Social organization in the classroom.* Cambridge, MA: Harvard University Press.

Merleau-Ponty, M. (1962). *Phenomenology of perception* (C. Smith, Trans.). London: Routledge & Kegan Paul.

Mezirow, J., & Associates. (1990). *Fostering critical reflection in adulthood. Guide to transformative and emancipatory learning.* San Francisco: Jossey-Bass.

Miller, J. (1981). *Assessing language production in children.* Baltimore: University Park Press.

Minskoff, E., Wiseman, D., & Minskoff, J. (1972). *The MWM program for developing language abilities*. Ridgefield, NJ: Educational Performance Associates.

Mishler, E. (1986). The analysis of interview narratives. In T. Sarbin (Ed.), *Narrative psychology: The storied nature of human conduct* (pp. 233–255). New York: Praeger.

Montgomery, J. (1992). Implementing collaborative consultation perspectives from the field. *Language, Speech, and Hearing Services in Schools, 23*, 363–364.

Montgomery, J. (1996). Sentence comprehension and working memory in children with specific language impairment. *Topics in Language Disorders, 17*(1), 19–32.

Moore-Brown, B., & Montgomery, J. (2001). *Making a difference for America's children: Speech–language pathologists in public schools*. Eau Claire, WI: Thinking Publications.

Morrisette, M., & Gierut, J. (2002). Lexical organization and phonological change in treatment. *Journal of Speech, Language, and Hearing Research, 45*, 143–159.

Morrow, L., & Smith, J. (Eds.). (1990). Assessment for instruction in early literacy. Englewood Cliffs, NJ: Prentice-Hall.

Mount, B. (1994). Benefits and limitations of personal futures planning. In V. Bradley, J. Ashbaugh, & B. Blaney (Eds.), *Creating individual supports for people with developmental disabilities* (pp. 97–108). Baltimore: Brookes.

Muhlenhaupt, M. (2001). *More frequently asked questions about school-based OT and PT*. Available: *http://216.239.39.100/search?q=cache:pXbdmFtWkxgC: www.kidsot.com/FAQ2.pdf+cognitive+referencing&hl=en&ie=UTF-8*.

Murphy, S., & Smith, M. (1991). *Writing portfolios: A bridge from teaching to assessment*. Markham, Ontario, Canada: Pippin.

Myklebust, H. (1952). Aphasia in childhood. *Journal of Exceptional Children, 19*, 9–14.

Naremore, R. (1980). Language disorders in children. In T. Hixon, L. Shriberg, & J. Saxman (Eds.), *Introduction to communication disorders* (pp. 177–215). Englewood Cliffs, NJ: Prentice-Hall.

National Institute of Neurological Disorders and Stroke. (2001). *NINDS Williams Syndrome Information Page*. Available: *http://www.ninds.nih.gov/ health_and_medical/disorders/williams.htm*.

Nelson, K. (1986). *Event knowledge, structure, and function in development*. Hillsdale, NJ: Erlbaum.

Nelson, K., & Gruendel, J. (1981). Generalized event representations: Basic building blocks of cognitive development. In M. Lamb & A. Brown (Eds.), *Advances in developmental psychology* (pp. 131–158). Hillsdale, NJ: Erlbaum.

Nelson, N. (1998). *Childhood language disorders in context: Infancy through adolescence*. (2nd ed.). New York: Maxwell Macmillan International.

Nisbet, J. (Ed.). (1992). *Natural supports in school, at work, and in the community for people with severe disabilities*. Baltimore: Brookes.

Norris, J., & Hoffman, P. (1990). Comparison of adult-initiated vs. child-initiated interaction styles with handicapped prelanguage children. *Language, Speech, and Hearing Services in Schools, 21,* 28–36.

O'Brien, J., Mount, B., & Lyle O'Brien, C. (1990). *The personal profile.* Lithonia, GA: Responsive Systems Associates.

O'Connor, S. (1996). *Will my name be shouted out?: Reaching inner city students through the power of writing.* New York: Touchstone Books.

Oliver, M., & Barnes, C. (1993). Discrimination, disability and welfare: From needs to rights. In J. Swain, V. Finkelstein, S. French, & M. Oliver (Eds.), *Disabling barriers—enabling environments* (pp. 267–277). London: Sage.

Olswang, L., Bain, B., & Johnson, G. (1992). Using dynamic assessment with children with language disorders. In S. Warren & J. Reichle (Eds.), *Causes and effects in communication and language intervention* (Vol. 1, pp. 187–215). Baltimore: Brookes.

Osgood, C. (1953). *Method and theory in experimental psychology.* New York: Oxford University Press.

Oswald, D. P., Coutinho, M. J., Best, A. M., & Nguyen, N. (2001). Impact of sociodemographic characteristics on the identification rates of minority students as having mental retardation. *Mental Retardation, 39,* 351–367.

Owens, R. (1999). *Language disorders: A functional approach to assessment and intervention.* Boston: Allyn & Bacon.

Paley, V. (1981). *Wally's stories: Conversations in the kindergarten.* Cambridge, MA: Harvard University Press.

Paley, V. (1990). *The boy who would be a helicopter.* Cambridge, MA: Harvard University Press.

Paley, V. (1992). *You can't say you can't play.* Cambridge, MA: Harvard University Press.

Paley, V. (2001). *In Mrs. Tully's room: A childcare portrait.* Cambridge, MA: Harvard University Press.

Paley, V., & Delpit, L. (2000). *The Merrow Report: "Does a teacher's race matter?"* Available: *http://www.pbs.org/merrow/tmr_radio/transcr/race.pdf.*

Pannbacker, M. (1975). Diagnostic report writing. *Journal of Speech and Hearing Disorders, 40,* 367–379.

Parish, T. (2000). *Disparities in the identification, funding and provision of special education.* Available: *http://www.law.harvard.edu/civilrights/conferences/ SpecEd/parrishpaper2.html.*

Parker, R. (1990). Points of development, not points of failure. In L. Morrow & J. Smith (Eds.), *Assessment for instruction in early literacy* (pp. 62–74). Englewood Cliffs, NJ: Prentice-Hall.

Parr, S., Byng, S., & Gilpin, S. (1997). *Talking about aphasia: Living with loss of language after stroke.* Buckingham, UK: Open University Press.

Paul, R. (2001). *Language disorders: From infancy through adolescence: Assessment and intervention.* Baltimore: Mosby.

Pearson, D. (1998). Standards and assessment: Tools for creating effective instruction. In J. Osborn & F. Lehr (Eds.), *Literacy for all: Issues in teaching and learning* (pp. 264–288). New York: Guilford Press.

Pennington, B. (1999). Dyslexia as a neurodevelopmental disorder. In H. Tager Flusberg (Ed.), *Neurodevelopmental disorders* (pp. 307–330). Cambridge, MA: MIT Press.

Peterson, C., & McCabe, A. (1983). *Developmental psycholinguistics: Three ways of looking at a child's narrative.* New York: Plenum Press.

Piaget, J. (1955). *The construction of reality in the child.* New York: Routledge & Kegan Paul.

Pinker, S. (2001). Talk of genetics and vice versa. *Nature, 413,* 1–2.

Polanyi, L. (1989). *Telling the American story: A structural and cultural analysis of conversational storytelling.* Cambridge, MA: MIT Press.

Pollan, M. (2001, May 13). Behind the organic–industrial complex. *New York Times Magazine.* Available: *http://www.nytimes.com/2001/05/13/magazine/130organic.htm.*

Pope, D. C. (2001). *"Doing school": How we are creating a generation of stressed out, materialistic, and miseducated students.* New Haven, CT: Yale University Press.

Pore, S., & Reed, K. (1999). *Quick reference to speech–language pathology.* Gaithersberg, MD: Aspen.

Pound, C., Parr, S. & Byng, S. (1999, September 14). *Triumphs, tragedies and miracles: Media representations of aphasia and aphasia therapy.* Paper presented at the meeting of the British Aphasiology Society, London.

Pound, C., Parr, S., & Duchan, J. (2001). Using partners' autobiographical reports to to develop, deliver, and evaluate services in aphasia. *Aphasiology, 15,* 477–493.

Pound, C., Parr, S., Lindsay, J., & Woolf, C. (2000). *Beyond aphasia: Therapies for living with communication disabilities.* Oxon, UK: Winslow Press.

Prelock, P. (2002). Communication with peers in the classroom context: The next steps. In K. Butler & E. Silliman (Eds.), *Speaking, reading and writing in children with language-learning disabilities* (pp. 259–271). Mahwah, NJ: Erlbaum.

President's Commission for Excellence in Special Education. (2002). *Executive summary.* Available: *http://www.ed.gov/inits/commissionsboards/whspecialeducation/reports/summ.html.*

Pressley, M. (1998). *Reading instruction that works: The case for balanced teaching.* New York: Guilford Press.

Pressley, M., Almasi, J., Schuder, T., Bergman, J., Hite, S., El-Dinary, P., & Brown, R. (1994). Transactional instruction of comprehension strategies: The Montgomery County, Maryland, SAIL program. *Reading and Writing Quarterly: Overcoming learning difficulties, 10,* 5–19.

Prizant, B., & Duchan, J. (1981). The functions of immediate echolalia in autistic children. *Journal of Speech and Hearing Disorders, 46,* 241–249.

Prizant, B., Wetherby, A. & Rydell, P. (2000). Communication intervention issues for children with autism spectrum disorders. In A. Wetherby & B. Prizant, *Autism spectrum disorders: A transactional developmental perspective* (pp. 193–224). Baltimore: Brookes.

Prutting, C., Bagshaw, N., Goldstein, H., Juskowitz, S., & Umen, I. (1978). Clinician–child discourse: Some preliminary questions. *Journal of Speech and Hearing Disorders, 43,* 123–139.

Prutting, C., & Kirchner, D. (1983). Applied pragmatics. In T. Gallagher & C. Prutting (Eds.), *Pragmatic assessment and intervention issues in language* (pp. 29–64). San Diego, CA: Singular.

Purcell-Gates, V. (1998). Growing successful readers: Homes, communities, and schools. In J. Osborn & F. Lehr (Eds.), *Literacy for all: Issues in teaching and learning* (pp. 51–72). New York: Guilford Press.

Rao, P., Blosser, J., & Huffman, N. (1998). Measuring consumer satisfaction. In C. Frattali (Ed.), *Measuring outcomes in speech–language pathology* (pp. 89–112). New York: Thieme.

Read, C. (1971). Preschool children's knowledge of English phonology. *Harvard Educational Review, 41,* 1–34.

Reddy, M. (1979). The conduit metaphor: A case of frame conflict in our language about language. In A. Ortony (Ed.), *Metaphor and thought* (pp. 164–201). New York: Cambridge University Press.

Reeves, D. B. (2001). *Crusade in the classroom: How George W. Bush's education reforms will affect your children, our schools.* New York: Simon & Schuster.

Reichle, J., & Wacker, D. (1993). *Communicative alternatives to challenging behavior: Integrating functional assessment and intervention strategies.* Baltimore: Brookes.

Rice, M. (1996). *Toward a genetics of language.* Mahwah, NJ: Erlbaum.

Rice, M., & Wexler, K. (2001). *Test of Early Grammatical Impairment.* San Antonio, TX: Psychological Corporation.

Riessman, C. K. (1993). *Narrative analysis.* Newbury Park, CA: Sage.

Ripich, D., & Panagos, J. (1985). Accessing children's knowledge of sociolinguistic rules for speech therapy lessons. *Journal of Speech and Hearing Disorders, 50,* 335–344.

Ritchie, J., & Wilson, D. (2000). *Teacher narrative as critical inquiry: Rewriting the script.* New York: Teachers College Press.

Robertson, C., & Salter, W. (1995). *The Phonological Awareness Test.* East Moline, IL: Lingui-Systems.

Roemer, M. (1995). *Telling stories: Postmodernism and the invalidation of traditional narrative.* Lanham, MD: Rowman & Littlefield.

Rogoff, B. (1995). Observing sociocultural activity on three planes: Participatory appropriation, guided participation, and apprenticeship. In J. V. Wertsch, P. del Rio, & A. Alvarez (Eds.), *Sociocultural studies of mind* (pp. 139–164). Cambridge, UK: Cambridge University Press.

Roller, E., Rodriquez, T., Warner, J., & Lindahl, P. (1992). Integration of self-contained children with severe speech–language needs into the regular education classroom. *Language, Speech, and Hearing Services in Schools, 23,* 365–366.

Rosch, E. (1981). Prototype classification and logical classification: The two systems. In E. Scholnick (Ed.), *New trends in cognitive representation: Challenges to Piaget's theory* (pp. 73–86). Hillsdale, NJ: Erlbaum.

Rosenthal, R., & Jacobson, L. (1992). *Pygmalion in the classroom*. New York: Irvington.

Rosner, J. (1975). *Helping children overcome learning difficulties*. New York: Walker & Co.

Rothstein, R. (2002, June 19). A voucher program flunks special ed. *New York Times*, p. 7.

Sacks, O. (1996). *An anthropologist on Mars: Seven paradoxical tales*. New York: Vintage Books.

Sacks, P. (1999). *Standardized minds: The high price of America's testing culture and what we can do to change it*. Cambridge, MA: Perseus.

Sadker, M., & Sadker, D. (1995). *Failing at fairness*. New York: Touchstone Books.

Safe and Responsive Schools Project, I. U. (2000). *Minority disproportionality*. Available: *http://www.indiana.edu/~safeschl/minor.html*.

Salinger, T., & Chittenden, E. (1994). Focus on research analysis of an early literacy portfolio: Consequences for instruction. *Language Arts, 71,* 446–453.

Sanders, D. (1977). *Auditory perception of speech: An introduction to principles and problems*. Englewood Cliffs, NJ: Prentice-Hall.

Santosh, P., & Baird, G. (2001). Pharmacotherapy of target symptoms in autistic spectrum disorders. *Indian Journal of Pediatrics, 68,* 427–431.

Scarborough, H. S. (2001). Connecting early language and literacy to later reading (dis)abilities: Theory and practice. In S. Neuman & D. Dickinson (Eds.), *Handbook of early literacy research* (pp. 97–110). New York: Guilford Press.

Scarborough, H. S., & Dobrich, W. (1994). On the efficacy of reading to preschoolers. *Developmental Review, 14,* 245–302.

Schank, R., & Abelson, R. (1977). *Scripts, plans, goals, and understanding*. Hillsdale, NJ: Erlbaum.

Schiffrin, D. (1987). *Discourse markers* (2nd ed.). New York: Cambridge University Press.

Schön, D. (1983). *The reflective practitioner: How professionals think in action*. New York: Basic Books.

Schön, D. (1987). *Educating the reflective practitioner: Toward a new design for teaching and learning in the professions*. San Francisco: Jossey Bass.

School Zone Publishing Company. (2002). Available: *http://shop.store.yahoo.com/schoolzone3/04062.html*.

Schraeder, T., Quinn, M., Stockman, I., & Miller, J. (1999). Authentic assessment as an approach to preschool speech–language screening. *American Journal of Speech–Language Pathology, 8*(3), 195–200.

Schulz, J. (1985). Growing up together. In H. Turnbull & A. P. Turnbull (Eds.), *Parents speak out: Then and now* (2nd ed., pp. 11–20). Columbus, OH: Merrill.

Scribner, S. (1988). Literacy in three metaphors. In E. Kintgen, B. Kroll, & M. Rose (Eds.), *Perspectives on literacy* (pp. 71–81). Carbondale: Southern Illinois University Press.

Searle, J. (1969). *Speech acts: An essay in the philosophy of language.* London: Cambridge University Press.

Seattle Public Schools (2002). *Developmental stages of reading.* Available: *http://www.seattleschools.org/area/acastan/full/append_a.pdf.*

Sedaris, D. (2000). *Me talk pretty one day.* New York: Little, Brown.

Segal, E. (1995). A cognitive–phenomenological theory of fictional narrative. In J. Duchan, G. Bruder, & L. Hewitt (Eds.), *Deixis in narrative: A cognitive science perspective* (pp. 61–78). Hillsdale, NJ: Erlbaum.

Segal, E., Duchan, J., & Scott, P. (1991). The role of interclausal connectives in narrative structuring: Evidence from adults' interpretations of simple stories. *Discourse Processes, 14,* 27–54.

Shaywitz, S. (1996). Dyslexia. *Scientific American, 275,* 98–104.

Shprintzen, R. (1997). *Genetics, syndromes, and communication disorders.* San Diego, CA: Singular.

Silliman, E. R., Badr, R. H., Wilkinson, L. C., & Turner, C. (2002). Language variation and struggling readers: Finding patterns in diversity. In K. Butler & E. Silliman (Eds.), *Speaking, reading, and writing in children with language learning disabilities* (pp. 109–148). Mahwah, NJ: Erlbaum.

Silliman, E., Butler, K., & Wallach, G. (2002). The time has come to talk of many things. In K. Butler & E. Silliman (Eds.), *Speaking, reading, and writing in children with language, learning disabilities* (pp. 3–25). Mahwah, NJ: Erlbaum.

Sinatra, G. M., Brown, K. J., & Reynolds, R. E. (2001). Comprehension strategies instruction: Implications of cognitive resource allocation. In C. C. Block & M. Pressley (Eds.), *Comprehension instruction: Research-based best practices.* (pp. 62–76) New York: Guilford Press.

Sinclair, K., & Tse, H. (2001). Writing reflective journals. In D. Kemper (Ed.), *Reflective teaching and learning in the health professions* (pp. 84–99). Malden MA: Blackwell Science, LTD.

Singer, B., & Bashir, A. (1999). What are executive functions and self-regulation and what do they have to do with language learning disorders? *Language, Speech, and Hearing Services in Schools, 30,* 265–273.

Sleeter, C., & Grant, C. (1991). Race, class, gender, and disability in current textbooks. In M. Apple & L. Christian-Smith (Eds.), *The politics of the textbook* (pp. 78–110). New York: Routledge, Chapman & Hall.

Smith, J. (1990). Measurement issues in early literacy assessment. In L. Morrow & J. Smith (Eds.), *Assessment for instruction in early literacy* (pp. 75–82). Englewood Cliffs, NJ: Prentice-Hall.

Smith, M., & Dickinson, D. (2002). *User's guide to the Early Language and Literacy Classroom Observation Toolkit* (research ed.). Baltimore: Brookes.

Snow, C. (1996). Toward a rational empiricism: Why interactionism is not behaviorism any more than biology is genetics. In M. Rice (Ed.), *Toward a genetics of language* (pp. 377–396). Mahwah, NJ: Erlbaum.

Snow, C., Burns, S., & Griffin, P. (Eds.). (1998). *Preventing reading difficulties in young children.* Washington, DC: National Academy Press.

Snow, C., & Goldfield, B. (1981). Building stories: The emergence of information structures from conversation. In D. Tannen (Ed.), *Analyzing discourse: Text and talk* (pp. 127–141). Washington, DC: Georgetown University Press.

Snow, C., & Ninio, A. (1986). The contracts of literacy: What children learn from learning to read books. In W. Teale & E. Sulzby (Eds.), *Emergent literacy: Writing and reading* (pp. 116–138). Norwood, NJ: Ablex.

Sparks, S. (1984). Speech and language in fetal alcohol syndrome. *ASHA, 26,* 27–31.

Spradley, J. P. (1980). *Participant observation.* New York: Holt, Rinehart & Winston.

Stackhouse, J., & Wells, B. (1997). *Children's speech and literacy difficulties: 1. A psycholinguistic framework.* London: Whurr.

Stark, R., Tallal, P., & McCauley, R. (1988). *Language, speech and reading disorders in children: Neuropsychological studies.* Boston: Little, Brown.

Stehli, A. (1991). *Sound of a miracle: A child's triumph over autism.* New York: Doubleday.

Stein, N., & Glenn, C. R. (1979). An analysis of story comprehension in elementary school children. In R. Freedle (Ed.), *New directions in discourse processing* (Vol. 2, pp. 53–120). Norwood, NJ: Ablex.

Stern, D. (1985). *The interpersonal world of the infant: A view from psychoanalysis and developmental psychology.* New York: Basic Books.

Sternberg, R. J. (1990). *Metaphors of mind: Conceptions of the nature of intelligence.* New York: Cambridge University Press.

Stiegler, L. (in press). Two-culture collision: The diagnosis of autism spectrum disorders from the perspectives of parents and speech–language pathologists. In J. Duchan & D. Kovarsky (Eds.), *Diagnosis as cultural practice.* Hawthorne, NY: De Gruyter.

Stone, C. (1993). What is missing in the metaphor of scaffolding? In E. Forman, N. Minick, & C. A. Stone (Eds.), *Contexts for learning: Sociocultural dynamics in children's development* (pp. 169–183). New York: Oxford University Press.

Stone, C. (2002). Promises and pitfalls of scaffolded instruction for students with language learning disabilities. In K. Butler & E. Silliman (Eds.), *Speaking, reading and writing in children with language learning disabilities* (pp. 175–198). Mahwah, NJ: Erlbaum.

Stout, M. (2000). *The feel-good curriculum: The dumbing down of America's kids in the name of self esteem.* Cambridge, MA: Perseus.

Stuart, C. (2002). *California Trail Junior High: Seventh Grade Language Arts.* Available: *http://teachers.olathe.k12.ks.us/~cstewart/assessmentinst.htm.*

Tager Flusberg, H. (Ed.). (1994). *Constraints on language acquisition: Studies of atypical children.* Mahwah, NJ: Erlbaum.

Tallal, P. (1976). Rapid auditory processing in normal and disordered language development. *Journal of Speech and Hearing Research, 19,* 561–571.

Tallal, P., Miller, S., Bedi, G., Byma, G., Wang, X., Nagarajan, S., Schreiner, C., Jenkins, W., & Merzenich, M. (1996). Language comprehension in language-learning impaired children improved with acoustically modified speech. *Science, 271,* 81–84.

Tashie, C., Shapiro-Barnard, S., Schuh, M., Jorgensen, C., Dillin, A., Dixon, B., & Nisbet, J. (1993). *From special to regular, from ordinary to extraordinary.* Concord, NH: University of New Hampshire, Institute on Disability.

Thagard, P. (1986). Parallel computation and the mind–body problem. *Cognitive Science, 10,* 301–318.

Thagard, P. (1999). *How scientists explain disease.* Princeton, NJ: Princeton University Press.

Threats, T. (2001). New classifications will aid assessment and intervention. *ASHA Leader, 6*(18), 12–13.

Tierney, R., Carter, M., & Desai, L. (1991). *Portfolio assessment in the reading-writing classroom.* Norwood, MA: Christopher-Gordon.

Torgesen, J., & Bryant, B. R. (1998). *Test of Phonological Awareness.* Austin, TX: Pro-Ed.

Torgesen, J., Wagner, R., & Rashotte, C. (1997). *Test of Word Reading Efficiency.* Evanston, IL: Cognitive Concepts.

Tough, J. (1977). *The development of meaning.* New York: Halstead Press.

Trabasso, T., & Magliano, J. (1996). How do children understand what they read and what can we do to help them? In M. Graves, P. van den Broek, & B. Taylor (Eds.), *The first R: A right of all children* (pp. 160–188). New York: Columbia University Press.

Travis, L. (1978). The cerebral dominance theory of stuttering, 1937–1978. *Journal of Speech and Hearing Disorders, 43,* 278–281.

Treiman, R., & Bourassa, D. (2000). The development of spelling skill. *Topics in Language Disorders, 20,* 1–18.

Tucker, J. (1985). Curriculum-based assessment: An introduction. *Exceptional Children, 52,* 119–204.

Turnbull, H. R. (1985). Jay's story. In H. R. Turnbull & A. P. Turnbull (Eds.), *Parents speak out: Then and now* (pp. 109–118). Columbus, OH: Charles E. Merrill.

U.S. Department of Education Office of Special Education and Rehabilitative Services. (2002). *A New Era: Revitalizing Special Education for Children and Their Families.* Washington, DC: Author. Retrieved November 24, 2002, at *http://www.ed.gov/inits/commissionsboards/whspecialeducation/reports/info.html.*

Van Riper, C. (1939). *Speech correction, principles and methods.* New York: Prentice-Hall.

Vargha-Khadem, F., Watkins, K., Price, C., Ahburner, J., Alcock, K., Connelly, A., Frackowiak, R., Friston, K., Pembrey, M., & Mishkin, M. (1998). Neural bases of inherited speech and language disorders. *Proceedings of the National Academy of Sciences, 95,* 12695–12700.

Vygotsky, L. (1978). *Mind in society: The development of higher psychological processes.* Cambridge, MA: Harvard University Press.

Vygotsky, L. (1981). The genesis of higher mental functions. In J. Wertsch (Ed.), *The concept of activity in Soviet psychology* (pp. 144–188). Armonk, NY: Sharpe.

Wagner, R., Torgesen, J., & Rashotte, C. (1999). *Comprehensive Test of Phonological Processing (CTOPP)*. Austin, TX: Pro-Ed.

Warren, S., & Kaiser, A. (1986). Generalization of treatment effects by young language-delayed children: A longitudinal analysis. *Journal of Speech and Hearing Disorders, 51,* 239–251.

Wells, G., & Claxton, G. (2002). *Learning for life in the 21st century: Sociocultural perspectives on the future of education.* London: Blackwell Science.

Wilhelm, J. D. (1995). *You gotta be the book: Teaching engaged and reflective reading with adolescents.* New York: Teachers College Press.

Williams, J. (2002). Using the theme scheme to improve story comprehension. In C. Block & M. Pressley (Eds.), *Comprehension instruction: Research-based best practices* (pp. 126–139). New York: Guilford Press.

Wink, J. (2000). *Critical pedagogy: Notes from the real world* (2nd ed.). New York: Longman.

Wolfensberger, W. (1972). *Normalization: The principle of normalization in human services.* Toronto: National Institute of Mental Retardation.

Wolfensberger, W. (1992). *A brief introduction to social role valorisation as a high order concept for structuring human services* (rev. ed.). Syracuse, NY: Training Institute for Human Service Planning, Change Agency, and Leadership.

Wood, D., Bruner, J., & Ross, G. (1976). The role of tutoring in problem solving. *Journal of Child Psychology and Psychiatry, 17,* 89–100.

Wood, D., & Middleton, D. (1975). A study of assisted problem solving. *British Journal of Psychology, 66,* 181–191.

Woodcock, R. (1998). *Woodcock Reading Mastery Tests—Revised.* Circle Pines, MN: American Guidance Service.

World Health Organization. (2001). International classification of functioning, disability and health (ICF). Available: *www3.who.int/icf/icftemplate.cfm.*

Yopp, H. (1995). *Yopp–Singer Test of Phoneme Segmentation.* California State University. Available: *http://teams.lacoe.edu/reading/assessments/yopp.html.*

Zenderland, L. (1998). *Measuring minds.* New York: Cambridge University Press.

Zipes, J. (2001). *Sticks and stones: The troublesome success of children's literature from Slovenly Peter to Harry Potter.* New York: Routledge.

Ziskin, L. (1985). The story of Jeannie. In H. R. Turnbull & A. P. Turnbull (Eds.), *Parents speak out: Then and now* (pp. 65–73). Columbus, OH: Merrill.

Index

Author index can be found at *http://www.acsu.buffalo.edu/~duchan*.